FAMILIAR AND FOREIGN

FAMILIAR AND FOREIGN

IDENTITY IN IRANIAN FILM AND LITERATURE

Edited by
Manijeh Mannani and Veronica Thompson

AU PRESS

Published by AU Press, Athabasca University
1200, 10011 – 109 Street, Edmonton, AB T5J 3S8

ISBN 978-1-927356-86-9 (print) 978-1-927356-87-6 (PDF) 978-1-927356-88-3 (epub)
doi: 10.15215/aupress/9781927356869.01

Cover design by Marvin Harder, marvinharder.com.
Interior design by Sergiy Kozakov.
Printed and bound in Canada by Friesens.

Library and Archives Canada Cataloguing in Publication

Familiar and foreign : identity in Iranian film and literature / edited by Manijeh Mannani and Veronica Thompson.

Includes bibliographical references.
Issued in print and electronic formats.

1. Persian literature—History and criticism. 2. Motion pictures—Iran—History. 3. National characteristics, Iranian, in literature. 4. National characteristics, Iranian, in motion pictures. 5. Persian literature—Western influences. 6. Motion pictures—Iran—Western influences. I. Thompson, Veronica, 1963-, editor II. Mannani, Manijeh, 1964-, editor

PK6412 I34 F34 2015 891'.5509 C2015-904428-6
C2015-904429-4

We acknowledge the financial support of the Government of Canada through the Canada Book Fund (CFB) for our publishing activities.

Canadian Heritage Patrimoine canadien

Assistance provided by the Government of Alberta, Alberta Multimedia Development Fund.

Alberta Government

Contents

Remember the flight

The bird is mortal

Forugh Farrokhzad

[illegible]

[illegible]

[illegible]

Library and Archives Canada Cataloguing in Publication

[illegible] / edited by Manijeh Mannani and Veronica Thompson.

Includes bibliographical references [illegible]
Issued in print and electronic formats.

1. Persian literature—History and criticism. 2. Motion pictures—Iran—History. 3. National characteristics, Iranian, in literature. 4. National characteristics, Iranian, in motion pictures. 5. Persian literature—Western influences. 6. Motion pictures—Iran—Western influences. I. Thompson, Veronica, [illegible], editor II. Mannani, Manijeh, [illegible], editor

[illegible]

We acknowledge the financial support of the Government of Canada through the Canada Book Fund (CBF) for our publishing activities.

Canadian Heritage / Patrimoine canadien

Assistance provided by the Government of Alberta, Alberta Multimedia Development Fund.

Alberta Government

Familiar and Foreign

An Introduction

Manijeh Mannani and Veronica Thompson

At a time when the Iranian government figures prominently in mainstream media for its foreign policy and nuclear program and when a diversity of voices and perspectives is lacking in the West, it seems pertinent to engage with artistic and literary works that offer more nuanced depictions of Iranian society than are generally available. In the face of predominantly simplistic and monolithic representations of Iran as a repressive, profoundly patriarchal, and politically intractable nation full of religious fanatics imbued with a hatred of the West and prone to terrorism, Iranian artists reveal a very different society, one whose cultural traditions are rooted in a lengthy and complex history that sometimes sit uneasily with the demands of modernity. The artists under consideration in this volume engage with Iranian culture and Western responses to Iran in two ways: their works question the strategies—and in some cases, the ideology—that have been imposed internally on Iranian society, and they challenge the new Orientalist discourse that defines the character of Western conceptions. The essentialist approach of Western media, governments, and even financial institutions that underlies their responses to an Islamic government demonizes Iranians in Iran who have no say in the dealings of the government, as well as Iranians in diaspora with no ties to or interest in political matters.

The artists represented in this collection tackle a range of issues in response to internal and external constructions of Iranian identity, or *hoviyyat*.[1] The question of identity is at the heart of Persian literature and was central to classical Persian poetry, which is essentially spiritual in nature. In the poems of Attar, Jami, Rumi, and Hafiz, to name just a few, the central theme is a spiritual quest, the goal of which is to gain proximity to the Beloved. The first requirement for the individual on a spiritual quest is to "annihilate his ego (*nafs*) and become selfless. . . . It is only after he has divorced himself from his material needs and the worries of his own existence and the world that the seeker can approach the Divine" (Mannani 162). The annihilation of *nafs*, as well as the ongoing Manichaean tensions between the demands of "heart and mind" and "body and mind" that are the defining characteristics of the not-yet-unified Self in Sufi poetry, prefigure modern conceptions of the fragmented Self. In classical poetry, the spiritual quest ultimately culminates in a unified Self, while the modern Self remains divided and insecure.

Spirituality, once the defining characteristic of Persian poetry (which was, until recently, the pre-eminent genre of Persian literature), has partially given way to more secular preoccupations in modern Iranian literature. As Ramin Jahanbegloo argues, "the conflict between traditional and modern understandings of the relationship among religion, state, and society" has dominated the Iranian intellectual agenda particularly during the past decades (15). Tradition and Eurocentric modernity collided following both the Constitutional Revolution (1906–11) and the 1979 Islamic Revolution in particular and distinct ways, as each encounter was inflected by the specifics of its historical moment. The Constitutional Revolution introduced Western modalities of thought, and this political change was subsequently reflected in social and cultural narratives.[2] Subsequently, the anti-imperialist Islamic Revolution vehemently opposed all Western values and thoughts. Over the past three decades, the Iranian government has been adamantly, but unsuccessfully, pursuing its anti-Western principles and imposing strict conformity to religion. The widespread embracing of a Western lifestyle among most Iranians, especially the younger generation, and the 2009 Green Movement illustrate the failed attempts to excise Western influence. This apparent infatuation with Western culture exists in juxtaposition with a nostalgic pride in Persian tradition. Perhaps no critic has identified this duality and the arising complications better than Dariush Shayegan, who, in *Cultural Schizophrenia: Islamic Societies Confronting the West*, delineates the underlying contradictions in Iranian society and the way in which Iranians are caught between the desire to be "modern and archaic, democratic and authoritarian, profane and religious, ahead of the time and behind it" (22). In his 2011 monograph, *Modernity, Sexuality, and Ideology in Iran*, Kamran Talattof takes the issue to a higher level and explicates the reasons behind Iran's failure to achieve modernity in its Western denomination.

He proposes the use of a different "approach," which he calls "modernoid, or resembling modernity," to clarify why "its culture has become unstable, changing constantly in a chaotic fashion" and consistently lacking "a modern conceptualization of sexuality" (9).

Within Iranian discourse, *modernity* remains a fluid term. Although there is no consensus among scholars of Iranian studies about the precise implications of modernity, it is still important to be aware of the distinctions that have been made among its various derivatives. Talattof has identified various definitions of the concept: "'modernity' proper as an epochal or historical category; 'modernité' as a state of mind and being or a human experience; 'modernisation' as material development, industrialisation, or development in technology and economic relationships; and 'modernism' as a realm of cultural and aesthetic values and practices" (22). Babak Rahimi, too, has described "modernization" as a "restrictive set of socioeconomic and state policies for 'modernizing' a perceived 'backward' society, in contrast to 'modernity' as a broad interpretative and institutional field of contention with multiple historical trajectories on a global scale" (451). Abbas Milani has added his voice to the debate. Modernism, Milani argues,

> refers to a moment of aesthetic renovation—where form was content. Modernization is an attempt to buy piecemeal into the modern age (and is usually concurrent with the attempt to maintain some form of authoritarianism). Modernity, on the other hand, is an organically inter-related series of changes in the economic, political, spiritual, epistemological and aesthetic domains. It begets secularism and democracy, rationalism and individualized aesthetic and spiritual realms. It expands the private domain and catapults politics to the public domain. ("Said Amir Arjomand" 578–79)

Moreover, Abbas Milani contends that "rationalism and the rule of law," ideas considered "modern" today, and the quest for "human ideals like democracy and freedom," as primarily secular notions, have occupied the minds of Persians for more than a thousand years, and certainly "long before the Renaissance in Europe" (*Lost Wisdom* 9). Milani, à la Sohrab Sepehri, speaks of the importance of "washing the eyes" and "removing the dust of custom and old beliefs" from them in thinking that modernity is essentially a Western, Eurocentric concept.[3] In the face of the demonization of Iran in Western media, Milani reminds us of the opulent and wide-ranging cultural legacy of a country that has had a decisive role in shaping Western consciousness. His comprehensive overview starts with the Bible—specifically, the book of Ezra, which is "replete with profuse praise for Persia and its kings," primarily Cyrus (*Lost Wisdom* 11–12).[4] Milani then carries on with a detailed discussion of the dominance and influence of Persian progressive thoughts and beliefs on Western consciousness until the long and complicated encounter between Iran and the West in the nineteenth century. He discusses the impact of Zoroastrian, Mithraic, and Manichaean concepts on Greco-Roman and Judeo-Christian thought systems; on the natural and human sciences, including philosophy, geography, mapping, medicine, historiography, mathematics, architecture, and linguistics; and on some prominent figures of the Western tradition such as St. Augustine, Dante, Chaucer, and Shakespeare (12–20).

Concurring with Hans Blumenberg, who defines modernity as "a secular form of critical cultural Gnosticism," Milani lists a wide range of important Persian texts, such as Rumi's *Mathnawi* and Beyhaqi's historical narratives, as "a rich repository of the very ideas that have been assumed 'Western' since the nineteenth century" (18). "Between the tenth and thirteenth centuries," Milani argues, "many of the ideas we now consider the quintessence of modernity—rationalism, secularism, individualism, urbanism, limited government—began to evolve in Iran and helped shape a naïve 'Renaissance'" (18). He specifically mentions three Western philosophers and critics—Hegel, Nietzsche, and Harold Bloom—who have noted the importance of Persian and Zoroastrian thought on Western consciousness. For instance, in *The Philosophy of History*, Hegel states:

> Persians are the first Historic people. . . . In Persia first arises that light which shines itself and illuminates what is around; for Zoroaster's 'Light' belongs to the World of Consciousness—to Spirit as a relation to something distinct from itself. We see in the Persian World a pure exalted Unity, as the essence which leaves the special existences that inhere in it, free; —as the Light, which only manifests what bodies are in themselves; —a Unity which governs individuals only to excite them to become powerful for themselves—to develop and assert their individuality. Light makes no distinctions: the Sun shines on the righteous and the unrighteous, on high and low, and confers on all the same benefit and prosperity. . . . The principle of development begins with the history of Persia. This therefore constitutes strictly the beginning of World-History (173).

While recognizing the precedence of notions such as "democracy" in Persian culture, Milani takes note of the universal nature of these concepts and warns of any misapplication of these discussions by supremacist, nationalist, and religious zealots (20–21).

In a similar vein, many historians and gender theorists have indicated that the causes of modern transformations within Iranian society cannot be limited to external factors. In probing the history of interactions between Europe and Iran, especially as it concerns cultural relations, Afsaneh Najmabadi asserts that these exchanges, which date back to at least the sixteenth century, played a profound role in transforming sexuality and gender in nineteenth-century Iranian society, although she insists that the "internal causes" cannot be ignored either (5). Najmabadi highlights the importance of remembering the "innumerable contingent events and concepts that transformed genders and sexualities" and the difficulty in making "a separation between internal and external developments" as they are progressively "intermeshed" at the turn of the century (5). In Najmabadi's estimation, "much cultural hybridization was . . . mediated through the increasing interactions between Iran and the Indian subcontinent and the Ottoman Empire," and "on the cultural level, more so than on the economic, administrative, and military levels, the interactions were a two-way street" (5). Inspired by the research of Mendus and Randall and that of Bleys, Najmabadi concludes that "just as this cultural traffic transformed Iranian gender and sexual sensibilities, European gender and sexual mores were also changed through interactions with other societies that Europe 'discovered.' . . . Neither Iranians nor Europeans invented themselves out of whole cloth" (5).[5]

Sexuality and gender inequality have been major components of the discourse on Iranian modernity and identity. In this predominantly patriarchal culture, some Persian women have played decisive roles in shaping the history of the country (Taghi 165–201; Kohl, Witt, and Welles 198). It is equally important to note that the patronizing view of most Iranian men toward women has an uneven and fluctuating precedence according to many historical accounts, including Herodotus's *Histories*. Milani recounts history from the viewpoint of Herodotus, who, despite his estimation of the Persians as "barbarians" and "the other," notes that Persian men took the seizure of their young women by foreign armies much more lightly than did their Greek counterparts, for whom their women were key constituents of their Greek "honor" (*Lost Wisdom* 14). The subtle differentiation that Milani is expressing here is the nonpatronizing attitude toward women at that time in Persian history, an attitude in explicit contradiction to that of the Greeks. Of course, throughout different historical periods and as the result of various sociopolitical upheavals, Iranian women have gained, lost, and, in certain cases, regained some of their basic rights.

In *Sexual Politics in Modern Iran*, a study of the role of gender relations and politics in modern Iranian life, Janet Afary lays bare the persisting patriarchal norms in contemporary Iran, drawing upon Michel Foucault's theories about societal controls exercised upon individual bodies (Foucault 103–11). In the same study, Afary invokes Erich Fromm, who delineates how the freedom from social hierarchies and the changes in social orders that came with the abrogation of the rigid class system in Western societies resulted in feelings of displacement, disconnectedness, and trauma by individual members of society (Fromm 123–29). Afary claims that the shift from a primarily agrarian to an urban lifestyle amplified similar feelings of displacement and insecurity, which Iranians were already feeling in the face of modernity (201). These factors all led to the embracing of Islamic values, which further perpetuated the patriarchal and patrimonial principles within Iranian society (201). Iranian women, who had made much progress following the Constitutional Revolution in claiming equal status and rights, saw many of these advances revoked after the Islamic government came to power.

Closely related to Afary's study of gender politics in Iran are Nayereh Tohidi's views. Tohidi approaches the issue from a sociopsychological perspective by outlining how Iranian men responded to modern forces. According to Tohidi, Iranian men alleviated the insecurity, anxiety, and helplessness they were feeling in the face of modernity by exercising even more power over their families, and especially over the female members of their families—that is, their wives, daughters, and sisters. These feelings of inferiority—in conjunction with the deeply embedded notions of *gheyrat* and *namus*, which define a man's sense of honour in protecting the purity and integrity of his female kinship—compound the societal pressures experienced by Iranian women. These constructions and performances of gender circumscribe both women and men.[6]

The tradition-modernity dialectic, which is central to modern Iranian identity, is encountered in the chapters in *Familiar and Foreign* and is embodied in a number of recurring motifs, such as alienation, exile, memory and history, geographic and linguistic displacement, liminality, loss and longing, gender and sexuality, and generational disparities.[7] In addition to these motifs, the choice of genre, from confessional poetry to the graphic novel to film, deliberately reflects the collision of and resulting dialogue between past and present.

Iranians felt the bind between tradition and modernity acutely after 1979. The political situation, economic factors, and the increasing lack of opportunity for women, artists, and political dissidents to exercise their rights and express their views and opinions led many Iranians to leave the country, and many remain in diaspora. Diasporic identity is characterized by experiences of exile, displacement, and dispossession. As Gina Wisker writes, "For people silenced and dispossessed, writing back against that silence often involves the crucial need to explore and express history, and most importantly, the self." She adds that "semi-fictionalized autobiography and life writing" have become "particular favorites of many women writers in response to the double experience of silencing" (164). Illustrating this trend, the past two decades have seen a sharp rise in the publication of many Iranian autobiographies that "write back against the silence" as a form of resistance. Among recent publications, the works of three Iranian women—Marjane Satrapi, Azar Nafisi, and Fatemeh Keshavarz—have drawn critical attention and are the subject of examination in several chapters in this collection. These narratives deal with a complex array of issues, the most important of which is the representation of women under the Islamic, post-imperialist regime. The memoirs have received a wide range of responses from both within and outside Iran, but most notably, from Iranian academics abroad who have questioned the legitimacy of exposing the internal weaknesses of the Islamic regime vis-à-vis the West through the sharing of personal stories and experiences. Abedinifard, Goldin, and Mannani attend to the nuances of self-writing, where confrontation with the Self is inevitable. In his article on Iranian autobiography, Abedinifard argues that Satrapi, in her two *Persepolis* volumes, "unveils the self" as a way of pushing back against the repressive measures, particularly as they apply to women, during the formation years of the Islamic Republic. In contrast, Mannani discusses how Keshavarz, in her response to Nafisi's memoir, *Reading Lolita in Tehran*, reveals her internalization of the regimentation and censorship of the post-1979 state in her own self-regulated and self-censored memoir, in which an idealized Self is constructed. Similarly, Goldin, by examining the misogynistic use of selective hybrid words and idioms, maintains that Arabic has negatively impacted the Persian language and provides a comprehensive overview of Persian as "linguistically egalitarian" before the advent of Islam. Goldin's evaluation of language extends to what she believes is an inherent discursive control of Iranian women's life-writing.

The construction of Self is also problematized in the essays in this volume that focus on fiction. The common motif in these narratives is alienation, regardless of whether the setting encompasses Iran or Europe or, in Goli Taraqqi's case, both. The essays provide analyses of illustrations of an alienation that is twofold: the exilic alienation experienced as a result of geographic and linguistic displacement and what might be called "domestic alienation" within the realm of the home and family in Iran. Zoya Pirzad, as shown by Madeleine Voegeli, illustrates the complexities of establishing selfhood in a culture in which patriarchy is institutionalized. As Voegeli argues, the rigidly prescribed gender roles in Pirzad's fiction strip both women and men of individual identity, leaving them estranged and empty within their familial milieu. Blake Atwood, too, probes gender roles, but his discussion concentrates on homoeroticism and homosexuality and on how the difference between the two within the Iranian context is informed by Eve Sedgwick's notion of "homosexual panic," which functions as a different way of "coming out of the closet." What Atwood describes as the "failed emotional passage" of male characters into adulthood in the fiction of Alizadeh and Taraqqi and those writers' reliance on two female characters (the two sides of the mother figure) explain the suspension of male characters' "ascendance" to heterosexuality.

The exploration of exilic alienation is the subject of Babak Elahi's chapter on Kader Abdolah's *My Father's Notebook*, where the motifs of spatial and linguistic dislocation figure prominently. As Elahi observes, Abdolah's "novel is a metafictional account of a son's attempt to translate his father's notebooks from an unknown language into Dutch." The essay analyzes how the cultural displacement of diaspora is mediated through the interplay between the language of the host country and a universal sign language—Abdolah's father is both deaf and mute—and how "migration involves a transformation of self" through the narrator's inability to use his Persian mother tongue to write. The use of sign language in the narrative is a communicative catalyst when the "home and host" languages are incompatible.

Laetitia Nanquette's essay, too, explores exile as theme, style, and genre in Goli Taraqqi's short stories. According to Nanquette, identity is redefined in the state of exile, where confrontation with the Other is mandatory. She uses Peyman Vahabzadeh's theory that exile and immigration are not dichotomous in Persian literature to argue, in her analysis of the stories, that emigrants and exiles "have come to terms with their permanent conditions of alterity and foreignness" (Vahabzadeh 496). In the narratives that Nanquette studies, the protagonists embody varied stages of exilic experience, from the liminality of the newly exiled to the hybrid Self that incorporates both Western and Iranian values. Nanquette does note Taraqqi's repeated use of the term *Farang*—the subject of Goulia Ghardashkhani's essay, which also examines Taraqqi's short fiction. *Farang*, as Ghardashkhani explains, derives etymologically from the word *France*; however, over the years, the term has come to refer to "the West and Westerners" and "more specifically to the lands and peoples of Europe and North America" (Ghanoonparvar 2–3). In Ghardashkhani's problematization of the concept, the signification of the word *farang* becomes dependent on the geographical location and psychological condition of the narrating subject. In other words, the meaning is multiple and spatially determined.

The motifs of history and memory are dealt with most fully in the articles on film. Khatereh Sheibani, in her analysis, explores how Bahram Beizai deconstructs and reformats "formal history" and "national identity." After Sheibani's acknowledgement of the *mellat-ommat* dichotomy, she dismantles these concepts to challenge the construction of history as a "monological, cultural explanation" in both its Iranian and Islamic accounts.[8] She shows how Beizai's films undermine the rigid lining up of historical events. Anselmi and Wilson return to Satrapi's *Persepolis*, albeit the film adaptation by Paronnaud and Satrapi, and compare it to Ari Folman's *Waltz with Bashir*. They argue that both films "resist and subvert the history that is visually offered to us" in an effort to "reclaim different social memories . . . and reformulate individual identity paradigms in relationship to conceptions of national histories." In foregrounding the complex relationship between film and television, Anselmi and Wilson demonstrate how both movies emphasize the fragmented Self.

It is important to note that only one essay in the collection deals with poetry despite the prominence of the genre in classical Persian literature and its ongoing importance. The small space that poetry occupies in this volume explains the positioning of Mohaghegh Neyshabouri's chapter, which opens the book and elucidates the tradition-modernity collision that underscores the entire collection. This ongoing discord between past and present is reinforced by the subject of her chapter, which deals with the confessional work of Forugh Farrokhzad. As Mohaghegh Neyshabouri argues, Farrokhzad's poetry demonstrates the struggle for Self "in the lives of progressive women artists of her generation." In her poems, Farrokhzad expresses an individualized female Self defined against societal norms and expectations by presenting intimate details of female experience, a trend that remains nascent even four decades after her tragic death and, at the same time, reinforces our critical stance that tradition still exerts a powerful grasp on Iranian minds.

The essays presented here engage with the complex imbrication of the discourses of religion, patriarchy, and politics within the overarching paradigm of tradition and modernity. The various and diverse depictions of Self presented by the artists examined in these essays indicate the ongoing construction, deconstruction, and reconstruction of identity. These fictive narratives problematize the one-dimensional and shallow representations of Iranians that circulate unexamined in the West. Moreover, these films and literary texts not only challenge the neo-colonialist stereotypes but also reveal the limitations of collective identity as figured within and outside of Iran. Iranian identity as reflected in art, be it classical or modern, is informed by duality. A duality that was once metaphysical in nature has given way to a more politicized schism as a result of the country's long, complex, and revolutionary history. The ongoing quest for equality for all members of Iranian society and the fight for personal and political expression remain among the many legitimate aspirations of the Iranian nation.[9]

NOTES

1 We have adopted the system of transliteration used by the journal *Iranian Studies* for Persian words and names, except in the case of proper names (such as those of cities) for which a familiar English spelling exists.

2 For more information on the Constitutional Revolution, see Afary, *Iranian Constitutional Revolution*.

3 Within the Iranian intellectual milieu, Milani believes, three separate groups of ideologues have fostered this essentially colonialist view: whereas enchanted Iranian secular intellectuals and most Iranian Marxists embraced Eurocentric and Western liberating and modern ideas, the religious forces that constituted the third group rejected them on the basis of their origin (*Lost Wisdom* 10–11).

4 "Cyrus, King of Persia . . . is often referred to as God's 'anointed' and the 'chosen' ruler," notes Milani, adding, "Cyrus was in fact the first ruler to issue a declaration of human rights . . . and the first ruler to create a truly multi-cultural empire by affording his conquered peoples the liberty to maintain their own linguistic, religious, and cultural autonomy" (*Lost Wisdom* 11–12).

5 Mohamad Tavakoli-Targhi, too, contends that "in the interplay of looks between Asians and Europeans, there was no steady position of spectatorship, no objective observer. . . . The field of vision and the making of meaning were perspectival, contestatory, and theatrical" (*Refashioning Iran* 36).

6 It is important to recognize that although today women are discriminated against by laws that govern institutions such as marriage, child custody, inheritance, and court testimony, they do have equal access to education (Mongabay). The World Bank reports that, in Iran, "[t]he female-to-male ratio in primary school is the world's highest, with 1.2 girls enrolled for every boy. The number of women in secondary school as a percentage of the eligible age group more than doubled from 30 percent to 81 percent, and in 2009,

more than half of all Iranian university students, 68 percent of the students in science, and 28 percent in engineering were women" (60).

7 None of the works in this collection subscribes strictly to postmodernism proper. However, postmodernism resonates intensely with Iranian intellectuals because its irrationality evokes the same absence of rationality that is, in this traditional culture, deeply rooted in mysticism (Haghighi 10–12). Afshin Matin-Asgari suggests that as an "'intellectual style,' postmodernism arguably has occupied the leading place that Marxism enjoyed in Iran a generation ago" (113). Nietzsche and Foucault, considered by many Iranians as pioneers of postmodern thought, were popular because of the former's seminal work, *Thus Spoke Zarathustra*, and the latter's work on the 1979 Iranian Revolution. This popularity has extended to Heidegger, Lyotard, and Derrida, among others, whose "fashionable philosophical jargon" Iranian intellectuals like Babak Ahmadi use loosely without having a thorough understanding of the concepts behind it (Haghighi 276). Haghighi takes issue with writers like Ahmadi who argue that "all interpretations of the truth are equal. . . . They have the same degree of credibility and are equally problematic" (279). In the words of Matin-Asgari, it is precisely this thesis that Haghighi opposes—seeing postmodernism as "a confused crossover between postmodern rhetoric and irrational tendencies of Iranian intellectual 'tradition'" (114).

8 *Mellat-ommat* refers to a dichotomy between Iranians who share language and culture and Iranians for whom their shared religion of Islam takes precedence over nationality. Mohamad Tavakoli-Targhi argues that, in order to recover from historical and cultural amnesia, Iranians reinvented a pre-Islamic past, one in which Iran became "a lost Utopia with . . . Mazdak as a theoretician and practitioner of freedom and equality, Kavah-'i Ahangar as the originator of 'national will' (*himmat-i mellii*), and Anushirvan as a paradigmatic just-constitutional monarch." In what Tavakoli-Targhi describes as "a conscious effort to *dissociate* Iran from Islam and the Arabs,"

> [i]t was argued that the veiling of women and polygamy were non-Iranian customs promulgated by the Arabs after the conquest of Iran. These "historical facts" were used rhetorically in the Constitutionalist discourse in order to project Iran's "decadence" on to Arabs and Islam and introject the desirable attributes of Europeans on the pre-Islamic Self. This double process of projection and introjection provided mechanisms for the recasting of the *millat* and articulating a secular nationalist discourse and identity. The modernist dissociation of Iran from Islam intensified the Islamist desire to essentialize Islam in the constitution of Iranian identity. In the political struggle between Islamists and secularists in the twentieth century, the allegorical meanings of ancient history figured into the competing rhetorics of cultural authenticity. ("Contested Memories" 175; see also "Refashioning Iran" 77)

9 The editors would like to acknowledge Leila Pazargadi's assistance in formulating the first call for papers that led to this publication.

WORKS CITED

Afary, Janet. *Iranian Constitutional Revolution, 1906–1911*. New York: Columbia UP, 1996.

———. *Sexual Politics in Modern Iran*. Cambridge: Cambridge UP, 2009.

Blumenberg, Hans. *The Legitimacy of the Modern Age*. Trans. Robert M. Wallace. Cambridge, MA: MIT P, 1983.

Foucault, Michel. *The History of Sexuality*. Vol. 1. 1978. New York: Vintage Books, 1990.

Fromm, Erich. *Escape from Freedom*. 1941. New York: Discus Books, 1965.

Ghanoonparvar, M. R. *In a Persian Mirror: Images of the West and Westerners in Iranian Fiction*. Austin: U of Texas P, 1993.

Haghighi, Shahrokh. *Gozar az moderniteh? Nicheh, Fuko, Lyotar, Derida* [*Beyond Modernity? Nietzsche, Foucault, Lyotard, Derrida*]. Tehran: Agah, 2001.

Hegel, Georg Wilhelm Friedrich. *The Philosophy of History*. Trans. J. Sibree. Buffalo, NY: Prometheus, 1991.

Jahanbegloo, Ramin. "Two Concepts of Secularism." *Comparative Studies of South Asia, Africa, and the Middle East* 31.1 (2011): 13–22.

Kohl, Benjamin G., Ronald G. Witt, and Elizabeth B. Welles. *The Earthly Republic: Italian Humanists on Government and Society*. Philadelphia: U of Pennsylvania P, 1978.

Mannani, Manijeh. "The Metaphysics of the Heart in the Sufi Poetry of Rumi." *Religion and Literature* 42.3 (2010): 161–68.

Matin-Asgari, Afshin. "Iranian Postmodernity: The Rhetoric or Irrationality?" *Critique: Critical Middle Eastern Studies* 13.1 (2004): 113–23.

Milani, Abbas. *Lost Wisdom: Rethinking Modernity in Iran*. Washington, DC: Mage, 2004.

———. "Said Amir Arjomand, *After Khoemini: Iran Under His Successor*." *Iranian Studies* 45.4 (2012): 577–81.

Mongabay. "Country Profile: Iran Government and Politics." N.d. 8 Nov. 2012. http://www.mongabay.com/reference/country_profiles/2004-2005/2-Iran.html.

Najmabadi, Afsaneh. *Women with Mustaches and Men Without Beards: Gender and Sexual Anxieties of Iranian Modernity*. Berkeley: U of California P, 2005.

Rahimi, Babak. "Ali Mirsepasi, *Political Islam, Iran, and the Enlightenment: Philosophies of Hope and Despair*." *Iranian Studies* 45.3 (2012): 449–53.

Shayegan, Dariush. *Cultural Schizophrenia: Islamic Societies Confronting the West*. 1992. Syracuse, NY: Syracuse UP, 1997.

Taghi, Shokoofeh. *Zan-azari dar qesse-ha va tarikh* [*Abuse of Women in Stories and History*]. Sweden: Nashr-i Baran, 2008.

Talattof, Kamran. *Modernity, Sexuality, and Ideology in Iran: The Life and Legacy of a Popular Female Artist*. Syracuse, NY: Syracuse UP, 2011.

Tavakoli-Targhi, Mohamad. "Contested Memories: Narrative Structures and Allegorical Meanings of Iran's Pre-Islamic History." *Iranian Studies* 29.1/2 (1996): 149–75.

———. "Refashioning Iran: Language and Culture During the Constitutional Revolution." *Iranian Studies* 23.1/4 (1990): 77–101.

———. *Refashioning Iran: Orientalism, Occidentalism, and Historiography*. New York: Palgrave, 2001.

Tohidi, Nayereh. "Mas'ale-ye zan va roshanfekran teye tahavvolat-e daheh-ye akhir" ["The Woman Issue and Intellectuals During the Upheavals Within the Past Few Decades"]. *The Feminist School*, 12 Shahrivar 1390 (3 Sept. 2011). 8 Nov. 2012. http://www.feministschool.com/spip.php?article6940.

Vahabzadeh, Peyman. "Where Will I Dwell? A Sociology of Literary Identity Within the Iranian Diaspora." *Comparative Studies of South Asia, Africa, and the Middle East* 28.3 (2008): 495–512.

Wisker, Gina. *Key Concepts in Postcolonial Literature*. Basingstoke, UK: Palgrave Macmillan, 2007.

World Bank. *World Development Report 2012: Gender Equality and Development*. Washington, DC: World Bank, 2011. 9 May 2012. http://siteresources.worldbank.org/INTWDR2012/Resources/7778105-1299699968583/7786210-1315936222006/Complete-Report.pdf.

[illegible] the various and diverse depictions of Self presented by the [illegible] contained in [illegible] attest to the ongoing construction, deconstruction, and [illegible] of identity. [illegible] problematize the [illegible] representations of Iranians that circulate unexamined in the West. Moreover, these films and literary texts not only challenge the [illegible] stereotypes but also reveal the limitations of collective identity as figured [illegible]. Iranian identity, reflected in its best classical [illegible] equality. A [illegible] that was [illegible] metaphysical in nature has [illegible] politicized schism as a result of the country's long, [illegible] history. The ongoing quest for equality for all members of [illegible] and the fight for personal and political expression remain among the [illegible] of the Iranian nation.[illegible]

NOTES

1. We have [illegible] the system of transliteration used by the journal *Iranian Studies* for Persian [illegible] names, except in the case of proper names such as those of cities for which a familiar English spelling exists.
2. For more information on the Constitutional Revolution, see Afary, *Iranian Constitutional Revolution*.
3. [illegible] three separate groups of [illegible] as enchanted Iranian [illegible] embraced [illegible] and Western [illegible] the religious forces that constituted the third group rejected them on the basis of their origin (*Lost Wisdom* 10–11).
4. Cyrus [illegible] often referred to as God's 'anointed' and the 'chosen' ruler [illegible] in fact the first ruler to issue a declaration of human rights [illegible] create a truly multicultural empire by affording his [illegible] to maintain their own linguistic, religious, and cultural autonomy [illegible].
5. Mohamad [illegible] contends that "in the interplay of looks between Asians and Europeans [illegible] position of spectatorship, no objective observer. . . . The field [illegible] of the making of meaning were perspectival, contestatory, and [illegible]" ([illegible]).
6. It is important to recognize that although today women are discriminated against by laws [illegible] such as marriage, child custody, inheritance, and court testimony, [illegible] access to education (Mong[illegible]). The World Bank reports that in Iran [illegible] the female-to-male ratio in primary school is the world's highest, with 1.2 girls enrolled for every boy. The number of women in secondary school as a percentage of the eligible [illegible] has doubled from 30 percent to 81 percent, and in 2009,

CHAPTER ONE

The Development of the Artistic Female Self in the Poetry of Forugh Farrokhzad

Safaneh Mohaghegh Neyshabouri

Between the views of those critics who value the literary merit of Forugh Farrokhzad's poetry and those who consider it mere erotic verse, there is a significant interface: they all agree that her poetry drastically changed the path of self-expression in Iranian women's literature. Farrokhzad daringly expressed herself on taboo topics, and the rebellious quality of her work undermines the patriarchal rules of Iranian culture. She presented her intimate experiences, and by doing so created the image of a lonely genius in a patriarchal world too indifferent to a woman's sufferings. To some readers, she has become an accessible idol whose personal experiences of nervous breakdowns and divorce, along with her tragic sudden death in 1967 at the age of only thirty-two, define the value of her poetry. As American critic Jasmin Darznik writes: "During her own lifetime, critics tended to conflate Farrokhzad's poetry with the poetic persona of her verses, and when Forugh Farrokhzad is remembered today, it is still most often as a confessional poet, one who drew directly from her life to her art or, more pointedly, from her sex life to her erotic verses" (104).

The similarities between Farrokhzad and the persona she created have made her life story a point of reference in interpreting her work. The same can be said of the importance of Farrokhzad's life story in the feminist movement of Iran. Her struggle both in life and in art to balance socially accepted roles for women with their personal aspirations and inner desires has made her the symbol of resistance to patriarchal power. While I concede that her life experiences made her the epitome of the progressive Iranian woman at the turn of the twenty-first century, I believe that she moved beyond this struggle into a realm of universal human experience. In trying to express her femininity, Farrokhzad found, defined, and constantly redefined her artistic self. The incorporation of personal experiences into art demonstrates this struggle in the lives of progressive women artists of her generation and places Farrokhzad among the poets of the confessional school.

The term "confessional poetry" was first used by critic M. L. Rosenthal, in a review of Robert Lowell's *Life Studies* published in 1959 (154). The broad acceptance of the term resulted in some critics giving more weight to the candour of the poems than to their artistic qualities. Robert Phillips insists that "a true confessional poet places few barriers, if any, between his self and direct expression of that self, however painful that expression may prove," arguing that confessional poetry "dispenses with a symbol or formula for an emotion and gives the naked emotion direct, personally rather than impersonally" (8). He suggests that the more directly the poet exposes her inner feelings and desires, the greater the artistic value of her work. However, Bruce Bawer expresses a completely contrasting view, writing that "the best of confessional poetry is marked by balance, control, a sense of form and rhythm, and even a degree of detachment" (8). Bawer's position is that confessional poetry should be more than simply an emotional outpouring that reflects the poet's personal life and experiences. Nonetheless, as the poetry of the personal "I," confessional poetry often reveals private experiences and feelings about a great range of issues, including death, depression, and love. The "I" of Farrokhzad's poetry invites the reader to bear witness to the sufferings of the persona and to join her as she goes through distressing experiences. Through the use of personal material, she ventures into areas of female consciousness and feeling that had rarely been touched on by other forms of Persian poetry produced by women. To make her voice heard, Farrokhzad needed to break through the limitations and challenge societal expectations of her as a woman and as an artist.

In the course of discussing the poetry of another female confessional poet, Sylvia Plath, with whom Farrokhzad has been compared many times, Sandra

Gilbert also explores the work of Charlotte Brontë, referring to her novel *Jane Eyre* as a Bildungsroman. She states that Brontë "couldn't write the serious, straightforward, neo-Miltonic account of the 'growth of the poet's mind' that Wordsworth produced." Primarily for psychosocial reasons, "[w]omen as a rule, even sophisticated women writers, haven't until quite recently been brought to think of themselves as conscious subjects in the world. Deprived of education, votes, jobs, and property rights, they have also, even more significantly, been deprived of their own selfhood" ("A Fine, White Flying Myth" 249). In an earlier study of confessional poets, Gilbert aptly observes the difference between male and female confessional poetry:

> The male confessional poet—Lowell, Berryman, Yeats—writes in the certainty that he is the inheritor of major traditions, the grandson of history, whose very anxieties, as Harold Bloom has noted, are defined by the ambiguities of the past that has shaped him as it shaped his fathers. The female poet, however, even when she is not consciously confessional like Plath or Saxton, writes in the hope of discovering or defining a self, a certainty, a tradition. ("My Name Is Darkness" 448)

Gilbert does not use the term *Bildungsroman* for the work of the female confessional poets but states that "[c]onsidering and discarding different metaphors, different propositions of identity," the female confessional poet "seem[s] to be straining to formulate an ontology of selfhood, some irreducible and essential truth about her own nature" (448). However, Farzaneh Milani considers "[t]he whole canon of Farrokhzad's poetry . . . as a kind of Bildungsroman." Milani believes that the term "best embodies Farrokhzad's emergence from cultural conditioning and her struggle to come to self-realization, warranting its adaptation to her journey and to her awakening" (136). Although Bildungsroman is a genre of novel and has most often been associated with the development of a male protagonist's mind and character, the concept—or rather its subtype, Künstlerroman—can be used to study the development of the persona in the poetry of Farrokhzad. In what follows, I trace the formation of the female self in samples of Farrokhzad's poetry. I begin by introducing the forces that shape the selfhood of the artistic female self; this is followed by a discussion of whether and how the persona goes through rebirth and recreation of her artistic self.

Autocratic political systems and cultural obstacles have prevented the freedom of expression in different periods of Iranian history and have resulted in the formation of a complex system of metaphors and layers of meaning in Persian poetry. A cursory look at the history of Persian literature reveals how poetry has helped many in expressing their most radical criticism of cultural, social, religious, and political matters without facing any serious consequences. However, this situation has been the privilege of male poets, and the female experience has been glaringly absent from Persian poetry. In the mid-twentieth century, with certain cultural developments and the creation of more opportunities for women to participate in society, a new tradition of women's poetry came into being that was highly self-reflective and self-revelatory. It was a new school of poetry by women, in which they openly expressed their feelings and emotions, braving stigmatization by the patriarchal and religious society. In what appeared as a sudden change in Iranian society's cultural spirit, female poets shed their veils and raised their voices. Up to this point in the history of Persian poetry, there is almost no trace of female experience, but, as Farzaneh Milani describes this new generation of women poets, "with body unveiled and pen in hand, they led the reader behind walls and veils to the domain of the private" (127). Unlike the obedient traditional woman who, as the Persian proverb says, "suffered and suppressed [*besuz va besaz*]," the women of this generation broke their silence and shared their complaints, emotions, and most intimate experiences with others.

Women who claimed their right to express themselves publicly challenged the patriarchal values of the Iranian society. The presence of these new voices was even hard for many enlightened male thinkers to accept (Milani 128–30). Religious institutions, which greatly influenced public opinion, equated female emancipation to women being physically exposed. Modernism was associated with technology, education, and progress, on one hand, and unrestrained sexual expression of women, on the other. Many artists and thinkers of the time reflected in their work the dual ideals of having roots in traditional values yet aspiring for change. Even fifty years after her death, the literary life of Forugh Farrokhzad exemplifies this state of cultural uncertainty in the Iranian mind.

Farrokhzad worked with two different conflicts, personal and sociocultural, that grew from the same root. As Kamran Talattof argues, while the general consensus among scholars is that her work can be divided into two distinct categories (the unrefined personal poetry of her early work and the valuable social poetry of her last two collections), elements of personal and social conflict can be observed in both her early and later poems. Also, according to Talattof, the structural and philosophical changes in her later poetry reveal "the natural flourishing of a sensitive mind" (89). I believe that it was through this constant shuttling between the old values and the new, the personal conflicts and the social restrictions, that Farrokhzad's artistic voice emerged and developed.

Farrokhzad's first three collections—*The Captive* (*Asir* 1952), *The Wall* (*Divar* 1956), and *Rebellion* (*Esyan* 1957)—were, and still are, interpreted primarily in sexual terms (Milani 132). Their erotic nature prevented many early readers and critics from observing in them the evolving voice of a female artist. The publication of *The Captive* was a breath of fresh air and introduced new possibilities to women artists in Iran. As Michael Hillmann rightfully notes, the open expression of a woman's emotion in *The Captive* was unprecedented in the Persian literary tradition (3–6). In a culture where women were expected to be silent and invisible, Farrokhzad's outspokenness became controversial. Her search for autonomy and freedom and her harsh criticism of cultural and social ills begin here. The persona in the poems of *The Captive* is a young woman frustrated by limitations and haunted by feelings of loss and guilt. In the title poem, the woman is held motionless by her expected roles of mother and wife. The home—or to be more specific, the "house"—is a place of confinement and silence:

> I think about it and yet I know
> I do not have the strength to leave this cage
> Even if the prisoner would let me go
> I am short of breath to fly away.
>
> From behind the bars, each bright morning
> A smiling child looks at me
> As I start to sing the happy song
> His kissing lips near mine.
>
> Oh endless sky if one day I choose to fly
> Away from this silent prison
> How will I answer the child's crying eyes?
> Let me be for I'm a captive bird.[1] ("The Captive" 13–24)

The image of a "captive bird," which represents the persona's aversion to the forced immobility within her home, recurs in Farrokhzad's first three collections. Also, although the portrayal of men changes through the course of Farrokhzad's poetic career, they are depicted in her early poetry as emotionally unavailable. They objectify women, reducing them to a commodity:

> He asks for winey kisses
> What should I say to my hopeful heart?
> He thinks about pleasure and ignorant of how
> I think about that everlasting bliss. ("Stranger" 13–16)

While Farrokhzad constantly rejects this objectification, I agree with Simidchieva's observation that there are "instances in which the *dramatis persona* looks at herself exclusively through the prism of paradigmatic patriarchal mores, which lay upon women the entire responsibility for sexual misconduct" (23). She is the one whose "fiery eyes" invite the man to a sinful pleasure ("Bitter Tale" 30). Despite this association with temptation, her role falls within the other stereotypical presentation of the female, that of the "angel in the house": the caring mother and patient wife/beloved who suffers but keeps silent to avoid disturbing her man and her child. In accordance with this image, it is the man who is an active agent:

> There is a city beside that river
> Where my heart is held captive, in a proud man's fist
> . . .
> On the sandy shore, and under palm trees
> He has stolen kisses, from my eyes and lips ("Remembering the Past" 3–8)

As Shimidchieva argues, the persona in these poems is "a beguiling recipient of the man's caresses, rather than his partner in passion" (26). Like Shahrzad (Scheherazade) of *One Thousand and One Nights*, her role is that of a caregiver and domesticator, but she lacks the legendary character's determination and courage. Nonetheless, we should give credit to Farrokhzad because the description of intimate moments and the blunt expression of a woman's feelings were textually rebellious moves in Persian literature. Had the young Farrokhzad taken *The Captive* to a publication house in an earlier time, it would have been rejected, but at a time of great cultural change, the daring and explicit content of her poetry justified its circulation.[2]

Farrokhzad's defiant declaration of independence through the expression of sexual freedom continues through her second collection, *The Wall* (*Divar*), which starts with the infamous "Sin." The breathless metre of the poem, its passionate tone, and the fact that it describes a sexual encounter from a woman's perspective have made it taboo. But in addition to challenging the limits of sexual description, Farrokhzad pushes the textual boundaries by questioning the representation of women/the beloved in Persian literature. Symbolized in the character of "Leili," the quintessential sweetheart is portrayed in Islamic-Persian literature as a disinterested, aloof beloved for whom the lover has to go through extremes. She is mysterious, cunning, and merciless. But in Farrokhzad's "On Leyli's Grave," the beloved/poetic persona is no longer perplexing and unapproachable. If "in Leyli's surreptitious eyes [. . .] night had blossomed" (9) and her feelings were unclear, in the eyes of the beloved in this poem, "the fiery flower of love has bloomed" (10). The speaker does not understand why Leyli's disinterest in love is counted as a virtue; she asks: "Who was Leili? What's the tale of her dark eyes?" (6). Unlike Leyli, the persona is active in love: she is not just a beloved; she is also a lover who meets her beloved in honesty and calls herself "the bride of lasting thoughts and imaginations" (18). Her candour results in her infamy among the crowd of people who do not accept a woman's outspokenness. The walls function as a synecdoche for the house that imprisons her and, by extension, a metonym for the society that restrains her. It is with this perception of society that the persona looks at art as a realm of infinite freedom.

"The Wall," which also lends its title to the collection, reflects the liberation inherent in artistic creation. On the surface, the poem is a feminist objection to the cultural limitations placed on women's freedom of movement, but at a deeper level, it criticizes the patriarchal view of women:

> In the hasty passing of cold moments
> Your wild eyes in their silence
> Build walls around me.
> From you I run to untrodden paths. (1–4)

It is not what Farrokhzad does or says but how she is perceived that brings about her limitation. To bypass these obstacles, she turns to a way left rather untried by her predecessors: that of poetic creation.

The critique of the male gaze and the liberating force of artistic creation introduced by Farrokhzad in her earlier poems continue in her third collection, *Rebellion*. Furthermore, in John Zubizarreta's words, this collection moves "from an acknowledged captivity to a self-conscious awareness of the nature of the particular barriers and then to a rebellious, complex struggle with wide-ranging issues of human value and human identity" (423). In other words, Farrokhzad's concern with women's freedom and her search for a female identity—formed in spite of social norms—turns into a lament about the human condition and a poetic rebellion against it. "Servitude Mutiny," "Godly Mutiny," and "God's Rebellion" are direct objections to the human condition and to the God who, detached from human experiences, maintains his power by casting fear on people and reminding them of the punishments of the day of justice. She calls herself "the child of one pleasure-filled night" (37) and the result of "a body entwined around another body" (39) that had no choice in coming into being. In "Godly Mutiny," she sees God as the "insidious laughter of death" (85) who does not understand human misery. A woman's quest for personal identity and freedom expands and becomes more inclusive: she addresses both the human condition and human identity.

It is in *Another Birth*, her fourth collection, that Farrokhzad enters a new phase of her artistic creativity and depicts the birth of a liberated and autonomous self. "Rebirth," which is a reflection on life and being, starts with this line: "My entire being is a dark chant" (1). *Ayeh*, translated here as "chant," refers to the lines of the Quran. The religious connotation of *ayeh* indicates the persona's view of herself as sacred and divine. She has built a sacred self through the projection of life in art:

> I
> Know a sad little fairy
> Who takes abode in an ocean
> And who ever so softly
> Plays her heart into a wooden flute;
> A sad little fairy
> Who dies with a single kiss every night
> And is born every morn with another. (62–69)

The persona's identity is constantly reformed through art. To use Foucauldian terminology, it is in the free space provided by art that she is able to nourish her agency and try different modes of being a self: to die and be reborn. There is also a change in the tone of the poems that address sociocultural issues. In Farrokhzad's first three collections, the poems have a predominantly personal tone. In *Another Birth*, even in the poems that specifically address women's issues, like "Windup Doll," the tone is no longer admonishing or defiant. Rather, it is descriptive of a situation in which a woman's agency can play an important role. As mentioned earlier, in "On Leyli's Grave" (from *The Wall*), Farrokhzad challenges the age-old representation of the woman as beloved; in "My Beloved" (from *Another Birth*), she goes further and both switches and surpasses the man/woman, lover/beloved dichotomies.

In the first three collections, both men and women are depicted as caught in their stereotypical gender roles, but the man in "My Beloved" is beyond masculine clichés. As Milani observes, "[a]fter centuries of posing as the lover, man finally becomes the beloved" (141). He is not a fragment of an imagination or an emotionally unavailable man too concerned with his image. He is personable and simple:

> He is wildly free
> Like a healthy instinct
> In the heart of an inhabited island.
> He cleans
> With the strips torn from Majnun's tent,
> The street's dust
> From his shoes. (23–28)

Just as she questions Leyli's portrait in an earlier poem, in "My Beloved," Farrokhzad criticizes the image of Majnun as a lover whose unrequited love has made him miserable. Not only are the man's feelings reciprocated, but he also grows in this love and, in an unprecedented turn in Persian literature, he becomes the beloved as well as the lover. "He is a simple man" who "loves purely" the simple little joys of life, "a tree / a dish of ice-cream" (50–53), and it is with this man that the persona conquers the garden of life. "The Conquest of the Garden" describes an Edenic place in which, confident about her choices and way of life, the speaker discards her doubts. Empowered by love, she has put aside all conventions:

> Everyone is afraid
> Everyone is afraid, but you and I
> Joined the lamp, water and mirror
> And we were not afraid. (12–15)

This Edenic garden is also a place of equality in which the lovers have "picked the apple / from that distant playful branch" (10–11), a place where they were not lured into picking it but chose to do so. The speaker is no longer feeling unsure or guilty. Her feelings and her intellect are in harmony with each other. Even the spear-like cry of the crow (a bird that represents an ill omen and a spreader of gossip) that flew over them and took the news of their unconventional union to the city (lines 1–5) cannot affect her. She is no longer confined within the invisible walls of tradition and norms. Her partnership and equality with the man in the matter of love, the most natural and basic relationship between the sexes, demonstrate her freedom from social and personal restrictions.

The persona's voice in the personal and social arenas is best reflected in Farrokhzad's last collection, *Let Us Believe in the Dawning of the Cold Season*, which was published posthumously. In the personal arena, the voice is that of a strong and defiant artist no longer in need of a muse; it is the voice of a woman who does not even need the security of a simple man's love and who is completely reliant on her own strength and aspirations. She asks:

> Why should I stop, why?
> The birds have flown in search of a blue dimension.
> The horizon is vertical
> The horizon is vertical and motion: fountained. ("It Is Only the Voice That Remains" 1–4)

She celebrates life, motion, and artistic creativity. The persona comes to the understanding that it is only her voice, her artistic creation, that remains and brings about her boundless freedom; accordingly, she refuses to be silenced and stopped. In "Remember the Flight," the persona presents a wholesome and formed identity. She is no longer concerned with physical limitations or engaged in the numerous aspects of her newly found freedom. She has established her identity independently:

> No one
> Will introduce me to the sun
> No one will introduce me to the sparrows' feast.
>
> Remember the flight,
> The bird is mortal. (7–11)

Outside the confining veils and borders, in the realm of artistic creation, she has constructed a personal autonomous self.

In this collection, Farrokhzad also ventures into the social arena. In the poem "I Grieve for the Garden," she combines her accessible and simple diction with allegory and symbolism and a prophetic yet innocent tone to create an urgent voice. In this poem, the garden represents the Iran of the time when the Shah, rather than expressing concern about the country's needs, was engaged in justifying his autocracy by celebrating the history of the monarchy:

> Father says:
> "It's past my time
> It's past my time
> I've carried my load
> And I've done my job"
> And in his room from dawn to dusk,
> He reads Shahnameh
> Or Nasekh-al-tavarikh.[3] (20–27)

While "Father" represents the monarchy, "Mother" stands for another important institution of power in society: religion. Mother thinks that praying and observing religious doctrines can solve all the nation's problems. To her, the garden's infection is a punishment from God for the sins and disbelief of the people—the sins that are the result of Iran's modernization and introduction to Western culture:

> Mother always looks at the bottom of things
> She seeks the signs of some transgression
> And thinks the garden is infected
> By the blasphemy of a plant. (37–40)

The brother represents the elite group of people who criticize the way modernization is imposed on the society yet remain apathetic and impractical:

> My brother calls the garden "a graveyard"
> He laughs at the confusion of herbs
> And counts
> The number of

Dead fish rotting
Under the sick surface of water. (49–54)

The sister stands in opposition to the brother, as she is mesmerized by superficial modernization and takes pleasure and pride in material affluence:

She lives on the other side of the city
Inside her fake home
With her fake goldfish
Under the loving protection of her fake husband
And under the branches of a fake apple tree
She sings fake songs
And makes natural children. (74–80)

The brother and sister represent the young generation, drowned in a modernization that is taking place on a superficial and materialistic level. But the persona, the artist woman, thinks there is a chance to save the garden that is slowly decaying:

I think the garden can be taken to the hospital
I think . . .
I think . . .
I think . . .
And the heart of the garden is swollen under the sun
And the mind of the garden is very slowly draining
Of green memories. (111–17)

The garden is left unplowed. The speaker is the only one who has confidence in the forgotten potential of the garden. The hope that the persona displays in Farrokhzad's later poetry is far from the disappointments of the speaker of her earlier poems, who had surrendered to society's expectations.

Farrokhzad's journey toward an autonomous poetic self can be traced from her early collections to her later ones. The limited and confined "I" moves toward the free, expanded, and universal "self." The representation of this free woman affected Forugh Farrokhzad's own reputation and continues to influence the reading of her poetry today. In Goli Taraqqi's words: "[T]ired of being a captive in the prison of traditions of a society which condemns her true identity and her womanhood, Farrokhzad breaks traditional and moral rules and finds her freedom in what others call 'disgrace' and 'stigma'" (54). She continues to be criticized for her nonconformity to traditional poetic forms and themes and is stigmatized for her choices in personal life. Like the persona in her poetry, Farrokhzad was excessive and restless. She had an internal urge for a life filled with pure and unprecedented moments and with experiences beyond the daily engagements and cautious uncertainty and dismay.

Through poetry, Farrokhzad recorded the progress of an artistic female self. She celebrated the experience of motherhood and, in her early works, attempted to create a balance between the outer/social role of mother and wife and the inner, personal desire to be an artist. The poems document the struggles between her inner and outer selves, her traditional responsibilities and artistic desires. In her early poetry, achieving equilibrium between these roles is close to impossible, since the persona looks at herself solely through a patriarchal lens. She is in need of the male gaze and is thoroughly dependent on it for the realization of herself and her place in the world. Farrokhzad's revolt and her declaration of independence are manifested through her support for the freedom of poetic expression, partly reflected in the sexual exposure in her poems. Poetry was the space of liberty where she explored her selfhood, defined and redefined it. Rahimi Bahmany notes that, for Farrokhzad, "self-realization is closely related to self-narration" and "non-productivity" equals "non-existence" (81). "Love" is a central theme; it is a human prerogative and highly desirable. However, its value and its effect on the human mind are equal to the value and effect of art. Art became Farrokhzad's friend; it became the love, the lover, and the beloved she had long desired. Poetry gave her strength to resist the normalizing effect of society and its negative power, and a space to try different modes of selfhood. Artistic creation and celebration of the female experience resulted in the rebirth of a persona who was not limited to gender roles dictated by society.

NOTES

1 Throughout, I quote from Farrokhzad's collected poems (*Panj Ketab*). Unless otherwise indicated, translations are my own, and numbers in parentheses refer to lines, not pages.

2 See Shoja'odin Shafa's preface to *Asir* (*The Captive*).

3 *Shahnameh* (*The Book of Kings*) is Iran's national epic written by Ferdowsi. *Nasekh-al-Tavarikh* is a multi-volume history book composed by court historian Mohammad Taghi Sepehr in the nineteenth century.

WORKS CITED

Bawer, Bruce. "Sylvia Plath and the Poetry of Confession." Bloom 7–20.

Bloom, Harold, ed. *Sylvia Plath*. Updated ed. Bloom's Modern Critical Views. New York: Infobase, 2007.

Brookshaw, Dominic Parviz, and Nasrin Rahimieh, eds. *Forugh Farrokhzad, Poet of Modern Iran: Iconic Woman and Feminine Pioneer of New Persian Poetry*. London: I. B. Tauris, 2010.

Darznik, Jasmin. "Forough Goes West: The Legacy of Forough Farrokhzad in Iranian Diasporic Art and Literature." *Journal of Middle East Women's Studies* 6.1 (2010): 103–16.

Farrokhzad, Forugh. *Panj Ketab: Majmoueh Ash'ar-e- Forugh* (Five Books: The Collected Poems of Forugh). Tehran: Shaqayeq, 1999.

Gilbert, Sandra M. "A Fine, White Flying Myth: The Life/Work of Sylvia Plath." *Shakespeare's Sisters: Feminist Essays on Women Poets*. Ed. Sandra M. Gilbert and Susan Gubar. Bloomington: Indiana UP, 1979. 245–60.

———. "'My Name Is Darkness': The Poetry of Self-Definition." *Contemporary Literature* 18.4 (1977): 443–57.

Hillmann, Michael C. *A Lonely Woman: Forugh Farrokhzad and Her Poetry*. Washington, DC: Three Continents and Mage, 1987.

Milani, Farzaneh. *Veils and Words: The Emerging Voices of Iranian Women Writers*. Syracuse, NY: Syracuse UP, 1992.

Phillips, Robert. *The Confessional Poets*. Crosscurrents/Modern Critiques. Carbondale: Southern Illinois UP, 1973.

Rahimi Bahmany, Leila. "Bewildered Mirror: Mirror, Self and World in the Poems of Forugh Farrokhzad." Brookshaw and Rahimieh 69–82.

Rosenthal, M. L. "Poetry as Confession." *Nation* 189.8 (1959): 154–155.

Shafa, Shoja'odin. Preface to Forugh Farrokhzad, *Asir* (*The Captive*). 1955. Tehran: Amir Kabir, 1973.

Simidchieva, Marta. "Men and Women Together: Love, Marriage and Gender in Forugh Farrokhzad's *Asir*." Brookshaw and Rahimieh 19–33.

Talattof, Kamran. "Personal Rebellion and Social Revolt in the Works of Forugh Farrokhzad: Challenging the Assumptions." Brookshaw and Rahimieh 83–99.

Taraqqi, Goli. *Bozorg banu-ye hasti* [*The Great Mother Archetype*]. Tehran: Nilufar, 2007.

Zubizarreta, John. "The Woman Who Sings No, No, No: Love, Freedom, and Rebellion in the Poetry of Forugh Farrokhzad." *World Literature Today* 66.3 (1992): 421–42.

CHAPTER TWO

Overcoming Gender

The Impact of the Persian Language on Iranian Women's Confessional Literature

Farideh Dayanim Goldin

The idea that language embodies patriarchal thought processes, severing women writers from the written language and from their own words, was first elaborated by the French feminist theorists Luce Irigaray and Hélène Cixous. Irigaray argues, for example, that language generally denies women a distinct subjectivity, with the result that the voice of women has largely been excluded from mainstream cultural discourse (Donovan). In this chapter, I juxtapose this theory to the obstacles faced by Iranian women writers of life narratives. Is it possible that Persian could have impeded Iranian women's literary aspirations, especially in the genre of life narratives? Conscious of the limitations of examining Iranian culture through a Western cultural gaze, I do not depend on Western theorists alone. Instead, I analyze the roots of the language as much as possible.

Many feminist critics argue that language is structured according to patriarchal thought processes, resulting in the silencing of women and the locking away of their inner thoughts. In *Beyond God the Father*, Mary Daly blames men for stealing the language and urges women to reclaim its power (8–11). Irigaray and Cixous consider language to be phallocentric, excluding and repressing women (see Tong 217–33). Cixous writes:

> I shall speak about women's writing: about *what it will do*. Woman must write her self: must write about women and bring women to writing, from which they have been driven away as violently as from their bodies—for the same reasons, by the same law, with the same fatal goal. Woman must put herself into text—as into the world and into history—by her own movement. (875)

The hypothesis that language affects thoughts and social behaviour is reflected in numerous feminist novels that attempt to overcome the phallocentric bias of language. In *Woman on the Edge of Time*, Marge Piercy replaces the pronouns *he* and *she* with *per* (124). In *Native Tongue*, Suzette Haden Elgin creates a woman-centred language, Laadan, to convey the female experience (242–63). Similarly, Doris Lessing uses Dari, a dialect of Persian, in *The Marriage Between Zones Three, Four and Five*, a novel that envisions a parallel dimension in which women initiate the creation of a utopian world. Indeed, one might think that Persian would be an ideal feminist language. In contrast to most other Indo-European languages, as well as to Arabic, a Semitic language from which it has borrowed extensively, Persian is grammatically gender-neutral. There is no generic *he* in Persian: the pronoun *u* is gender-neutral, referring to both *he* and *she*. However, the gender-neutral grammar of Persian does not mean that the language is devoid of gender bias.

GENDER BIAS IN PERSIAN

The principle of linguistic relativity, more commonly known as the Sapir-Whorf hypothesis, proposes that "the structure of the language one habitually uses influences the manner in which one thinks and behaves" (Kramsch 11).[1] If we accept this hypothesis, then gendered terminology that encodes derogatory assumptions about women actively reinforces patriarchal attitudes and power structures. On this basis, one might argue that, in the wake of the Muslim conquest of Persian in the mid-seventh century, the absorption into Persian of gender-specific features of Arabic served to encourage a bias against women in Persian culture.

According to Farideh Tehrani, in the years following the conquest, the mullahs (Muslim religious leaders) supported the change of script from Persian to Arabic in hopes that it would facilitate the learning of Arabic and hence the study of the Quran (20). With this change of script, Arabic words and word-formation processes entered Persian, with the usual consequences: some Persian vocabulary was lost, and new words entered the language via Arabic. Especially in tandem with conversion to Islam, these linguistic changes may have influenced Iranians to alter their thought processes to resemble those of their Arab conquerors, including ideas concerning women.

In "Arabic Influences on Persian Literature," de Bruijn writes, "Classical Persian literature was born in an environment dominated by Arabic culture" (369) and proposes the term *literary bilingualism* to describe the relationship of Arabic and Persian (384). In other words, it is sometimes possible to express a single idea through two different words, one Persian, the other Arabic, with each word tied to its own linguistic roots and connotations. Writing in 1946, William Haas estimated that "about 50 percent of the Persian language consists of Arabic words" (186). According to John Perry, roughly 25 percent of Persian vocabulary—half of these borrowed words—have only a feminine form (270), a good example being *bakereh*, female virgin. Although the masculine version (*baker*) exists in Arabic, it has not entered the Persian vocabulary. It is also significant that, in their feminine form, many borrowed Arabic words have negative connotations. *Za'ifeh* has been an especially damaging word for Iranian women. In its masculine form, the Arabic word *za'if* means "weak," as in being weak from an illness. Although the word has been adopted in both forms in Persian, the masculine form does not have a strong negative connotation. In fact, to be used as a negative word, *za'if* needs the help of another adjective: for example, "he is *za'if* and *bi-eradeh*" means that he is weak and lacks willpower. However, when the Arabic suffix *-eh* is added, thereby creating the feminine form, the meaning of the word changes drastically. *Za'ifeh* (the weaker one) means a female slave or wife in Arabic. In Persian, the word is often used to demean one's wife and to emphasize her lower status in society.

While such words arguably imported a negative view of women to Iran, other Arabic words convey religious morality. Numerous borrowed Arabic words carry moral assumptions and are associated with women: for example, *esmat* (purity) and *effat* (chastity) are often used as female names. With the negating prefix *bi-*, as in *bi-esmat* and *bi-effat* (impure and unchaste), these words develop into linguistic tools that work to enforce moral codes. A relatively new loanword that has been added to this collection is *hejab*, meaning a woman's head covering. Wearing the *hejab* became mandatory when the Islamic government gained power in Iran in 1979. The word has come to connote more than a piece of clothing, however:

it symbolizes women's chastity and moral purity. Again, word *bi-hejab* does not simply represent a woman without a head covering; rather, it signifies a woman who lacks moral values, since she has dared to display her hair. When used in reference to men, the same concept is considered an insult. A traveller to Shiraz during the Iran-Iraq war reported seeing a banner hung by the gates of the city on which were the words *Be shahr-e lachak be-sar-ha khosh amadid* ("Welcome to the city whose people cover their hair"), meaning a city whose inhabitants are all women, that is, a city of cowards (Dayanim 1980). This deliberate insult was used to provoke the Shirazi men into action, since they had not volunteered in great numbers for the war with Iraq.

Considered within the context of the Sapir-Whorf hypothesis, the above examples might suggest that the insertion of Arabic words into Persian led to a change of linguistic patterns, which, in turn, encouraged patriarchal values. However, other theorists disagree with the theory that Islamic culture was responsible for the introduction of a bias against women into Persian culture. Mohamad Tavakoli-Targhi asserts that many scholars have wrongly promoted pre-Islamic Iran as "a lost Utopia," in part by arguing that "the veiling of women and polygamy were non-Iranian customs promulgated by the Arabs after the conquest of Iran." As he goes on to say, "These 'historical facts' were used rhetorically . . . in order to project Iran's 'decadence' on to Arabs and Islam and introject the desirable attributes of Europeans on the pre-Islamic Self" (175). Referring to the last Iranian empire before the rise of Islam, Mary Boyce lends support to this criticism, noting that "[d]espite Zoroastrian teachings about spiritual equality, in Sasanian law women were indeed held to belong to their nearest male relatives—father, husband, brother or son" (130).

Moreover, as Herbert Clark and Eve Clark observe, "when people lack a word for a useful concept, they soon find one" (265). Therefore, it is also possible that Iranians simply adopted foreign words in ways that accorded with existing attitudes. Such beliefs are evident in the word *arusi* (wedding), a derivative of the Arabic word *arus* (bride): the implication here is that marriage is an Iranian woman's raison d'être. More telling of the traditional patriarchal attitude toward Iranian women is the word *arusak*. The addition of the diminutive suffix *-ak* at the end of *arus* changes the meaning from "a bride" to "a small bride," an inanimate object, a doll, something to play with. Traditionally, Iranian men preferred their brides as young as nine years old, malleable children who would easily conform to life in their in-laws' homes. In fact, one of the first amendments to the legal system after the Islamic Revolution reinstated the marriage age for women at nine. This preference for young girls often brought female family members together before weddings for the custom of *band-andazi*: removing the bride's body hair, including the pubic hair, which signifies a woman's maturity. The custom of early marriages was so common that satirists like 'Ali Akbar Saber (1862–1911) criticized "chauvinist men," whom he held "responsible for the degraded state in which women find themselves," as Hasan Javadi notes (211). The custom of child marriage is illustrated in a sketch titled "The Young Bride," in which a groom carries his bride home in his arms as if she were his child, as well as in "The Young Girl and Her Old Husband," which depicts a child-bride, decorated and bejewelled, shrieking at the sight of her much older husband and attempting to hide in her aunt's arms (see figs. 2.1 and 2.2).

Figure 2.1. "The Young Bride" (from the journal *Mulla Nasr al-Din*, reprinted in Javadi 223)

Additionally, Persian (unborrowed) titles and words addressing women reflect the importance of marital status for women and their dependence on men. For example, the words *zan* (a woman) and *khanom* (lady) also mean "wife." The equivalent of the title "Miss," *dushizeh*, also denotes virginity, dictating the moral code of a woman's sexual life before marriage. In other words, the acceptable status of a woman is that of eternal dependence: as a girl, on her father, and as a wife and mother, on her husband and male children. In contrast, the parallel words for men—*mard* (man), *aqa* (gentleman, Mr.), and *shohar* (husband)—are separate words, indicating men's independence and sovereignty. This dichotomy in the importance of marriage for women but not for men is also evident in Persian proverbs (*zarb-ol-masal*) that Iranians use often in their everyday speech. *Zan nadari gham nadari*, "No wife no strife," says one proverb (Haim 250). Yet another suggests the longevity of a man's sexual life: *Mard-e chel saleh tazeh aval-e chelchel-esheh*, "At the age of forty, a man only has just begun his fling" (652). In contrast, another proverb deplores the unmarried status of a young woman: *Zan keh rasid be bist be hal-esh bayad gerist*, "When a woman reaches the age of twenty, one must cry for her" (249).

Figure 2.2. "The Young Girl and Her Old Husband," from Saber, *Hop Hop Nama* (reprinted in Javadi 222)

This preoccupation with women's youth is also evident in the words used to describe old women. At best these words are neutral, as in *pir-e-zan* or *zal*. Other terms for aged females, such as *ajuzeh* (old hag, crone) and *pacheh-var-malideh* (old pest) have negative connotations. An old Persian proverb says: *Pir zan namord ta ruze barani*, "The old woman would not die, and when she did, it was on a rainy day, an inconvenient day" (148). In contrast, aging and old age have positive connotations for men. For example, *pir-e-mard* (an old man) is also *rish sefid* (white-bearded), connoting a leader whose advanced age is synonymous with experience and wisdom. In fact, the word *rish* (beard) is the root of many words that suggest dignity, credit, experience, and wisdom. *Rish sefid* (white-bearded) can also mean "a wise man, an "elder"; *rish nadashtan* (not to have beard), "to lack dignity"; *rish dar asiab sefeed kardan* (to have one's beard made white in a flour mill), "to lack experience"; and the list goes on. In comparison, the only word that refers to a woman's body hair is *gis-borideh*, meaning "the one whose hair is cut off, a shameless woman."

There are yet other words in Persian that imply a difference in status between men and women. For example, whereas the word *zan* (woman) is, at best, neutral, the word *mard* (man) connotes many positive qualities. To be a *mard* is to be strong, generous, humane, and capable; *na-mard* (not to be a man) is therefore to be inhuman or a coward. Moreover, the word *mard* has been used to compensate for the lack of a gender-specific pronoun. Ferdowsi, the famous Iranian epic poet of the tenth century, employs the term in a generic sense in a famous poem often used by Iranians as a proverb:

> *Zeniru bovad mard ra rasti*   *ze sosti dorugh ayad o kasti*
> Strength brings man truthfulness, while falsehood creates weakness. (Haim 250)

The choice of the word *mard* betrays patriarchal habits of thought: women are denied the attributes of strength and truthfulness. It seems ironic that Ferdowsi would use a masculine word in this way, given that in composing his great Persian national epic, *Shahnameh*, he strove to cleanse the language of Arabic words.

Borrowings from Arabic also reflect the expectation that women belong within domestic (rather than public) space and that they should be silent and submissive. For example, a woman who is *khyaban-gard* (who roams the streets) or *harjaii* (who has known many places) is a prostitute. Women are not to speak too much: a noisy and chaotic room is compared to *hamam-e zananeh*, a communal bath for women, a place where women traditionally socialized and gossiped. A *zan-e zaban deraz*, a woman with a long tongue, is a woman who cannot stop talking and is therefore to be avoided. When a woman answers back, rather than remaining quiet and docile, she is a *patiareh*, a shrew, an argumentative woman. A woman who dares to observe, who does not look down, is a *chashm darideh*, a woman with "torn eyes," the result of her habit of opening them too often or too wide. In addition, women need to be kept under control. A Persian proverb says, *Zan-e saliteh sag-e b-qalladeh ast*, "A woman who is a bitch is a dog uncontrolled by a collar," while another proverb reminds men, *Zan-e saliteh shohar-e mard ast*, "A woman who is a bitch rules her husband—she is the husband" (Haim 249). In *Shahnameh*, Ferdowsi enumerates the necessary qualifications for the ideal woman:

> Three qualities make a woman
> Fit for the throne of superiority
>
> The first is her *sharm* and her wealth
> With which to adorn her husband's house
>
> The second is her procreation of auspicious sons
> Who will increase her husband's delight
>
> The third is her face and her figure
> Coupled with her covered hair. (535; qtd. in Milani, *Veils and Words* 52)

On the basis of the evidence that has come down to us, it is not possible to draw definitive conclusions about the origin of patriarchal attitudes in Persian culture. Although it may be that contact with Arabic enabled and encouraged the expression of such attitudes, it is also quite likely that these attitudes were present in the culture, at least to some degree, prior to the Arab conquest. One way or another, though, despite its gender-neutral grammar, Persian is today replete with words, phrases, and proverbial sayings that reflect and reinforce patriarchal values. Whether borrowed or constructed as compound words and phrases, these features of Persian serve either to discriminate against women or simply to exclude them. As part of the foundation of a culture and its thought processes, patriarchal language has the power to kill women's creative thoughts and words.

FORBIDDEN FEELINGS: IRANIAN WOMEN AND POETRY

Michel Foucault writes that "in every society the production of discourse is at once controlled, selected, organised and redistributed according to a certain number of procedures" (216)—rules that serve the purposes of exclusion. As he explains, "We know perfectly well that we are not free to say just anything, that we cannot simply speak of anything, when we like or where we like; not just anyone, finally, may speak of just anything" (216). Language, in other words, gives privileged or exclusive rights to selected members of the society to speak and to exercise control over discourse. Iranian women autobiographers have had a dual obstacle to overcome: the existence, in Persian, of language that demeans women and inherited cultural taboos against sharing personal stories.

Given that Arabic is linguistically unrelated to Persian, it is often very difficult for Iranians to pronounce Arabic words. As a result, formal Persian, which is used in literature and in writing generally, contains a great many more Arabic words than does the spoken language. Moreover, as David Crystal points out, "One of the most important functions of language variations is to enable individuals to identify with a social group or to separate themselves from it" (42). As Iranians writers came under pressure to include Arabic words as a mark of literary sophistication and to accept Islamic values as standard codes of morality, not only did literary Persian diverge from the spoken language, but men came to rule the realm of literature, while women remained silent behind culturally imposed walls.

In addition, under the autocratic dynasties that ruled many generations of Iranians, wrong words could destroy lives. Even in more prosperous times—during the reign of Mohammed Reza Shah Pahlavi (1941–79), for example—the members of the secret service, SAVAK, penetrated every corner of Iranian lives, forcing parents to teach their children from a very young age not to trust even their closest friends. Words were dangerous tools. Iranians, therefore, learned to be discreet. "[S]erious writers," Rivanne Sandler notes, "made use of allegory and symbolism and allusion, even vague writing that could be taken in a hundred different ways, to say what they had to say." She adds, "Their readers, after all, had had a long apprenticeship in deciphering evasive and symbolic language" (249). The language became so indirect that the speaker could deny its content as needed. Circuitous expression became a part of the culture to the point where even parents and children had to speak indirectly and tentatively. Consequently, candidness, the core of autobiographical writing, came to be considered unacceptable and rude, and even became dangerous.

In her autobiography *Daughter of Persia*, Sattareh Farman Farmaian writes of her meeting with a minister of education concerning the expansion of a social services school of which she was a founder. Political and social stagnation in Iran forbade them to talk directly of business matters. Instead, the government official spoke through "allegories and examples from history" (274). Articulate Iranians adopted this style of ambiguity in order to guard the private realm. In fact, in contrast to English, a well-spoken Iranian has traditionally been not one who communicates directly, using the fewest words possible, but rather one who can hide the message in a web of poetry (*zarb-ol masal*), stories, and allegories. It is up to the listener to decipher and disambiguate the message from the long, indirect speech.

This pressure to use indirect language separated women further from involvement in society. Unable to voice discontent, they suppressed their thoughts. Farman Farmaian, for example, remembers her mother demanding that good girls control their tongues. "For this reason," she writes, "I learned not to reveal my heart in my speech." She goes on to say: "By the time I was ten [. . .] I had become accustomed to shutting my feelings" (19). Recollecting her childhood, Farman Farmaian expresses the same sentiment that so many Western feminists have articulated: there were no acceptable words in her native tongue to express her sense of frustration and her thoughts, even to her own mother. Similarly, in her novel *Zendegi bayad kard* (*One Must Live*), Mansoureh Etehadi quotes a grandmother's words of advice to her crying teenaged granddaughter, Zari: "A respected woman would never allow her feelings to surface!" (24). At the same time, the grandmother is proud of Zari's *khuy-e aram va sar be zir*, her timidity and shyness, which contrasts with her outspoken mother's unacceptable air of independence and openness (20). The indirectness and formality of Persian suppressed Iranians, in general, and women, in particular, from self-expression in both life and literature.

However, the same system of ambiguous and indirect communication may have ultimately helped Iranian women. They disguised their literary creativity as a simple means of communication. Kate Millet's book *Going to Iran* contains a picture of an Iranian woman demonstrator at the beginning of Khomeini's reign holding a placard that reads (210):

> *Dar tolu-e azadi*
> *Jaye to zan khali*

"In the sunrise of freedom," the rhymed couplet declares, "a woman's place is forgotten." These simple lines, undoubtedly created at the last minute for the freedom march, illustrate how Iranians often turn to poetry to communicate a strong message that, if stated directly, would be less effective, and possibly even offensive, to Iranian ears. Poetry thus allowed for the expression of self in a way that would have been impossible for women in direct, simple words.

One of the earliest female poets in Iran was Aqabaji, the wife of the Iranian king Fatali-shah Qajar. In Moshir-Salimi's *Zanan-e sokhanvar*, she is portrayed as a beautiful woman who had many suitors (1: 349–53). She was married off to the king, who had a harem of 150 wives. On the wedding night, the king visited her in the bridal chamber, the *hejleh*, but left after a few minutes without consummating the marriage, for unknown reasons. Terribly hurt, Aqabaji decided to leave for her father's house. This made the king angry: he ordered her not to leave the *andarun*, the inner quarters. Being afraid to speak directly to her husband, Aqabaji instead composed a poem for him:

Yaram shab amad, shab mand o shab ham raft
Hich namidanam omram cheguneh amad o cheguneh raft

My beloved came to me at night, but also left at night
I don't know what became of my life, how I found and how I lost it. (1: 350)

The poem softened the king's heart. She was allowed to go back to her family, and she remained a virgin the rest of her life.

Another early female poet, Tuni, also complained to her husband through her poetry. She was born in Shiraz but her birth and death dates are unknown. Her story, as it appears in Moshir-Salimi's *Zanan-e sokhanvar* (2: 148), portrays a woman of extraordinary humour and command of words. When she discovered her husband's infidelity and homosexual relationship with a lover, she wrote a poem about her deep emotional wounds and left it on her husband's pillow. He was embarrassed and returned to her, realizing that his wife's chastity had not allowed her to talk of such subjects directly. In this way, the restriction on women's freedom of expression led to the emergence of Iranian women poets.

Classical Persian poetry reflected this social appreciation for indirectness. The love poetry often spoke to an ideal figure, genderless and distant. Hillmann points out that in classical poetry, "poetic speakers are male, of course. But, for the most part, so are the beloveds addressed and described" (*Iranian Culture* 146). About the construction of Iranian "lyric poetry," or *ghazal*, Heshmat Moayyad writes:

> The tacit acceptance of amorous feelings toward male companions, combined with the inferior social status and seclusion of women in Islamic Iran, discouraged men from expressing positive feelings for women, naming their names,

publicly associating with them, or treating them as equals. Under such circumstances, how could a poet talk about his love for a woman . . . ? (137)

In essence, women were barred not only from writing poetry but also from becoming poetic subjects. However, this style of love poetry with its gender confusion eventually enabled the development of women's poetry.

By the beginning of the twentieth century, women, like Parvin E'tesami, had composed many poems covering subjects such as motherly love, friendship, and the traits of a chaste wife. Women composed poetry to show the importance of education for girls and young women—quite a revolutionary message. Women composed poetry to reveal their suffering and to plead for consideration from men. They avoided, however, writing about their personal feelings and concentrated instead on didactic and moral issues. In a place where the pen was often viewed as a weapon of corruption, it is amazing that Iranian women managed to write at all. The writings of these courageous women resulted in a literary tradition that paved the way for the most talented poets of twentieth-century Iran.

It was not until the middle of the twentieth century, however, that the classical mould of women's poetry was broken. Forugh Farrokhzad crossed the boundaries of both the language and the culture, writing in a simple, colloquial style, rather than in the classical language of poetry, and giving voice to her outrage against the restrictions imposed on women in Iranian society. In her autobiographical poetry, she wrote openly about sexual desire and physical love, or what Farzaneh Milani calls "feminine lust" (145), transforming women into active participants in erotic encounters. In the opening stanza of "Mashuq-e man" ("My Beloved"), for example, the man's body is described through the eyes of the woman, rather than the other way around:

My lover
with naked, shameless body
on his strong legs
stood like death. (Ranjbaran 50)

The inversion of culturally sanctioned gender roles is evident even in the title of this famous poem, "Mashuq-e man." In classical Persian poetry, male poets used *mashuqeh*, the feminine form of the Arabic loanword *mashuq*, to refer to the female beloved. As the "beloved," the *mashuqeh*, women were depicted as the passive objects of the poet's sexual desires. Women were absent as active lovers, their desires unknown, unthinkable. In "My Beloved," Farrokhzad brazenly claims possession of her male partner, her *mashuq*, making him the object of her own sexual passion.

Elsewhere, like Ferdowsi, Farrokhzad used the words *zan* (woman) and *mard* (man) to mark the gender in her poetry. In "Nagshe penhan" ("The Hidden Plan"), for example, she again suggests that the traditionally submissive female—the "crazy" victim of male desire—is herself alive with sexuality:

ah, ey mardi keh labha-ye mara	Oh, you man who my lips
az sharar-e buseha suzandeh-I	You have set on fire with your kisses
gofteand an zan zani divaneh ast	They say that that woman is crazy
kaz labanash buseh asan midahad	Because kisses are easily taken.
ari, ama buseh az labhaye to	Yes, but kisses from your lips,
bar labane morde-am jan midahad	Give life to my lifeless lips.
(Farrokhzad 115–16)	

Appalled by Farrokhzad's daring, open poetry that exhibited her unbridled sexuality, Qaem Maqami, like many other critics, criticized Farrokhzad for "shamelessly" displaying her sexuality (149), suggesting that she had wasted her talent on "lewd" poetry when she could have tried to improve society as E'tesami had (150). But Farrokhzad continued her writing despite such criticism. In "The Sin," Farrokhzad openly admits to committing adultery:

gonah kardam gonahi por ze lezat	I sinned a sin full of pleasure,
kenare peykari larzan o madhush	Next to a shaking, stupefied form.
khodavanda che midanam che kardam	O God, who knows what I did
dar an khalvatgah-e tarik o khamush	in that dark and quiet seclusion.
(qtd. in Hillmann, A Lonely Woman, 77)	

Rosemarie Tong suggests that one strategy for combatting patriarchy, proposed by Luce Irigaray, is "to mime the mimes men have imposed on women. If women exist only in men's eyes, in images, women should take those images and reflect them back to men in magnified proportions" (228). In a similar fashion, Farrokhzad reversed the image of woman in Persian poetry, daring to manifest herself as a complete human being with a full range of desires. Farrokhzad was fortunate to live during the reign of Mohammed Reza Pahlavi, who granted an unprecedented degree of freedom to Iranian women. Although she was criticized, she was not prosecuted, exiled, or forbidden to publish her poetry. She was allowed to have an impact and a voice. In her brief life—she died in a car accident in February 1967, at the age of thirty-two—she freed poetry to move in new directions, paving the way for autobiographical writing that reveals a woman's life and inner thoughts.

Commenting on Persian literature in 1975, the Iranian scholar Sa'id Nafisi wrote that "the artist has always preferred imagination to observation" (15–16), thus excluding the art of memoir, of self-revelation and observation of one's personal life, from the artistic realm. Similarly, a decade after the Revolution of 1979, other scholars of Iranian women writers lamented the rarity of autobiographies and even biographies by Iranians, and fewer still by Iranian women. In a 1990 essay, for example, Farzaneh Milani wrote, "Granted the part played by humility, self-censorship, discretion, and unfavorable living conditions, the fact remains that whereas male writers have produced a handful of life narratives, no woman literary figure has ever published an autobiography" ("Veiled Voices" 10). Two years later, she reaffirmed that statement: "Avoiding voluntary self-revelation and self-referentiality, most Iranian writers have turned their backs on autobiography" (*Veils and Words* 201). That same year, William Hanaway went even further to suggest that maybe autobiography was a culture-bound genre, "too Western-centered and culture-bound for Iranians to make use of it" (62) and that, as a literary genre, life narrative simply did not interest Iranians. These critics pointed to the continuing political oppression of freedom of speech and literary expression, the indirect style of writing in Persian, and the spiritual veiling of women as the factors responsible for this absence of literary memoirs.[2]

Iranian Women's Life Narratives

One might expect that the reversal of women's legal rights and independence that accompanied the Revolution of 1979 would indeed work to silence women's literary voices. However, in the decades following the Revolution, women in Iran have published a large number of short stories and novels. Once a genre rarely attempted by women, prose literature now attracts numerous female writers. More significantly, although most female Iranian writers historically resorted to evasion and ambiguity, in the decades following the Revolution women have dared to write confessional narratives—perhaps the most self-revealing and direct form of literature. Since 1990, the year that the articles by Milani and Hanaway appeared, the situation has thus changed quite dramatically, calling into question the argument that Iranian culture does not lend itself to life narratives.

Iranians often use the Persian word *khaterat* somewhat casually to refer to any autobiographical narrative. *Khaterat* can include Forugh Farrokhzad's books of poetry, or Homa Sarshar's *In the Back Alleys of Exile* (1993), a two-volume collection of essays and poetry, or Zohreh Sullivan's *Exiled Memories: Stories of Iranian Diaspora* (2001), a documentation of her interviews or "story gathering" (xiii)—all very valuable books, although not literary life narratives. Also categorized as *khaterat* are memoirs written mostly by members of the Qajar and Pahlavi royal families: for example, Ashraf Pahlavi's *Faces in a Mirror: Memoirs from Exile* (1980) and Farah Pahlavi's *An Enduring Love: My Life with the Shah* (2004), as well as Soraya Esfandiari's *Le palais des solitudes* (1991) and Satareh Farman Farmaian's *Daughter of Persia* (1992). These memoirs—some produced with the help of another author—quite obviously seek to present a particular version of history.[3] Supposedly written to correct misunderstandings, they interpret events in a way that flatters the author. In addition, *Khaterat-e Tajol Moluk* (*The Memoirs of Tajol Moluk*), allegedly the autobiography of Reza Shah Pahlavi's wife, and Farideh Diba's *My Daughter, Farah*, are actually forgeries, published to achieve the political aim of discrediting the Pahlavis. On her website, Farah Pahlavi—the wife of Mohammed Reza Pahlavi, the last shah of Iran—warns readers that *The Memories of Mrs. Farideh Diba*, a memoir supposedly written by her mother, is a "fabrication by malicious people" (Pahlavi). All the same, in a convoluted way, these works affirm that memoirs by Iranian women find an audience. In addition, some sixteen books have appeared that are actually literary memoirs, eight of which were published between 2003 and 2005. This surge of self-revelation is impressive. In the following pages, I examine the circumstances that enabled these women to write in a genre that has traditionally been the most forbidding in Iranian literature.

In the 1920s, a Qajar princess, Taj al-Saltana, wrote an account of her life, *Khaterat-e Taj al-Santana*. The volume was not published during her lifetime, as Golbarg Bashi notes ("'Boom' in Prose" 8), and quite possibly the writer may never intended it for publication. Nonetheless, her memoir—subsequently translated into English under the title *Crowning Anguish*—stands not only as the first effort of an Iranian woman to record her autobiography but as one of the few originally written in Persian. For the most part, however, virtually all literary memoirs by Iranian women have been written not in Persian but in languages of exile. Although Marjane Satrapi, famous for using the medium of comics for her two

Persepolis volumes, and the lesser known Ladane Azernour and Nahal Tajadod write in French, the preferred literary language of these memoirists is English.

Why would any writer choose a language other than her own to tell the story of her people, her own story? There are, of course, commercial considerations: these memoirs reach wider audiences if written in English. Azar Nafisi's *Reading Lolita in Tehran*, for example, a bestseller in the United States, could also have inspired other Iranian women to record and publish their life narratives in languages other than Persian. Moreover, even if it is not the spoken language, English is understood in many areas of the world, especially since it has become the language of computer technology and international business. Anita Desai, an Indian author, said that to her, English is "the key to a world literature" (Desai, Phillips, and Stavans 80). But perhaps the unprecedented number of life narratives created by Iranian women in exile also reflects their comfort with English and French as languages that are more suitable for carrying their voices, languages not delimited by Iranian cultural boundaries. At the same time, through writing memoirs, the new generation of hybrid Iranians, who often do not read Persian but are fluent in English, are able to connect with their parents' experiences of Iran.

The Iranian Revolution of 1979 provided the foundation for almost all these memoirs, propelled as they were by the shock of displacement, the longing for a lost homeland, and the suffering of those left behind. Moreover, the nostalgia among Iranians in exile and the curiosity of Westerners about Iran reinforce this momentum. Away from their homeland and in the languages of their exile, Iranian women memoirists write of a world lost to them. My memoir *Wedding Song* was originally a collection of stories written for my daughters, who wanted to know about their mother's life in a country they have never visited. The cover page to Shusha Guppy's *The Blindfold Horse* describes the book as an "evocation of a way of life that has been destroyed forever." In *Snake's Marble*, Mehry Reid expresses the hope that her "memoirs will help keep those [Iranian] traditions alive in the minds and hearts of Persians wherever they might be" (cover page). Her first chapter, in fact, is named "Window to the Past." Reid writes, "For many years, I thought about writing the memoirs of my childhood, but when my daughter . . . told me that she was carrying my first grandchild, this was the catalyst that got me started. I wanted to leave for him and his descendants a family history of sorts and a feeling for the customs, traditions, and way of life of the country where half of his forebears were born" (ix). In their zeal to recapture the Iran they knew for their children, many Iranian women memoirists tend to record parts of their past, or rather Iran's past, as if for an encyclopedia, reaching back to the Iran that is forbidden to many, trying to paint it with words. The popularity of women's memoirs in the West has enabled these Iranian women writers, who are often well read in Western literature, to treasure seemingly mundane details of life. The custom of cleaning sour grapes for Passover or visiting women's *hamam* in *Wedding Song*, the *sizdeh-bedar* picnic in Gelareh Asayesh's *Saffron Sky*, and "Sleeping on the rooftops under the desert sky," the recipe for Nowruz food of *sabzi-polo* and dried fish in Rouhi Shafii's *Scent of Saffron* are common scenes in Iranian women's memoirs. These women show the importance not just of historical events but also of everyday life, home details, and women's work. Women's memoirs celebrate women's worlds (Goldin, "Iranian Women" 32).

Throughout most of Iranian literary history, modesty and secrecy prevented Iranian women from recording their life narratives. Writing about self can also be frightening; it has consequences. Life narratives cannot possibly explain the author's life without involving other family members and friends. Even before I decided to write a book about my life, I received messages from family members threatening lawsuits if I spoke about family matters in my lectures. When Firoozeh Dumas told her father that she was writing a memoir, he responded, "Great! Just don't mention our name" (63). We have imported to the West the taboo against speaking and writing candidly from our Iranian past. However, although Iranian women traditionally shied away from writing, and especially from writing memoirs, telling of one's own or ancestral lives has always been a part of Iranian women's oral tradition. I remember vividly the winter nights when my mother, grandmother, and aunts gathered around a space heater, sharing life stories of women's past and present.

This tradition of storytelling has inspired many contemporary Iranian-American women fiction writers. For example, Gina Nahai started writing her first novel, *Cry of the Peacock*, after a summer she spent at home, often in the kitchen with her mother, grandmother, and aunt listening to them retell old stories of life in Iran, of events in the lives of family members and neighbours (Nahai). However, recording these stories in the form of nonfiction required time away from Iranian cultural sensibilities. Nahid Rachlin, an Iranian-American fiction writer, contemplated fictionalizing her life story (Rachlin). Undoubtedly, the publications of life narratives by other Iranian women encouraged Rachlin to write her own memoir, *Persian Girls*. As with many other women writers, she had to overcome the fear of baring her soul, of sharing her private life. In *When Memory Speaks*, Jill Ker Conway asserts, "For the woman autobiographer the major question becomes how to see one's life whole when one has been taught to see it as expressed through family and bonds with others" (4). The amazing explosion of memoir writing by Iranian women in recent years could be a consequence of the fact that, in Jill Ker Conway's terminology, we are finally willing to take "agency" for our life stories (14). We realize that our stories do matter, that these *khaterat*, these memories, are worth the risk.

Another factor has been the West's curiosity about a country that was labelled an "axis of evil" by the Bush administration. In response to the West's increasing curiosity about Iran, it has become possible to write a life narrative that is not merely confessional but conveys a political message. Such autobiographies allow rare glimpses of life through a lens largely uncoloured by the stereotypes promoted in Western media. Describing the writing of Firoozeh Dumas, the author of *Funny in Farsi*, Congcong Zheng writes:

> In the face of cultural differences, we have a choice. We can either choose to be cosmopolitan; accepting and welcoming the differences, or choose resistance, fear, and isolation from others. Ms. Dumas chooses the former, showing readers that our similarities far outweigh our differences. Her life experiences reflect that our similarities are what bind us together and that our differences can make us smile and sometimes laugh out loud. Diversity makes this world beautiful, amazing, and exciting, not scary. (12)

In a similar vein, in a review of Marjane Satrapi's *Persepolis*, Jumana Farouky comments, "From the start, Satrapi makes it clear that her mission is to dispel the Western notion of Iran as a land of fundamentalists and terrorists." Indeed, Satrapi takes pride in her Iranian heritage, imploring "all Iranians who say they love Iran to show it. I ask that those Iranians who are now hyphenated to always remember their heritage because everything we are today comes from our culture" (Ahkami and Ahkami 57). Speaking about *Persepolis* in an interview with the *Los Angeles Times*, Satrapi said, "I wrote this book to give the image of Iran that I knew." She added, "Anytime I was outside my country and saw pictures of Iran, it was pictures of women in chadors and guys with guns" (Saidi). In the book, Satrapi portrays her parents as Westernized intellectuals: her mother wears pants, not a chador, and her father shaves his beard despite the Islamic rules enforced in Iran.

To alleviate the West's fear of the Islamic Republic of Iran, many writers look for metaphorical images to reveal the Western side of Iran, showing the familiar, friendlier aspects of the country and recognizing that Iranians are often victims themselves. In *The Dance of the Rose and the Nightingale*, Nesta Ramazani uses "metaphors of movement," images of ballet, to fuse Iranian and Western traditions. Marjane Satrapi's comic-strip memoir displays many shared cultural emblems: a denim jacket with a Michael Jackson button, Nikes, and Western music—the BeeGees, Pink Floyd, and Stevie Wonder. Firoozeh Dumas, in *Funny in Farsi*, mingles her parents' Iranian ways, like their arranged marriage when her mom was seventeen, with their learned and practiced American lifestyle: for example, Firoozeh's adventures in babysitting or her father's affinity for forbidden ham. Azar Nafisi also brings her readers closer to Iranian life through her books. The message is, "We are more like you than you think. We are the same people, also the victims of Islamic fundamentalism and theocracy."

But can the language of the West, with its preconceived notions of Iranian culture and women—a language based on a Western patriarchal construct that views the East, including Iran, through distorted lenses—be used as the medium to define and defend Iranian culture and thoughts? About women's autobiographies, Jill Ker Conway writes: "If the autobiographer gazes at himself in the mirror of culture, just as the portrait painter must when working on his self-portrait, how should a woman use a mirror derived from the male experience?" (4). For Iranian women autobiographers, this question is doubly treacherous. How can they possibly write of their Iranian experiences through the prism of Western culture? At the same time, contemporary Iranian women memoirists have earned international recognition and wide readership because they write in a language that is widely read, a language that is probably more comfortable for them. Most Iranian women memoirists received a Western-style education. Azar Nafisi spent her high school years in England and received her higher education from Oklahoma University; Marjane Satrapi left for Vienna at age fourteen and finished her education in France; Gelareh Asayesh emigrated to the United States at age fifteen, Firoozeh Dumas at age seven; and Nesta Ramazani was sent to a boarding school in England as a child and later went to an English-speaking Presbyterian school in Tehran. Three decades after the Revolution, and living in exile, these women are at ease with their adopted languages and cultures. Their children have been raised to speak English or French with little or no Iranian accent. In their writings, female Iranian memoirists embrace the languages of their adopted countries, languages that do not constrain them.

But can these memoirs really be considered Iranian? Can a writer be Iranian if she does not write—or even worse, cannot write—in Persian? At a conference in 2004, the poet Simin Behbahani told her Iranian audience that they were not exactly Iranians any longer; that they had created a unique, hybrid culture of their own.[4] The question remains, however: have these hybrid writers turned their backs on their culture by forsaking their language? I asked Azar Nafisi if she had ever considered writing her memoir in Persian. She replied:

> I wanted to write this story when I lived in Iran, but I could not. There were many reasons why this book could not be written in Iran, not all of it political. There were too many restraints, too many rules, imposed by the government and many of the readers. I don't know if I would have written the same story, in the same style; even the language you write in can decide the way your book is shaped, but I know I had the same urges when I was in Iran.

In the same interview, I asked her if she would like her memoirs to be translated into Persian. She replied that she did, "but I want to have control over the translation. It is translatable as far as any book is. It is so difficult to capture the nuances, the lights and shades of a book in another language." Similarly, when asked about translating her book into Persian, Satrapi replied, "I will translate it myself" (Ahkami and Ahkami 55). However, that has yet to become reality. Of all these memoirs, only *Funny in Farsi* has been translated into Persian (albeit with slight censorship), perhaps because of its optimistic, positive view of Iranians. It is doubtful that most other memoirs, including and especially Nafisi's, would pass the strict cultural, political, and linguistic barriers to translation and publication in Iran. For now, memoirs by Iranian-American women writers survive and thrive in exile only. And so do their authors, who are making sure that their voices are heard and are thereby creating a literary canon of their own.

SILENCING IRANIAN WOMEN'S VOICES IN ENGLISH: AZAR NAFISI AND HER CRITICS

The attention given to memoirs written by women of Iranian heritage increased considerably with Azar Nafisi's bestseller, *Reading Lolita in Tehran*. Highly acclaimed by American critics, her voice is probably the loudest among all Iranian-American women memoirists. Her book, written in the language of exile, presents Western literature (mostly authored by "dead white men") as a contrast to the Iranian mentality in post-revolutionary Iran, especially in describing women's lives. Iranian critics did not receive the book as enthusiastically as did American reviewers. Fatemeh

Keshavarz gained fame by including the name of Nafisi's bestselling book in the title of her own memoir, *Jasmine and Stars: Reading More Than Lolita in Tehran*. Keshavarz sharply criticizes Nafisi's adoration of Western books while neglecting Persian literature. After summarizing much of Shahrnush Parsipur's *Women Without Men*, Keshavarz states that *Reading Lolita in Tehran* "does not mention Parsipur even in passing" (106). She also disapproves of Nafisi's presumed negative portrayal of Iranian men: "*Reading Lolita in Tehran* . . . presents fathers, brothers, and uncles primarily as a menacing group of people" (61–62). Keshavarz claims to bring the reader "an in-depth critical understanding of this eyewitness literature, which I dub the New Orientalist narrative" (2). She further chastises Nafisi: "I am interested in the making and impact of the perspective that RLT [*Reading Lolita in Tehran*], and works of its kind, represent. As a teacher and scholar of literature, I feel we should take very seriously the distorting and *silencing power* that such texts exercise on our culture and society" (7; my emphasis). Although Nafisi has largely remained silent about Keshavarz's criticism, she seems to have answered back in her subsequent memoir, *Things I've Been Silent About*, in which she demonstrates her knowledge and enjoyment of Persian literature. Additionally, presumably to refute Keshavarz's claim about her negative view of Iranian men, she shows unconditional love and support for her father despite his numerous infidelities in his marriage to Nafisi's mother.

However, Keshavarz is not the only critic who calls Nafisi a "New Orientalist" (4). In his scathing criticism of Nafisi's book, Hamid Dabashi blasts the author for advancing the cause of the United States, "the virtual empire," which lacks "long-term memory" of its colonizing actions around the world:

> A particularly powerful case of such selective memories is now fully evident in an increasing body of mémoire by people from an Islamic background that has over the last half a decade, ever since the commencement of its "War on Terrorism," flooded the US market. This body of literature, perhaps best represented by Azar Nafisi's *Reading Lolita in Tehran* (2003), ordinarily points to legitimate concerns about the plight of Muslim women in the Islamic world and yet put[s] that predicament squarely at the service of the US ideological psy-op, militarily stipulated in the US global warmongering. (2)

Dabashi adds that "*Reading Lolita in Tehran* promotes the cause of 'Western Classics' at a time when decades of struggle by postcolonial, black and Third World feminists, scholars and activists has finally succeeded to introduce a modicum of attention to world literatures" (3). As legitimate as Dabashi's arguments might be, they also question Nafisi's right to write in her area of expertise, the literature of the West—yes, the literature of "dead white men." Even as a feminist, especially as a feminist, one cannot deny Nafisi the right to her voice, the right to speak about her Iranian students' enthusiasm to glean from her knowledge. She was, after all, a teacher of Western literature in Tehran. That was what she taught then; that is what she teaches now.

No memoir can include the entirety of a person's life and thoughts. To make sense, to be effective, a life narrative has to focus on a few elements of the author's life. Thus, Nafisi's first book explains her teaching of Western literature in Tehran, and her second focuses on her family life as a child and a young woman. In a chapter titled "Policing Truth," feminist theorist Leigh Gilmore writes: "When a writer is seen in relation to the dominant discourses of power s/he was simultaneously inscribing and resisting, the 'innocence' of autobiography as a naïve attempt to tell a universal truth is radically particularized by a specific culture's notion of what truth is, who may tell it, and who is authorized to judge it" (107). Dabashi claims that Nafisi betrays the efforts of "feminists," "scholars," and "activists" in order to promote "Orientalist" viewpoints; she is an agent of the West. However, one might also consider the fact that the efforts referred to by Dabashi do not intend to obliterate those literatures but rather to expand them and to make room for analysis of all literatures. That defines, after all, freedom of speech, even when we disagree. Edward Said describes Orientalism as a "style of thought based upon an ontological and epistemological distinction made between 'the Orient' and (most of the time) 'the occident'" (2). He further defines Orientalism as "a Western style for dominating, restructuring, and having authority over the Orient" (3). This is the argument Dabashi uses against Nafisi. A similar article by Mitra Rastegar, "Reading Nafisi in the West," also criticizes Nafisi's portrayal of women in Iran. Rastegar believes that Nafisi views "the 'West' as modern, rational, and dynamic and opposed to an 'East' that is static" (108). Similarly, inspired by Keshavarz, Laetitia Nanquette criticizes the autobiographical voices of two French-Iranian writers, Ladane Azernour and Chahdortt Djavann. Calling their books "new orientalist narratives," she writes,

> The end of the 1990s marks a change in Iranian cultural tradition, represented in the mass publication of memoirs by writers and intellectuals, a genre that was previously restricted to political figures. One can link this shift to the decline of the Iranian tradition of collectivism and the new direction toward individualism. It happened as a result of contact with the West, especially

> among Iranians living abroad. The "nobodies" of the Iranian diaspora, a term used by Lorraine Adams, have thus awakened, mainly in North America, to publish their lives. (269)

She concludes, "I hope that this article raises an awareness of French new orientalist narratives' flaws and dangers, as an attempt to *stop* them from flourishing in the French publishing market as they have flourished in the American one" (279; my emphasis). Although Rastegar, Dabashi, Keshavarz, and Nanquette make valid points, I wonder whether in exile, we have come to be overly protective of our *vatan*, the country we have left behind. In our Western enclaves that are second homes for now-hyphenated Iranian-Americans, we struggle with a "newly created culture outside Iran," in the words of Simin Behbahani. Should we feel guilty for having abandoned those still in Iran? Does such "guilt" forbid the voice of discontent against anything Iranian? If so, women's voices are silenced yet again.

IRANIAN WOMEN MEMOIRISTS: WILL THEY EVER WRITE IN PERSIAN?

Commenting on Persian literature in 1975, the Iranian scholar Sa'id Nafisi wrote that "the artist has always preferred imagination to observation" (15–16), thereby effectively excluding the art of memoir, of self-revelation and observation of one's personal life, from the Persian artistic realm. In an interview in 2008 for *Pars Arts: Iranian Diaspora Life/Culture/Identity*, Sepideh Saremi asked Shahrnush Parsipur for her thoughts on the English-language memoirs written by Iranian woman in recent years and on what appears to be a gradual shift toward fiction. Parsipur responded,

> Though I read many female authors, it's mostly Persian work. I am aware that many women write memoirs, and I think this is because writing fiction is very scary. Writing fiction is like being a god. Getting to this point is a little difficult. Women are tiptoeing to this creativity by putting down their memories first. They write their memoirs, and when the fears go away, they can write stories.

Perhaps for her own reasons, Parsipur does not comment on the dearth of memoirs written in Persian by Iranian women. Her own recollection of her lengthy imprisonment, in *Khaterat-e zendan* (*Prison Memoirs*), is banned in Iran. "Living in Los Angeles today, I think back," she wrote in her memoir, recalling that, in Iran, "the laws were such that they turned a person into stone—silent and immobile" (*Khaterat-e zendan* 5). Parsipur's memoir has not been translated into English, and

Parsipur does not list her life narrative among her publications on her website. In another interview, she said that many countries are hesitant to translate and publish her books for fear of retaliation by the Islamic government (Bashi, "Simply a Stunner").

This may not apply to the United States, but it is true that, even during the height of popularity of memoirs written by Iranian women, her *Khaterat-e zendan* remains virtually unknown. Her own recollection of her lengthy imprisonment, in *Khaterat-e zendan* (*Prison Memoirs*), is banned in Iran. "Living in Los Angeles today, I think back," she wrote in her memoir; "the laws were such [in Iran] that they turned a person into stone—silent and immobile" (*Khaterat-e zendan* 5). Parsipur's memoir has not been translated into English. In fact, Parsipur does not list her life narrative among her publications on her website. In an interview, she said that many countries are hesitant to translate and publish her books for fear of retaliation by the Islamic government (Bashi, "Simply a Stunner"). This obviously does not apply to the United States, but it is true that, even during the height of popularity of memoirs written by Iranian women, her *Khaterat-e zendan* remains virtually unknown. This supports my earlier assertion that because English has become an international language, a writer, especially an Iranian woman who is labelled *mamnu-ol qalam* (the one who is forbidden to write), would have difficulty succeeding financially without an English translation. Parsipur wrote to me, "The problem is that I have never found money from my work. This is the reason of my silence. I need to work so I can't write the books." In her interview with Saremi, however, Parsipur noted that her silence is a result of her separation from her heritage, her country:

> Now, in America, I'm away from my homeland and no one understands my language, and I don't understand theirs. When I publish a book now, ten people here read it and tell me it's interesting, but it's not a fortifying experience. If I was in Iran, the feedback would be more inspiring because it would come from a big community. For there to be a fire, there must be some fuel. When you live in exile, you burn yourself out. (Saremi)

Parsipur misses the feedback, the reaction that her fierce pen generated in Iran. In a way, the source of her literary creativity was Iran and its people, and now that she is away from both, she is silenced once again. I suggested to her that she try to arrange for an English translation of her memoir so as to make it accessible to a larger readership, including second-generation Iranians who might be fluent in spoken but not written Persian. Maybe a new readership in the United States can rejuvenate her literary voice. Similarly, the memoir of the Iranian human rights activist Mehrangiz Kar, *Gardanband-e moqadas* (*The Holy Necklace*), remains largely unnoticed. The book received one review, from Niloofar Beizai, who criticized Kar for her political views, while also commenting that she found it difficult to review the book objectively owing to its personal aspects. Kar's autobiographical essay "Death of a Mannequin," a haunting memoir of the rapid loss of women's rights under the Islamic government, was translated and published in the anthology *My Sister, Guard Your Veil; My Brother, Guard Your Eyes*, which received positive reviews. In a telephone conversation with me (9 Aug. 2010), Kar acknowledged the difficulties of finding good translators and publishers who would promote her books.

Of political memoirs written by three well-known Iranian women intellectuals, Shahrnush Parsipur, Mehrangiz Kar, and Shirin Ebadi, only Ebadi's book achieved financial and critical success. Since she is not a literary figure, Ebadi knew that, if her story was to be heard, she needed a well-known writer and translator. Her co-writer, Azadeh Moaveni, is a journalist and a writer of two of her own memoirs, *Lipstick Jihad* and *Honeymoon in Tehran*. Based on notes written in Persian by Ebadi, Moaveni and Ebadi produced a successful book, capitalizing on Ebadi's fame as a Nobel Peace Laureate, but the Iranian government's tight control on the press prevented the publication and distribution of *Iran Awakening*. When Ebadi faced a similar situation in the United Sates, she sued the American government for barring her book from publication, arguing that "restrictions on the publication of books by authors in countries subject to US sanctions are unconstitutional" ("Iranian Nobel Laureate"). During her visit to Brandeis University in 2008, I asked her whether she would consider translating her memoir into Persian and publishing it in Iran. She smiled and graciously told me, "You know that's impossible for now, unfortunately. One day—maybe." Indeed, political memoirs by anyone, especially women, are deadly in Iran. Ebadi's memoir succeeded largely because it is written in English and has found a wide readership. Of the three memoirs written by Parsipur, Kar, and Ebadi, the two written in Persian (including the only one written by a literary figure—Parsipur) remain largely unknown. Meanwhile, *Daughter of Persia*, a memoir written in English by a non-literary memoirist, Farman Farmaian, has been translated into many languages and claims wide readership. Language does matter.

As noted earlier, some scholars of Iranian women writers—such as Farzaneh Milani, Michael Hillmann, and William Hanaway—have argued that continuous political oppression against freedom of speech and literary expression and the indirect style of writing in Persian have been the main obstacles preventing Iranian women from writing memoirs. The dearth of memoirs written in Persian by Iranian women even today, and the lack of success of the few written in Persian in exile, testify to the truth of these scholars' assertions. I do not, however, agree with William Hanaway's suggestion that autobiography is a culture-bound genre, "too Western-centered and culture-bound for Iranians to make use of" (62). Literature and literary genres are shared and mimicked with cultural twists by writers around the world. I predict that the time will come for Iranian women memoirists to write successful, widely read memoirs in Persian. Just as Iranian women novelists have succeeded in writing large volumes of *roman* (the Persian term for "novel") since the Revolution, other Iranian women will find a way to manipulate the language and the genre to accommodate their thoughts and to record their life narratives.

NOTES

1 The so-called strong version of this hypothesis (the claim that the language we speak actually *determines* our thought processes) is now generally considered untenable: it is not that the scope of our thought is delimited by the language we speak or that it is impossible to express certain ideas in certain languages. However, a language's lexicon and grammatical structures facilitate the expression of certain concepts and relationships while complicating the expression of others. As Kramsch explains, "The way a given language encodes experience semantically makes aspects of that experience not exclusively accessible, but just more salient for the users of that language" (13).

2 I draw here and in the following section on an article I wrote for *Persian Heritage* in 2004, "Iranian Women and Contemporary Memoir."

3 Esfandiari's *Le palais des solitudes* (translated into English as *Palace of Solitude*) was written in collaboration with Louis Valentin, while Dona Munker is openly credited as a co-author of Farman Farmaian's *Daughter of Persia*.

4 Behbahani's remarks were made as part of an address delivered at the annual conference of the International Society for Iranian Studies (ISIS), Bethesda, MD, 28–30 May 2004.

WORKS CITED

Adams, Lorraine. "Almost Famous: The Rise of Nobody Memoir." *Washington Monthly* Apr. 2004. http://www.washingtonmonthly.com/features/2001/0204.adams.html.

Ahkami, Shahrokh, and Negar Ahkami. "An Interview with Marjane Satrapi." *Persian Heritage* 8 (Fall 2003): 54–57.

Asayesh, Gelareh. *Saffron Sky: A Life Between Iran and America*. Boston: Beacon, 1999.

Azernour, Ladane. *Les larmes de l'exil: L'Iran confisque* [*The Tears of Exile: Iran Confiscated*]. Paris: Les Quatre Chemins, 2004.
Bashi, Golbarg. "The 'Boom' in Prose Writing by Iranian Women Authors in the 1990s Within the Context of the Situation of Women in Contemporary Iran." Diss. U of Manchester, England, 2000.
———. "Simply a Stunner: The Proper Etiquette of Meeting Shahrnush Parsipur in the United States." *Iranian.com*, 9 July 2006. 12 Feb. 2011. http://iranian.com/Bashi/2006/July/Parsipur/index.html.
Beizai, Niloofar. "Gardanband-e moqadas: Hekayat-e roshanfekri sargardan, dar qafasi be bozorgi Iran!" ["The Holy Necklace: The Story of a Wandering Intellectual in a Cage the Size of Iran!"]. 23 Apr. 2003. 20 May 2010. http://www.nbeyzaie.com.
Boyce, Mary. *Zoroastrians: Their Religious Beliefs and Practices*. London: Routledge, 2001.
Cixous, Hélène. "The Laugh of the Medusa." Trans. Keith Cohen and Paula Cohen. *Signs: Journal of Women in Culture and Society* 1.4 (1976): 875–93.
Clark, Herbert H., and Eve V. Clark. "Language Processing." *Universals of Human Language: Method and Theory*. Ed. Joseph Greenberg and Edith A. Moravcsik. Vol. 1. Stanford: Stanford UP, 1998. 225–78.
Conway, Jill Ker. *When Memory Speaks: Exploring the Art of Autobiography*. New York: Vintage, 1998.
Crystal, David, ed. *The Cambridge Encyclopedia of Language*. Cambridge: Saw, 1984.
Dabashi, Hamid. "Native Informers and the Making of the American Empire." *Al-Ahram Weekly Online*, 1 June 2003. 5 June 2010. Available at http://www.hamiddabashi.com/articles/selected-newspaper-essays/.
Daly, Mary. *Beyond God the Father: Toward a Philosophy of Women's Liberation*. Boston: Beacon, 1993.
Dayanim, E. Personal interview. 25 Feb. 1980.
de Bruijn, J. P. T. "Arabic Influences on Persian Literature." *General Introduction to Persian Literature*. Ed. J. T. P. de Bruijn. Vol. 1 of A History of Persian Literature, ed. Ehsan Yarshater. New York: I. B. Tauris, 2009. 369–84.
Desai, Anita, Caryl Phillips, and Ilan Stavans. "The Other Voice: A Dialogue Between Anita Desai, Caryl Phillips, and Ilan Stavans." *Transition* 64 (1994): 77–89.
Djavann, Chahdortt. *Comment peut-on être français?* [*How Can One Be French?*]. Paris: Flammarion, 2006.
Donovan, Sarah K. "Luce Irigaray (1932–)." *Internet Encyclopedia of Philosophy*. N.d. 23 Mar. 2014. http://www.iep.utm.edu/irigaray.
Dumas, Firoozeh. *Funny in Farsi: A Memoir of Growing Up Iranian in America*. New York: Villard, 2003.
Ebadi, Shirin, and Azadeh Moaveni. *Iran Awakening: A Memoir of Revolution and Hope*. New York: Random House, 2006.
———. Personal interview. Waltham. 14 Apr. 2008.
Elgin, Suzette Haden. *Native Tongue*. New York: Daw, 1984.
Etehadi, Mansoureh. *Zendegi bayad kard* [*One Must Live*]. Tehran: N.p., 1996.

Farman Farmaian, Sattareh, with Dona Munker. *Daughter of Persia: A Woman's Journey from Her Father's Harem Through the Islamic Revolution*. New York: Crown, 1992.
Farouky, Jumana. "Common Grounds: Three Iranian Women Tell Their Stories." *Boston Phoenix* 15–21 August 2003. 5 Mar. 2004. http://www.bostonphoenix.com/boston/arts/books/documents/03084952.asp.
Farrokhzad, Forugh. *Asir* [*The Captive*]. Tehran: Orien, 1955.
Ferdowsi, Hakim Abolqasem. *Shahnameh* [*The Book of Kings*]. Tehran: Amir Kabir, 1966.
Foucault, Michel. "The Discourse on Language." *The Archeology of Knowledge and the Discourse on Language*. Trans. A. M. Sheridan Smith. New York: Pantheon, 1972. 215–37.
Gilmore, Leigh. *Autobiographies: A Feminist Theory of Women's Self-Representation*. Ithaca: Cornell UP, 1994.
Goldin, Farideh. "Iranian Women and Contemporary Memoirs." *Persian Heritage* 35 (Fall 2004): 32–35.
———. *Wedding Song: Memoirs of an Iranian Jewish Woman*. Hanover: UP of New England, 2003.
Guppy, Shusha. *The Blindfold Horse: Memories of a Persian Childhood*. London: Beacon, 1988.
Haas, William S. *Iran*. New York: Columbia UP, 1946.
Haim, S. *Persian-English Proverbs, Together with Idioms, Phrases, Glossarial Notes, Mother Stories*, Etc. Tehran: Beroukhim, 1956.
Hanaway, William. "Half-Voices: Persian Women's Lives and Letters." Najmabadi 55–63.
Hillmann, Michael Craig. "An Autobiographical Voice: Forugh Farrokhzad." Najmabadi 33–54.
———. *Iranian Culture: A Persianist View*. New York: UP of America, 1990.
———. *A Lonely Woman: Forugh Farrokhzad and Her Poetry*. Washington, DC: Mage, 1987.
"Iranian Nobel Laureate Winner Sues the US." *BBC News*, 2 Nov. 2004. 12 Feb. 2011. http://news.bbc.co.uk/2/hi/middle_east/3974099.stm.
Javadi, Hasan. "Women and Satire." *Satire in Persian Literature*. Rutherford, NJ: Fairleigh Dickinson UP, 1988. 198–225.
Kar, Mehrangiz. "Death of a Mannequin." *My Sister, Guard Your Veil; My Brother, Guard Your Eyes: Uncensored Iranian Voices*. Ed. Lila Azam Zanganeh. Boston: Beacon, 2006. 30–37.
———. *Gardanband-e moqadas* [*The Holy Necklace*]. Sweden: Baran, 2002.
Keshavarz, Fatemeh. *Jasmine and Stars: Reading More Than Lolita in Tehran*. Chapel Hill: U of North Carolina P, 2007.
Khayyam, Omar. *Rubaiyat-e Khayyam* [*The Rubaiyat of Khayyam*]. Tehran: Sherkate Sahami Chap, 1952.
Kramsch, Claire. *Language and Culture*. New York: Oxford UP, 1998.
Lessing, Doris. *The Marriage Between Zones Three, Four, and Five*. New York: Vintage, 1981.
Milani, Farzaneh. *Veils and Words: The Emerging Voices of Iranian Women Writers*. Syracuse, NY: Syracuse UP, 1992.
———. "Veiled Voices: Women's Autobiographies in Iran." Najmabadi 1–16.
Millet, Kate. *Going to Iran*. New York: Coward, McCann and Georghegan, 1982.

Moaveni, Azadeh. Honeymoon in Tehran: Two Years of Love and Danger in Iran. New York: Random House, 2009.
———. *Lipstick Jihad: A Memoir of Growing Up Iranian in America and American in Iran*. New York: Public Affairs, 2005.
Moayyad, Heshmat. "Lyric Poetry." *Persian Literature*. Ed. Ehsan Yarshater. New York: State U of New York P, 1998. 120–46.
Moshir-Salimi, Ali Akbar. *Zanan-e sokhanvar: Az yekhezar sal pish ta emrooz ke be zaban-e Parsi sohbat goftand* [*Women Writers: Those Who Have Spoken in Farsi from One Thousand Years Ago Until Today*]. 2 vols. Tehran: Orien, 1977.
Nafisi, Azar. Personal interview. 5 May 2004. E-mail.
———. *Reading Lolita in Tehran: A Memoir in Books*. New York: Random House, 2003.
———. *Things I've Been Silent About*. New York: Random House, 2008.
Nafisi, Sa'id. "A General Survey of the Existing Situation in Persian Literature." *Bulletin of the Institute of Islamic Studies* No. 1, Aligarh Muslim University, 1957.
Nahai, Gina. Personal interview. 6 July 1992.
Najmabadi, Afsaneh, ed. *Women's Autobiographies in Contemporary Iran*. Cambridge, MA: Harvard UP, 1990.
Nanquette, Laetitia. "French New Orientalist Narratives from the 'Natives': Reading More Than Chahdortt Djavann in Paris." *Comparative Studies of South Asia, Africa, and the Middle East* 29.2 (2009): 269–80.
Pahlavi, Farah. "A Warning Concerning a Fabricated Book." N.d. 10 Feb. 2011. http://www.farahpahlavi.org/book-warning.html.
Parsipur, Sharnush. *Khaterat-e zendan* [*The Memoirs of Prison*]. Stockholm: Baran, 1998.
———. Message to the author. 15 Aug. 2010. E-mail.
———. *Women Without Men*. Trans. Karman Talattof and Jocelyn Sharlet. New York: Feminist, 1998.
Perry, John R. *Form and Meaning in Persian Vocabulary: The Arabic Feminine Ending*. Costa Mesa, CA: Mazda, 1991.
Piercy, Marge. *Woman on the Edge of Time*. New York: Fawcet, 1976.
Qaem Maqami, Farhat. *Zan dar adabyat: Azadi ya esarat-e zan* [*Women in Literature: Women's Enslavement or Freedom*]. Tehran: Orien, 1977.
Rachlin, Nahid. Personal interview. 5 Oct. 2004.
———. *Persian Girls: A Memoir*. New York: Tarcher/Penguin, 2006.
Ramazani, Nesta. *The Dance of the Rose and the Nightingale*. Syracuse, NY: Syracuse UP, 2001.
Ranjbaran, Ecmail. Ed. *Iranian New Poetry: Road and River, Poems from 1960–1970*. Tehran: Azar, 1972.
Rastegar, Mitra. "Reading Nafisi in the West: Authenticity, Orientalism, and 'Liberating' Iranian Women." *Women's Studies Quarterly* 34 (Spring/Fall 2006): 108–28.
Reid, Mehry M., and Thomas R. Reid. *Snake's Marble: A Persian Memoir*. New York: Vintage, 1995.
Said, Edward. *Orientalism*. New York: Vintage, 1979.

Saidi, Janet. "Loosening Binds, Strengthening Ties: As Restrictions Ease, Iranian Women Are Telling Their Own Stories." *Los Angeles Times* 16 July 2003.

Sandler, Rivanne. "Literary Development in Iran in the 1960s and the 1970s Prior to the 1978 Revolution." *World Literature Today* 60 (1986): 246–51.

Saremi, Sepideh. "Interview with Shahrnush Parsipur, Author." 2 Jan. 2008. 12 Feb. 2011. http://www.parsarts.com/?s=Interview+with+Shahrnush+Parsipur.

Satrapi, Marjane: *Persepolis: The Story of a Childhood*. New York: Pantheon, 2003.

Shafii, Rouhi. *Scent of Saffron: Three Generations of an Iranian Family*. London: Scarlet, 1997.

Sullivan, Zohreh T. *Exiled Memories: Stories of Iranian Diaspora*. Philadelphia: Temple UP, 2001.

Taj al-Saltana. *Crowning Anguish: Memoirs of a Persian Princess from the Harem to Modernity.* Ed. Abbas Amanat. Trans. Anna Vanzan and Amin Neshati. Washington, DC: Mage, 1993.

Tavakoli-Taraghi, Mohamad. "Contested Memories: Narrative Structures and Allegorical Meanings of Iran's Pre-Islamic History." *Iranian Studies* 29.1/2 (1996): 149–79.

Tehrani, Farideh. *Negligence and Chaos: Bibliographic Access to Persian-Language Materials in the United States*. New York: Scarecrow, 1991.

Tong, Rosemarie. *Feminist Thought: A Comprehensive Introduction*. Boulder, CO: Westview, 1989.

Zheng, Congcong. "Laughter and Self-Reflection for Foreigners and Americans Alike: Reflections on *Funny in Farsi* by Firoozeh Dumas and Attending the Author's Talk at Carlsbad Library." *Peyk: Persian Cultural Center's Bilingual Magazine* 19.122 (July–August 2009): 12. Web. 29 June 2014. http://www.pccsd.org/peyk/No122/Peyk122-web.pdf.

CHAPTER THREE

Autobiomythography and Self-Aggrandizement in Iranian Diasporic Life-Writing

Fatemeh Keshavarz and Azar Nafisi

Manijeh Mannani

> If your image in the mirror is right,
> Yourself, not the mirror, you must smite.[1]
> Nezami Ganjavi

Although neither Azar Nafisi's *Reading Lolita in Tehran: A Memoir in Books* (2003) nor Fatemeh Keshavarz's *Jasmine and Stars: Reading More Than Lolita in Tehran* (2007) completely lends itself to discussion using the same tools that we usually adopt in analyzing Western modes of life-writing, both works still raise a question that is universally valid in this field: how much of the "true self" is disguised by the subject, the "I," in each memoir? The "true self" is generally understood as referring to the author's self, with the question concerning how far the author of an autobiographical work engages, whether consciously or unconsciously, in self-mythologizing. But the issue of subjectivity extends beyond an author's depiction of the autobiographical subject in the form of the author's own actions and emotions: it is the lens through which the author creates an image of the external reality in which he or she is embedded. This image, like that of the personal self, may also be distorted, typically in ways that support the author's autobiographical project. Drawing upon current theories in the genre of life-writing that tackle notions such as memory, selectivity, subjectivity, truth, and intention, I will argue that Keshavarz's memoir is more prone to processes of distortion than is Nafisi's—although Keshavarz and a host of other critics, including Hamid Dabashi, hold a different opinion in their criticisms of Nafisi.

Keshavarz's *Jasmine and Stars* opens with the ambitious claim that her book will help Westerners to see the humanity in "the Other"—here, the Iranians.Keshavarz's springboard for this daunting task is Azar Nafisi's memoir, *Reading Lolita in Tehran*, which Keshavarz criticizes for its apparent inaccuracies and distortions of various sorts. While these allegations may or may not be true—Nafisi's memoir (much like any other memoir) entails some exaggerations and omissions that reflect decisively on Iranian culture, religion, and politics—Keshavarz's response to Nafisi is far from objective. Yet the aspects from Iranian culture that are left out and those that are highlighted serve two completely different purposes for each writer. The weaknesses in *Reading Lolita* are mostly those that are typical of any type of memoir; they are, more often than not, inevitable. Keshavarz's memoir, however, fulfills a totally different purpose: it aims to project to people not familiar with Iran an image of Iranian society that is homogeneous, placid, and generally quite pleasant. In short, one might classify *Jasmine and Stars* as a work of creative nonfiction.

Keshavarz begins by recounting a well-known anecdote from Rumi's *Mathnavi*, a version of the famous fable of the blind men and the elephant, which cautions against "the dangers of partial or distorted vision" (Keshavarz 1).[2] In this version, those examining the elephant are not blind but are working in the pitch dark. The story concludes with the lesson that if these people had only had some candles, they would have been able to see that they were in fact all describing the same beast. As Keshavarz explains, in writing her memoir, she hopes to provide "a candle to remove—or at least to reduce—the depth of the dark" (4). Implicit in this hope is the claim that, with the aid of an apparently infallible memory, Keshavarz, as candle holder, will illuminate an accurate and comprehensive portrait of Iran:

> In *Jasmine and Stars*, I carefully and painstakingly weave a multihued tapestry of human voice and experience. I turn my narrating voice into a vehicle for the rainbow of the faces and words that filled my childhood and youth in

> Iran. I will not select any particular time period, target any specific political movement, privilege any class or gender, or handpick any specific social event. This is no ideological war for or against any. It is designed to be a meaningful excursion into modern-day Iran: a culture as charming, creative, humorous, and humane as any. A culture that has much to offer the world.
>
> You will laugh and cry with me and all the ordinary Iranians you will meet, some from my own family and many I could not myself have met. The compelling voices you will hear will not be those of politicians and ideologues, but of writers and poets as well as family members and friends. [. . .] If we have succeeded in transcending the I-know-the-elephant attitude, the recognition of the multiplicity of voices will empower us to resist all totalizing and silencing efforts. [. . .] The trick is to listen for the seemingly insignificant voices that carry the wisdom, tenderness, beauty, and humor in a culture, to open the door and let them into the safety of our recognition. If there are brighter candles, I have yet to find them. (5–6)

She goes on to declare that "*Jasmine and Stars* is a celebration of the common humanity shared among people of differing circumstances—religious, cultural, and geopolitical" (7).

Like any other society, that of Iran has both positive and negative sides. Keshavarz's efforts to deny or, failing that, to justify some of the less attractive sides of Iranian culture only undermine the credibility of her own narrative. In contrast, in her opening "Author's Note," Nafisi acknowledges the inherent subjectivity of any autobiographical narrative: "The facts in this story are true insofar as any memory is ever truthful." After all, as Sidonie Smith and Julia Watson observe, "In the act of remembering, the autobiographical subject actively creates the meaning of the past. Thus, narrated memory is an interpretation of a past that can never be fully recovered" (9). And as Daniel Schachter contends, "Memories are records of how we have experienced events, not replicas of the events themselves" (6). Nafisi's stance right at the beginning of her memoir attests to her familiarity with the principles and boundaries of the task she has undertaken; Keshavarz's claim to have written *Jasmine and Stars* with the aid of an unfailing memory only undermines the authenticity of her response to *Reading Lolita*.

Of the other major differences between Nafisi and Keshavarz, their widely different upbringing and backgrounds (educational and otherwise) reflect naturally and decisively on each author's perspective and approach. When Nafisi looks back at her life, she does so more as a Westernized Iranian, if not a Westerner. She is immersed in Western culture and literature as a result of her upbringing and education, which occurred, beginning at an early age, largely in the West. Keshavarz, however, looks back at her past as most Iranians would do; she is concerned with the image projected in the work (not just of herself, but also of Iranian society at large), since she spent her formative years in the country of her birth and left Iran as an adult.

In *Words, Not Swords*, Farzaneh Milani describes *Reading Lolita in Tehran* as "an innovative and complex blending of various genres—memoir, biography, autobiography, literary criticism, and political tract . . . as an art form that recognizes no geographical or temporal boundaries" (218). And yet autobiography, as we know it in the West, did not exist as a genre in Iranian culture until the past few decades. Despite this absence, a host of biographies and poems, both classical and modern, that contain autobiographical elements have in fact been produced by Iranians. There is, however, one main difference between all of these works (with the exception of some modernist poems) and their Western counterparts. William Hanaway notes that, in the work of a Western autobiographer, "weaknesses and darker aspects of the life are not suppressed." The emphasis in a Western autobiography, he argues, "is not on making a public image but rather on trying to understand the meaning of the life in its context" (58–59). In most of the Persian works, the objective is instead to put forward, in Ira Nadel's words, "an example or model of moral and didactic value for readers" (59–60).

A quick look at *Jasmine and Stars* provides us with numerous instances in which the author projects one such model, not just of herself but of Iranian society on a larger scale. Ironically, Keshavarz accuses Nafisi of presenting a "selective and exaggerated account of life in postrevolutionary Iran" (6). Describing *Reading Lolita* as a "New Orientalist" narrative, Keshavarz argues that Nafisi's account is "troubling" because "through its polarized vision of the world, it denies the value of listening. Instead, it contributes to the rising heat in the fiery East-West rhetoric." As she concludes, "The dehumanization of Muslims in the West and the diabolic representation of the West by Muslim extremists are both silencing narratives that have resulted from this heated polarization" (11). And yet the didactic stories in Keshavarz's own memoir almost always rest on exaggerations of their own. On the one hand, we have the beautification of Iranian culture, and on the other, the demonization of anyone who criticizes it. The narrative can be compared to a children's book in which some characters, usually those related to the narrating voice, are predominantly good, pious, and largely wronged and in which anyone who holds a different stance than the narrator is self-serving. This black-and-white dichotomy is foreshadowed in the first chapter of the book, in which Keshavarz uses the metaphors of jasmine and stars to refer to the good insiders, while the bad outsiders are "grasshoppers." She also refers to the different events in her childhood as "stations," undeniably alluding to the Sufi stages and stations. In addition to having elicited the wide range of adverse feedback usually invoked by such comparisons, the reference is considered by many to be blasphemous.[3] Keshavarz is, however, at ease in imbuing her childhood with a "mystical" aura.

No one in Keshavarz's family seems to have any serious flaws or shortcomings; indeed, she idolizes her uncle and, to a lesser extent, her parents, grandmother, siblings, friends, and neighbours. Speaking of her ex-husband, she shares no traits that are even slightly negative or improper for fear of damaging the unreal and highly subjective image she has projected of the "Muslim Iranian man." She explicitly compares her uncle to the great Sufi Bayazid Bastami. In her eyes, an individual who endeavours to free himself from seeking people's approval necessarily resembles Bayzaid Bastami (64–65). She likens her uncle to a shining star, alluding to the Sufi cosmology of love and the "classic metaphor" that compares wise guides and leaders to stars: "My uncle would simply enter the room, and everything would appear in a different light" (79). Toward the end of her the memoir, Keshavarz expands this description: "I can easily compare my uncle the painter to a saint. In fact, I have a hard time imagining a saint in any other way" (145). She goes on to draw a contrast with her father, who "was not a saint by any stretch of the imagination. He was emotional, demanding, and easily offended." But even her father is immediately issued a reprieve. A few lines later, she describes him using these words: "If I were to choose one adjective to describe Baba, I would say 'generosity' without a moment's hesitation" (145).

The use of sublime terminology and analogies in *Jasmine and Stars* is completely in accordance with the focus in some, if not most, Iranian biographies on figures who, as Hanaway notes, are "larger than life" (60), including poets, Sufis, and saints. Thus, for an Iranian writer like Keshavarz, who seems to have strong religious sentiments, it only makes sense to take advantage of these convenient models rather than attempt an alternative style with possible hazardous consequences. Hanaway's observations and the self-aggrandizement that is characteristic of the narrating voice in *Jasmine and Stars* are reminiscent of Michael Benton's description of biomythography: "a process of gathering and organising the scattered fragments of the past to meet the needs of the present" (224). My detailed analysis of *Jasmine and Stars* as a distinct example of what I am calling "autobiomythography" follows, to a large extent, the process in biomythographies that Benton outlines in his study of several biographies of prominent Western literary figures, such as the Brontë sisters, Byron, Dickens, and Sylvia Plath:

> (1) the first biographer is commissioned, selects and establishes a factual history, giving the "facts" a particular "spin";
> (2) the facts become fictionalized, typically through the writings of the subject as well as those of the biographer;
> (3) the fiction, in turn, becomes mythologized as its characters and landscape become symbols;
> (4) the myth is transmuted into a variety of "factions" in different media—stories accepted as based on fact but embellished with invented elements; and
> (5) modern biographers attempt to demythologize this process by returning to primary sources. (212)

Of course, not all of these steps are tightly applicable to the memoir in question: in addition to the main differences in the sub-genres to which *Jasmine and Stars* and the biographies listed by Benton subscribe, the subject in *Jasmine and Stars* is not a historical or prominent literary figure.

The figure of this autobiography is Keshavarz. The undesirable sides of life, as far as Keshavarz's selective memory aids her, are trivial, including, for instance, a female servant who fasts during her pregnancy because she is uneducated but very pious. There is also Keshavarz's "half-crazy" neighbour who murders her teenage daughter because she had "gotten pregnant" (30). Keshavarz balances this highly unusual and "undesirable" incident with the story of the poor charcoal seller, also living in the writer's neighbourhood, who, despite being illiterate, is open-minded enough to ask the Keshavarz family to help her daughters to learn to read and write.

In another part of her memoir, Keshavarz shares the story of her "prominent geneticist friend," an Iranian who had to leave his native country and his research incomplete because "his professional aspirations" that dealt with "controversial matters" had not been "received favorably by *certain clerical figures of a less liberal background*" (74; my emphasis). This tragic incident, which Keshavarz treats as a singular case, is actually highly representative of many Iranian experts who live abroad because of the limitations they have faced within the country; sadly,

Keshavarz euphemizes this incident as "professional aspirations" not having been "received favorably."

When Keshavarz criticizes Iranian society, she almost always has in mind the era before the 1979 Revolution. Indeed, her frustration extends back to the time of the Persian Empire and Cyrus the Great himself, who, in the author's words, "had freed the captive Jews of Babylon" (40). Keshavarz interprets this historic event as the root cause of Iranians thinking they are "genetically purified of racial prejudice forever" (40), a belief that she implies is expressed in *Reading Lolita*, despite there being no indication of it. Furthermore, Keshavarz regrettably fails to support this hypothesis about Iranians by presenting relevant examples. This statement also indicates that in her defence of her native culture, Keshavarz prioritizes Islamic culture over Iranian culture, which at other times, she uses interchangeably.

One of the reasons why Iranians have not adopted Western modes of life-writing is because autobiography, unlike all other genres, is more a cultural than a literary phenomenon (Hanaway 61). Moreover, in Farzaneh Milani's words, "its absence is perhaps the logical extension of a culture that creates, expects, and even values a sharply defined separation between the inner and the outer, the private and the public" and of the various types of censorship that could follow from it. "In short," Milani concludes, "it could be one more manifestation of strong forces of deindividualization, protection, and restraint" ("Veiled Voices" 2). If we read *Jasmine and Stars* against this observation, we begin to understand many of the omissions and exaggerations in the work. And reading the work in this light also elucidates the roots of Keshavarz's profound disillusionment with Nafisi's memoir. Keshavarz appears to be oblivious to the fact that in a memoir, one's private life and public image do not and should not necessarily correspond.

Moreover, *Jasmine and Stars*, following the tradition of most contemporary Iranian memoirs (Princess Ashraf Pahlavi's *Faces in a Mirror* is just one example), ends at exactly the same spot where the narrator started in terms of emotional and intellectual growth—Keshavarz, the professor of comparative literature today, remembers the details of her conversations about classical Persian poetry "at the age of five or six" with her parents as she discusses the matter in her concluding chapter. Following that tradition, the narrating voice in the memoir also delineates a "firm belief in the author's privileged knowledge of herself, of her 'real,' 'unified' self" and reveals "a totally different private self beneath the 'social' one" (Milani, "Veiled Voices" 14), as seen in numerous sections of the book, especially in the introductory chapter ("What Does the Elephant Look Like?") and the concluding one ("Tea with My Father and the Saints"). It is important to note, however, that Keshavarz almost nowhere in *Jasmine and Stars* charges Nafisi with being self-obsessed, although she is critical of many other aspects of *Reading Lolita*.

The reason behind the absence of the narcissism charge is twofold, in my view. First, there is little on which to base it, given that no indication of self-obsession can be found in Nafisi's memoir, and, second, Keshavarz may be cognizant of the explicit note of vanity associated with her own narrating voice in *Jasmine and Stars*. This self-admiration is nowhere as apparent as in the episode where Keshavarz discusses her radio show. As she makes a point of telling her readers, she has developed a "close relationship" with her audience, who are in the habit of writing to her "daily." On the occasion she recalls, she has just conducted an interview with the chancellor of a major university, during which she daringly asked him "bold questions." Fearing that her intemperate behaviour may have angered the show's producer, she goes looking for him, but he is nowhere to be found. She continues:

> I returned to the studio and threw myself on an armchair we used for resting between air times. A letter from a listener had been sitting on the side table since midday, and I opened it. A young carpenter was returning to school because my show had inspired him write his own poetry. Wow! Who cared about the outcome of the interview with the chancellor? I read the letter once more then lifted my head and noticed a red reflection in the glass parting the two sections of the studio. A beautiful bouquet of carnations was sitting on the table next to the entrance. It had been placed there when I was reading the letter. The note attached to it said, "Let's have him for a second interview. That is, if he survives this one! You were fabulous." (46–47)

Despite her opening claim that she will "carefully and painstakingly weave a multihued tapestry of human voice and experience," selectivity and bias inform, or rather misinform, Keshavarz's memoir. At one point, the narrating voice, perhaps naïvely, admits to the selective approach adopted in the memoir: "Too many good things fall through the cracks in many books written about the country of my birth and the people who nurtured me. So I have decided to write one that focuses on the good things, one that gives voice to what has previously been silenced and overlooked" (15–16). In other words, Keshavarz confesses that she is not going to portray an objective and neutral picture of the country of her birth. At the same time, Keshavarz criticizes *Reading Lolita* for "its slanted vision," condemning Nafisi's "partial and exaggerated portrayal of Iran and its Muslim inhabitants" (17).

Keshavarz also denounces Nafisi for portraying a static and threatening image of men in contemporary Iranian society, calling Nafisi's sharing of memories about several of her radical students at Tehran University a "dehumanization of Muslims" (62). Keshavarz apparently ignores the parts in *Reading Lolita* where Nafisi portrays a neutral, unthreatening, and even pleasant image of some Iranian men who were part of her life in Iran. Nafisi's "magician," her mentor, is only one example (139–40). Granted, Nafisi does paint an unfavourable portrait of her ex-husband, a Westernized Iranian who had attended university in the United States and brought her back there with him. He was, she writes, "insanely jealous," fixated on worldly success, and "wanted his wife to dress smartly, do her nails, go to the hairdresser every week"—wishes against which she rebelled by wearing "long skirts and tattered jeans" (83). As she later admits, "I chose to marry a man I despised deep down," someone who "wanted a chaste and virginal wife" but whose own morality was governed by a double standard: before returning to Iran for the summer and marrying Nafisi (who was not yet eighteen), "he had been living with an American girl he had introduced to everyone as his wife" (298). It thus appears that Nafisi's contempt for her first husband was rooted in his lack of integrity, the result of his only partial embrace of Western values. It is also surprising that Keshavarz passes judgment on Nafisi when the latter indicates that some revolutionary students, like Forsati, and some of the writer's colleagues, like Mrs. Rezvan, were opportunists (114). But why should Nafisi not have expressed this concern? We have all come into contact with opportunistic people at some point in our lives.

Keshavarz also takes issue with a scene in which Nassrin, one of the students in Nafisi's reading group, describes her mother, who came from an affluent family that espoused liberal values but who married a man whose own family was religious. Here, Keshavarz criticizes the idea that a deeply religious Muslim woman would not be likely to engage in making "fancy French food" or in teaching her children English (Keshavarz 62; cf. Nafisi 53–54). Keshavarz seems to be unaware of the attitude of most deeply religious people in Iran toward Western languages, cuisine, art, and so on, especially during the first decade following the Islamic Revolution—and of the fact that the English language was banned from most schools in that particular period. It is also perplexing that Keshavarz raises her eyebrow when Nassrin reveals that her mother never saw her American high school friends again following her marriage. In other words, in addition to restricting his daughter's movements, Nassrin's father evidently did the same to his wife. Keshavarz interprets the inclusion of this information as evidence of Nafisi's own hostility to Iranian culture generally and Iranian men in particular. But Nassrin is simply describing reality. Shirin Ebadi, in *Iran Awakening*, recounts a similar event concerning her neighbours, in which the "very religious father married his eldest daughter off to an even more pious *bazaari*" (described as "a trader or merchant, usually of deeply traditional background"), who "forbade her to visit her own parents unaccompanied" (106–07). One wonders whether, by querying the episode, Keshavarz is implying that Nafisi is fabricating these events in order to portray Iranian men in a negative light—or is she suggesting that she should not have written about such things?

Keshavarz's critique of *Reading Lolita* is imbued with uninformed anger (something that she accuses Nafisi of), flawed accusations, and unsubstantiated assertions and remarks. Had Keshavarz been in Iran during its early post-revolutionary period, she probably would not have so perfunctorily dismissed the factual accounts in Nafisi's memoir. If Keshavarz had referenced people and authorities like Shirin Ebadi, mentioned in *Jasmine and Stars* (116), more responsibly, her critique would have been more credible. If she had studied Ebadi's memoir, *Iran Awakening*, to learn about the Nobel Peace Laureate's similar, if not exact, recapturing of events during the period about which Nafisi was writing, she might have written a very different book.

Another of Keshavarz's unwarranted criticisms of Nafisi is that the latter refers to her (Muslim) male students by their last names. This more formal way of referring to these students, argues Keshavarz, prevents the reader from getting to know them (112). In contrast, the female students who visit Nafisi weekly at her home are called by their first names, and, as readers, we get to know them more thoroughly. Supposedly, this reveals a bias on the part of Nafisi against the male students. But this criticism merely speaks to Keshavarz's lack of familiarity with the academic world in Iran. Within Iranian post-secondary and secondary institutions, and even in some elementary schools, students—regardless of age, gender, religion, or ethnicity—are mostly referred to in a formal manner, by their surnames. The reason we know the first names of the female students is that they, as a group, visit Nafisi weekly at her house to discuss world literary masterpieces: Nafisi and these female students do have a more intimate relationship than usually exists between professors and their students in the formal and rigid setting of a classroom.

Keshavarz further accuses Nafisi of creating stereotypical categories of people, to which the actions of specific individuals then predictably conform (113). Nafisi's descriptions of certain public events, she argues, are filled with people who illustrate one such category, which Keshavarz chooses to label "the Ugly" (114). They are, she argues, mere caricatures, variations on a single theme, and are presented in a very unflattering light simply because they are, in one way or another, proponents of an Islamic culture. But if readers cannot attest to the credibility of Nafisi's descriptions through their first-hand experience, they can easily find photographs of the crowds of people that Nafisi describes eating on the roadsides during Khomeini's funeral and of Iranians picnicking daily outside the occupied American embassy (Nafisi 244, 104; cf. Keshavarz 114, 129). Anyone who has seen these images or experienced the events can confirm the accuracy of Nafisi's accounts; by criticizing Nafisi for depicting reality, Keshavarz once again undermines her own credibility. In a somewhat similar vein, Keshavarz takes exception to Nafisi's description of Persian dancing as highly seductive, "elusive," "sinewy," and "tactile" compared to Western dancing (131; cf. Nafisi 265). Although anyone who has seen Persian dancers perform would be unlikely to quarrel with Nafisi's description, Keshavarz argues that Nafisi views Persian dance from an "Othering" perspective, transforming it into an exotic object of scrutiny.

I used to live in the same quiet cul-de-sac in Tehran as Nafisi did. The hospital on the other side of our serene street was privately owned before the 1979 Revolution, as Nafisi describes it in *Reading Lolita*. After the Revolution, however, the hospital was confiscated by the government and the tranquility ended: throughout the week and especially on weekends, crowds of people would arrive to visit patients in the hospital. More often than not, these visitors had come from distant places, suburbs of Tehran and other cities, and more often than not, small children—often whining in the heat of summer or the cold of winter—could be heard playing and crying for hours on the street as their parents waited patiently just on the other side of the gates to our houses, which separated us from the hubbub outside. The visitors' vehicles, often parked quite literally in the middle of the street, made it difficult for residents to get in and out. Nafisi has captured this situation with much precision and truthfulness, recalling how, seated in her living room with her back to the window, she "could hear the sound of children shouting, crying and laughing, and, mingled in, their mothers' voices, also shouting, calling out their children's names and threatening them with punishments"—the world beyond her window coming to her "only through the disembodied noises emanating from below" (8).

Yet, again, this passage in her memoir has come under the criticism of Keshavarz, who sees it as evidence of Nafisi's elite disdain for ordinary humanity, implying that Nafisi should not have complained about this matter at all. She supports this critique with yet another flawed argument, stating that the eternal Forugh Farrokhzad—whom every student of Nafisi knows their teacher reveres—would have liked the commotion, as she "wrote about this hubbub in one of her most famous short poems" (139). And, as if this hijacking of Farrokhzad's take on the overall liveliness of crowds is not enough, Keshavarz also argues: "If you live in an apartment building in Tehran, Rome, or Istanbul, hearing the hubbub in the street is a joyful sound. It tells you that life is going on outside your window" (139). Here, Nafisi is being criticized for having recorded her thoughts honestly in response to the stimulants of her social world. But to criticize someone for speaking candidly, on the grounds that what is said fails to paint a sufficiently positive picture—to suggest that the person should instead have remained quiet—not only illustrates the very sort of "totalizing and silencing efforts" that Keshavarz claims must be resisted but also undermines the hope that one day Iranians will be able to tolerate criticism directed at them, whether personally and nationally. It certainly contradicts Michael Hillmann's hopeful assertion that "Farrokhzad's unveiled and unmasked poetic modernism and individuality have opened the way for Iranian poets henceforth to choose without inhibition specific poetic modes for their poetic effects and not to feel conventional fear of social, political, or cultural consequences" (52–53).

Keshavarz, in her argument, implies that Nafisi and others who have critiqued some aspects of Iranian society and politics are necessarily supportive of the idea of the superpowers invading Iran and that they have no objection to the wrong and unlawful invasion of Iraq (123). She has failed to realize that many people are against any type of conflict and war, let alone an invasion by the United States, but have the courage to voice their concerns about their countries of origin based on their experiences. The least the rest of us who are less daring can do is to allow others to express their constructive criticism.

Unfortunately, a similar opinion is held by some other critics of *Reading Lolita*. I do not know what Nafisi's political stance is regarding the idea of a regime change in Iran. I would be very disappointed, however, to discover that Nafisi has, in fact, been supportive of such a change, because, as we know, Iranians from all walks of life took part in the Revolution that resulted in the establishment of the Islamic Republic, which currently has the support of many Iranians within and outside the country. Despite weaknesses and mistakes committed by the Islamic Republic, many Iranians remain hostile to the idea of any type of interference, including a military interference or invasion by the United States. It would, indeed, be very disheartening to find that Nafisi supports such foreign interference. Yet, unlike most of my colleagues, that knowledge would not be helpful to me at all in my analysis of *Reading Lolita*; is it not one of the first and foremost rules of our discipline to judge literary works, including memoirs, by their content and style only and not by extra-textual factors? This issue brings to mind Phillippe Lejeune's assertion about autobiography:

> [A]s far as the author is concerned, there can be a shifting between the initial intention and that which the reader will finally attribute to him, either because the author misunderstands the effects induced by the mode of presentation that he has chosen, or because between him and the reader there exist other postures: many elements that condition the reading (subtitle, generic classification, publicity, publisher's blurb) may have been chosen by the publisher and already interpreted by the media. (126)

In their critiques of *Reading Lolita*, Keshavarz, Roksana Bahramitash, and Hamid Dabashi, among others, have indeed allowed themselves to be influenced by "elements that condition the reading," interpreting the text in the light of extra-textual factors. It is both illuminating and alarming that in her article "The War on Terror, Feminist Orientalism and Orientalist Feminism," Bahramitash draws conclusions on the basis of individuals who have endorsed *Reading Lolita*. To Bahramitash (as to many others who have been unable to see the big picture without being confused by extra-textual factors), the fact that Nafisi acknowledges the support of "her boss at the School of Advanced International Studies in Washington," Fouad Ajami, whom Bahramitash refers to as Nafisi's neo-conservative mentor, is reason enough to believe that *Reading Lolita* reinforces Bush's contemptuous and highly problematic description of Iran as "a member of an 'axis of evil' and an 'outpost of tyranny'" (Bahramitash 230; cf. Nafisi 347). Another individual with whom Bahramitash takes issue is Bernard Lewis, "the guru of the neo-conservatives," who praised the insight offered by *Reading Lolita* into "teaching Western literature" in "Revolutionary Iran"—a commentary that Bahramitash locates on the back cover of Nafisi's memoir. This does not exemplify scholarly and responsible criticism—judging the work by its endorsers and, even worse, condemning it because the author's parents "had political ties to the regime of the last shah" (Bahramitash 230) or discarding it on the grounds that Nafisi herself was "an upper-class woman" who had "a privileged life" (Keshavarz 136). This restrictive biographical mode of analysis has long been considered outdated and insufficient for objective, precise, and scholarly textual analysis.

In an interview that appeared not long after the publication of his "Native Informers and the Making of the American Empire," Hamid Dabashi was asked whether, in his condemnation of *Reading Lolita* as an "extension of American imperial hegemony," he was mainly referring to "the substance of the writing or the events surrounding its publication and popularity in the United States." He responded by insisting that his critique was "almost entirely directed at the substance of RLT, with a very minimum attention to its context" (Khosmood). He immediately followed this assertion with a description of *Reading Lolita* as "the portrayal of a figment of imagination called 'the West' as the arbiter of truth and salvation, and the dismissal of 'non-Western' cultures as banal and diabolical." Despite his insistence that his assessment of Nafisi's memoir is founded on its substance, his critique both in the interview and in his "Native Infomers" article suggests that even this competent critic is reading the text against the background of circumstances external to the memoir itself, namely, the political atmosphere and events following 9/11.

Like Bahramitash, Dabashi approaches Nafisi's memoir from a non-literary perspective, basing his critique primarily on extra-textual grounds, including what he calls Nafisi's "pathetic career opportunism and neocon connections" (Khosmood). Although Dabashi claims that he has remained focused on the "substance" in *Reading Lolita* and has not traded textual evidence for its irrelevant "context," consider the passage from his article in which Nafisi is described as "employed by the US Secretary of Defense Paul Wolfowitz, indoctrinated by the father of American neoconservatives Leo Strauss (and his infamous tract *Persecution and the Art of Writing*), coached by the Lebanese Shi'i neocon artist Fouad Ajami, wholeheartedly endorsed by Bernard Lewis (the most wicked ideologue of the US war on Muslims)," and as "an ex-professor of English literature with not a single credible book or scholarly credential to her name other than *Reading Lolita in Tehran*." He goes on to call Nafisi "an Oriental servant of a white-identified, imperial design" to make an extended argument on the basis of the photograph that appears on the cover of the book.

It is noteworthy that, in the interview, Dabashi admits that he is not privy to any information that would directly connect Nafisi with the proponents of the war in Iraq and a possible war with Iran. Indeed, there is not a single line in his original article that links textual evidence from the memoir with the contextual evidence that he and others have offered in their condemnation of Nafisi's ties with the neocons. Rather, as far as the memoir itself is concerned, his accusation that Nafisi serves as a "native informer" is based mainly on the fact that, as a professor of English and American literature in Iran, she supported students in reading Anglo-American literary classics. In Dabashi's interpretation, Nafisi's admiration for Western literature translates into a desire for an American imperialistic takeover of her country of birth.

I would like to reiterate here that Nafisi's political views can be critiqued by anyone who wishes to do so. However, this topic should be addressed within a framework suitable for that type of analysis, a framework most certainly separate from an analysis of *Reading Lolita*. As I have argued above, on the basis of the text itself, no critic has been able to support the idea that Nafisi's memoir was written to facilitate a takeover by the Americans—that, as Dabashi's critique would have it, the memoir seeks to "neutralise competing sites of cultural resistance to the US imperial designs both at home and abroad." Such a position cannot be defended except by drawing inferences from information external to the narrative, which are then imposed on the content of the memoir, in a process of reading meaning into a text rather than extracting meaning from it. But Iranian literary critics, however sincere and capable they may be, are making a grave error in deprecating Nafisi's memoir on the basis of mere inferences and, even worse, ad hominem arguments concerning Nafisi's "opportunism" and allegedly deficient scholarly credentials. And, after all, other academics, such as Farzaneh Milani, have openly praised Nafisi's "passion for literature, democracy, and human rights," as it animates *Reading Lolita* (*Words, Not Swords* 218).

Keshavarz argues, quite justifiably, that a trend can be seen in most of the works of fiction and nonfiction written about the Middle East in the West today. She calls this type of literature the "New Orientalist narrative," which, in accordance with the dominant political atmosphere in the West, especially after the events of 9/11, distorts the realities of life and the rich and complex cultures in the Middle East and vilifies its peoples, as did its predecessor. As she points out, the "old Orientalist" narrative sought to justify "the colonial presence of Europe in the Eastern Hemisphere," with or without actually advocating "a full military presence in the region" (2). The New Orientalist version, she argues, exhibits "many similarities to and a few differences from the earlier incarnation" (3). Both are marked, for example, by oversimplification, as is illustrated in the New Orientalist narrative's tendency to explain "almost all undesirable Middle Eastern incidents in terms of

Muslim men's submission to God and Muslin women's submission to men" (3). She further argues that while "the new narrative does not necessarily support overt colonial ambitions," neither does it "hide its clear preference for a western political and cultural takeover" (3).

Among the books that Keshavarz criticizes as examples of New Orientalist narrative are *Reading Lolita* and Khaled Hosseini's *The Kite Runner*. However, while Nafisi and Hosseini are highly critical of the governing administrations in Iran and Afghanistan, respectively, there is no suggestion in either work that the authors would necessarily want their countries to be redeemed by the West. Why can't artists take issue with problems they see in their countries of birth? What could the rationale be for not supporting or following potential Western models (on different levels) if they are practical, efficient, and more democratic? Is criticizing domestic and foreign policies necessarily a blind embrace of the West? There is no question that there are misconceptions about the Middle East and Islam and misrepresentations of Middle Eastern peoples and Muslims. It remains irrefutable that Orientalist views about the Middle East exist and that misconceptions, misunderstandings, and misrepresentations have particularly multiplied since 9/11 and the events that followed. There are most certainly books being written and movies (such as *Not Without My Daughter*) being produced today that further the vilification and demonization of the people of the Middle East and reinforce mainstream media reports. But the existence of these works does not necessarily make every critical work about the region treacherous and destructive.

Keshavarz's overarching thesis can be summarized as follows: New Orientalist narratives like Nafisi's and Hosseini's project distorted, oversimplified, and unduly negative images of Iran, Afghanistan, and other Middle Eastern countries, which only exacerbate tensions with the West. Therefore, writers who are originally from these parts of the world should strive to keep criticisms of their home countries mild and to a minimum, and, if they cannot do that, then they should remain silent. Keshavarz objects to Nafisi's memoir—which is based on its author's personal and professional experiences as an Iranian citizen, daughter, wife, mother, and university professor—because it calls attention to some of the less attractive aspects of post-revolutionary Iran. Yet, as Smith and Watson observe, an autobiographer's subjectivity is grounded in social realities:

> Experience is the process through which a person becomes a certain type of subject with certain kinds of identities in the social realm, identities constituted through material, cultural, economic, and interpsychic relations. . . . In

> effect, autobiographical subjects know themselves as subjects of particular kinds of experience attached to social statuses and identities. (9, 10)

Keshavarz, however, argues that a writer's fidelity to subjective experience must be tempered by "responsibility," in the form of due concern for the potential consequences of truth telling:

> One important issue that works such as *RLT* raise for those of us in the academy is the responsibility of the intellectual from the non-Western world representing the culture of her origin. Such an intellectual is caught between two equally uninviting prospects. The first is pushing the less desirable aspects of her native culture under the carpet, as it were, so as to avoid its further villainization. The downside of this is depriving her readers (particularly people of her native culture) of the fruits of her knowledge and criticism. The second is criticizing—and ideally improving—her native culture at the possible cost of making it more vulnerable to political, cultural—even military—attacks from the dominant culture. (29)

This comment goes a long way toward explaining Keshavarz's approach and objective in *Jasmine and Stars*. Keshavarz sees a need for Iranian intellectuals to carefully package their presentation of their country to the West, rather than telling the whole truth, as that might result in an invasion by the "dominant culture." Referring to Nafisi, Keshavarz states, "One is naturally proud of the success of a writer coming from one's culture of origin. Things get complicated, however, when the writing provides insider 'evidence' that we are by and large the underdeveloped 'Orientals' everyone had thought we were" (28). Again, one wonders whether Keshavarz can be unaware that her stance implies the need to practice self-censorship.

Nafisi supports an apolitical kind of Islam that was and still is practiced by many devout Muslims globally. There is no conflict between this approach to Islam and the structures and practices that prevail in Western democracies. Nafisi tells one of her radical Islamic students, Mr. Bahri, about her grandmother, whom she recalls as "the most devout Muslim I had ever known" but who also "shunned politics" (103). She remembers how her grandmother resented the fact that, during the reign of Reza Shah, her veil, "which to her was a symbol of her sacred relationship to God, had become an instrument of power" (103). Nafisi values respect and tolerance toward people of different faiths and ideological orientations, as is implied both in the above passage and elsewhere in *Reading Lolita*. This is indeed the attitude of many Muslim scholars and intellectuals, including Shirin Ebadi in *Iran Awakening* (see, for example, 39–40, 121–22, 204), about whom Keshavarz writes with reverence in *Jasmine and Stars*.

I do not mean to suggest that nothing of value can be found in *Jasmine and Stars*. Keshavarz's pride in her culture is clearly very genuine. She writes, for example, of Iranians' deep feelings for literature:

> I had lived, studied, and worked on three continents, and if there was a culture in which people expressed their enthusiasm for literature more publicly than in Iran, I could not think of one. It would be difficult to live in Iran and not see that this enthusiasm was not limited to the educated elite either. How many a baker, shopkeeper, or taxi driver had I heard whispering Omar Khayyam under his breath. (19)

Keshavarz goes on to narrate an incident in which a "lovely, elderly Buddhist lady" asks whether Iranians eat with their hands. Keshavarz describes why she was upset: "Not because eating with one's hands is such a disgrace. But because, despite all the stereotypes that I had encountered in Iran, and despite the way the Iranian Revolution had demonized America, I had not imagined the world in two irreconcilable halves of East and West" (25). She concludes that she "certainly was not prepared to accept that any particular part of the world would have a monopoly on sophistication" (25). Keshavarz also points to an erroneous assumption, common to most people in the West, that equates literacy with civilization. In Keshavarz's words, "In the print-dominated Western culture, illiteracy equals ignorance, lack of insight, and lack of refinement. As she thoughtfully observes, "We have an essentialist way of reducing civility and culture to technology and less institutionalized forms of education to savagery and crudeness" (45).

As Susanne Egan, a Western critic, acknowledges, autobiography is no longer the prerogative of "great men":

> From a far wider base of education and literacy than obtained a hundred years ago, and from a fuller recognition of the dignity inherent in every kind of human nature, we now find literary talent and a strong autobiographical impulse emerging from all walks of life. The palm has passed from white, middle-class men of distinction to the Jewish victims of the Nazi holocaust, to women, blacks, homosexuals, convicts, exiles, and the terminally ill, the minorities of our culture who write precisely because of their lack of other

kinds of power and their need to be heard. . . . For minorities, the dominant society establishes the norms by which they are rejected and which they, in turn, reject. The very effort to articulate a self becomes an expression of spirit; it asserts the value of an individual life by creating its literary experience. (23)

It is regrettable that Iranian academics like Keshavarz who live and teach in the West and who seem to be familiar with "the value of an individual life" and the importance of objective literary and social criticism should unfairly judge and deprecate the works of their fellow Iranians. Nor should the articulation of self, "the expression of spirit," be confined to what is comforting and positive. It is time to allow critics of Iranian society to voice their opinions without having to fear intimidation and judgment.

In her memoir, Nafisi recalls something she once told her students: "A great novel heightens your senses and sensitivity to the complexities of life and of individuals, and prevents you from the self-righteousness that sees morality in fixed formulas about good and evil'" (133). It remains for readers to determine which of the two authors, Nafisi or Keshavarz, has endeavoured to portray a more balanced, less biased view of herself and her native country. Paying close attention to the events covered and the images projected in each narrative, it is not hard to see why *Jasmine and Stars* has resonated with some Iranians. As Iranians, we are profoundly concerned with how we are viewed by others. As well, under the sensitive political circumstances and with all the negative propaganda that is being perpetuated against Iran, most of us understandably wish to avoid gratuitously enhancing the falsely sinister picture of ourselves that prevails in the West. But we must not sacrifice the capacity for critique. Despite this desire to counteract what some call the New Orientalist discourse, it is critical that we present all sides of our country boldly and truthfully.

NOTES

1 "Aiyneh chon aks-e to benmud rast / khod shekan, aiyneh shekastan khatast," from *Makhzan-ol Asrar* (*The Treasury of Mysteries*); the translation is one on which poet E. D. Blodgett and I collaborated. Nezami Ganjavi, a twelfth-century poet, stands as one of the most influential figures in Persian literature.

2 In this version of the story, an elephant is brought to a town the people of which have never seen an elephant. During the night, several townspeople examine the creature and, depending on the body part that each person touches, each describes it differently: one who touches the elephant's foot describes the animal as a "big, thick column"; another

insists that its trunk is a "drain pipe"; yet another individual describes its ear as a "large fan" (Keshavarz 1). While the story does caution against drawing conclusions on the basis of incomplete information, as an analogy, it also assumes that a culture is ultimately as simple as an elephant.

3 A Sufi's quest for proximity to the Beloved (God), which involves inward transformation, consists of various states and stations. William Chittick, in *The Sufi Path of Love*, describes the stations as "the spiritual and moral perfections, or the 'virtues' achieved by the traveler" and the states as "the spiritual graces bestowed directly by God and outside of man's power of acquisition" (12).

WORKS CITED

Bahramitash, Roksana. "The War on Terror, Feminist Orientalism, and Orientalist Feminism: Case Studies of Two North American Bestsellers." *Critique: Critical Middle Eastern Studies* 14.1 (2005): 221–35.

Benton, Michael. "Literary Biomythography." *Auto/Biography* 13 (2005): 206–26.

Chittick, William. *The Sufi Path of Love*. Albany: State U of New York P, 1983.

Dabashi, Hamid. "Native Informers and the Making of the American Empire." *Al-Ahram Weekly*, 1–7 June 2006. 27 Oct. 2012. http://weekly.ahram.org.eg/2006/797/special.htm.

Ebadi, Shirin. *Iran Awakening: From Prison to Peace Prize—One Woman's Struggle at the Crossroads of History*. Trans. Azadeh Moaveni. Toronto: Alfred A. Knopf, 2006.

Egan, Susanne. "Changing Faces of Heroism: Some Questions Raised by Contemporary Autobiography." *Biography* 10.1 (1987): 20–38.

Hanaway, William L. "Half-Voices: Persian Women's Lives and Letters." Najmabadi 55–64.

Hillmann, Michael Craig. "An Autobiographical Voice: Forugh Farrokhzad." Najmabadi 33–54.

Hosseini, Khaled. *The Kite Runner*. Toronto: Anchor Canada, 2003.

Keshavarz, Fatemeh. *Jasmine and Stars: Reading More Than Lolita in Tehran*. Chapel Hill: U of North Carolina P, 2007.

Khosmood, Foaad. "Lolita and Beyond: An Interview with Hamid Dabashi." ZNET, 4 Aug. 2006. 27 Oct. 2012. http://www.iran-heritage.org/interestgroups/politicalpublication2.htm.

Lejeune, Philippe. *On Autobiography*. Trans. Katherine Leary. Ed. Paul John Eakin. Minneapolis: U of Minnesota P, 1989.

Milani, Farzaneh. "Veiled Voices: Women's Autobiographies in Iran." Najmabadi 1–17.

———. *Words, Not Swords: Iranian Women Writers and the Freedom of Movement*. Syracuse, NY: Syracuse UP, 2011.

Nadel, Ira Bruce. *Biography: Fiction, Fact, and Form*. New York: St. Martin's, 1984.

Nafisi, Azar. *Reading Lolita in Tehran: A Memoir in Books*. 2003. New York: Random House, 2004.

Najmabadi, Afsaneh, ed. *Women's Autobiographies in Contemporary Iran*. Cambridge, MA: Harvard UP, 1990.

Pahlavi, Ashraf. *Faces in a Mirror: Memoirs from Exile*. Englewood Cliffs, NJ: Prentice Hall, 1980.

Rumi, Jalal al-Din. *The Analysis and Interpretation of Masnavi-ye Sharif*. Ed. Abdul-baqi Golpinarli. 3 vols. Tehran: Publication Press of the Ministry of Culture and Islamic Guidance, 1995.

Schachter, Daniel L. *Searching for Memory: The Brain, the Mind, and the Past*. New York: Basic Books, 1996.

Smith, Sidonie, and Julia Watson, eds. *Interfaces: Women, Autobiography, Image, Performance*. Ann Arbor: U of Michigan P, 2002.

[illegible] including Shirin Ebadi [illegible] Keshavarz [illegible]

[illegible] for example, [illegible]

[illegible] on these [illegible] and there was a culture [illegible] their enthusiasm for literature more publicly than [illegible] it would be difficult to [illegible] Iran and not [illegible] to the educated [illegible]. How many [illegible] whispering Omar Khayyam under [illegible]

Keshavarz [illegible] in which a "[illegible] elderly Buddhist lady" [illegible] with their hands [illegible] why she was [illegible] But because, despite [illegible] Iran, and despite the way the Iranian [illegible] She concludes that she "certainly [illegible] [the world] would [illegible] monopoly on [illegible] also points to an [illegible] common [illegible] West that equates [illegible] with civilization. In Keshavarz's [illegible] Western culture [illegible] equals ignorance, lack of [illegible] thoughtfully observes, "We have [illegible] and culture to technology and has institutionalized [illegible] (95).

[illegible] acknowledges, autobiography is no longer the [illegible]

[illegible] wider base [illegible] and literacy than obtained a hundred years ago, and [illegible] recognition of the dignity inherent in every kind [illegible] literary talent and [illegible] autobiographical impulse [illegible] from all walks of life. The path has passed from white, middle-class [illegible] to the Jewish victims of the Nazi holocaust, [illegible], black [illegible], convicts, exiles, and the terminally ill, the [illegible] write [illegible] because of their lack of other

CHAPTER FOUR

Graphic Memories

Dialogues with Self and Other in Marjane Satrapi's *Persepolis* and *Persepolis 2*

Mostafa Abedinifard

Born a decade prior to the Islamic Revolution, Marjane Satrapi grew up in the midst of turmoil. Her critically acclaimed graphic memoir *Persepolis: The Story of a Childhood*, which spans the years immediately before and after the Revolution, and its sequel, *Persepolis 2: The Story of a Return*, have found an abundant readership around the world. As Satrapi indicates in her introduction to the first volume, in creating this narrative of her life, she hoped to provide non-Iranians, particularly those in the West, with a more accurate perspective on Iran. Implicit in this aim is a distinction between the Iranian Self and the Western Other, with the latter constituting Satrapi's major implied audience. While the didactic aspects of the two *Persepolis* volumes cannot be denied, another, perhaps less appreciated, aspect of Satrapi's work resides in its critical dialogue with Iranian culture. Satrapi's assertion at the end of her introduction to *Persepolis*—"One can forgive but one should never forget"—applies as much to Iranians as to Western readers and reflects her attention to the Self as the other important implied audience for the text. Indeed, as Amy Malek notes, many Iranian readers have praised Satrapi's work "for preserving the communal memory of a generation" (375). In narrating her own memories, Satrapi critically intervenes in the culture and politics of censorship and compulsory veiling under the post-revolutionary Islamic regime and touches upon the important psychological consequences of such tactics of repression.

By choosing to present her story through the medium of comics, Satrapi further establishes a dialogue with the Other, in the form of her engagement with the established Western attitudes and aesthetic values that surround the production and reception of comics. Satrapi's relative unfamiliarity with comics before producing the *Persepolis* volumes seems to have contributed to her eclectic approach to the medium. Her style shows influences from various sources, not only the cartooning style of her mentor, David B., but also the tradition of Persian miniature painting and probably the satiric political cartoons that at one point appeared in newspapers and magazines in her native country. Yet Satrapi has clearly forged a cohesive, and very distinctive, style of her own, one that successfully deploys the expressive visual language of the medium.

UNVEILING THE SELF: SATRAPI'S REVOLUTIONARY AUTOBIOGRAPHY

In 1936, the ruler of Iran, Reza Shah Pahlavi (1878–1944), ordered women to abandon the veil; in 1980, a year after the revolution that brought the current regime to power, mandatory veiling was reinstituted. Ashraf Zahedi, in her essay "Concealing and Revealing Female Hair: Veiling Dynamics in Contemporary Iran," reminds us of the political meaning that attaches to these acts. Both have been used by Iranian women as political weapons for opposing the hegemonic discourses of the government, which have been obviously coercive during much of Iran's recent history. As Zahedi remarks, each regime has employed a combination of "encouragement, legal measures, and physical force to impose its political will on Iranian women" (250). In so doing, the Iranian government has consistently "deprived Iranian women of choice about their identity, self-presentation, and place in society"—violations that "have only intensified women's determination to challenge these regimes" (263). However, women in current Iranian society who are against mandatory veiling have essentially no recourse, because unveiling would undoubtedly result in physical reprisals.

Thus, it is no surprise that the most explicit oppositions to veiling and its politics during the past three decades have emerged not from inside the country but from outside, primarily from members of the Iranian diaspora or exilic community. Such a diasporic or exilic situation has provided Marjane Satrapi with an opportunity to challenge the issue of veiling, both in its literal and metaphoric sense, as a major hindrance to self-revelation. Compared to other memoirs and autobiographies written by diasporic and exiled Iranians, the *Persepolis* and *Persepolis 2* remain revolutionary in many respects. One revolutionary aspect is the very medium Satrapi has used: comics. This medium had never previously been used by any Iranian author, let alone an Iranian woman, perhaps partly because, as a mode of storytelling that relies on images as well as words, it might at times entail depicting women unveiled, which is taboo. Satrapi has repeatedly been asked why she chose to present her autobiography as a graphic work. Her answers usually refer either to the advantages of image-text over text or image alone or to matters of personal taste. (See, for example, Root 150, as well as her comments in Shaikh; Tully.) Yet, as far as the issue of self-revelation is concerned, her choice of comics as the medium for expressing her personal memories and life experiences has been of remarkable help to her in creating an innovative Iranian text, and particularly an Iranian autobiography.

In Iran, women's published autobiographies did not emerge until the mid-twentieth century (Milani 220). Furthermore, compared to the number of works in this genre in the West, few autobiographies have been published in Iran.[1] As Farzaneh Milani argues in detail, the major reason behind the long absence of such a genre in Iran—both for men and women—has been the deep-rooted concept of veiling, both in its literal and figurative meanings, and its surrounding cultural constructions in Iranian society (24, 131, 201–02). As for women's autobiography in particular, Milani points out, "In a sexually segregated society where access to a woman's world and words is limited, and the concept of honor is built around woman's virginity (the proof of her inaccessibility) women's autobiographies, with their assertive self-attention and self-display, cannot easily flourish, and they have not" (201).

As Bonnie Gunzenhauser observes, an autobiography is not simply a report of one's life story (77). One defining feature, she maintains, is that "autobiography has a psychological and philosophical dimension that requires its writer to balance the deeds of an active public self with the thoughts of a contemplative private one" (77). And yet, in the relatively few Iranian autobiographies written to date, the private self of the autobiographer often blurs with the public self. "Most of these life-scripts," Milani observes, "have a sense of self deeply rooted in the public domain, representing what Bakhtin calls rhetorical autobiography. They are devoted mainly to the defense of a political career, a religious cause, a notorious life" (221). Drawing on Helen Buss's distinction between "memoir" and "autobiography"—that "memoir writers are more concerned with making their lives meaningful in terms of the lives of others and in terms of their communities rather than in terms of individual accomplishments" (595)—we can deem such writings as the ones referred to by Milani to be more like memoirs of public life than personal autobiographies. Thus, ironically, such so-called autobiographies are efforts to veil, rather than unveil, their authors' selves.

In light of this argument, I believe that Satrapi's text is, without exaggeration, a turning point in the history of Iranian autobiographical literature for at least two reasons. First, if we take a certain degree of self-revelation to be one defining feature of autobiography, then Satrapi's self-revelation surpasses that of her Iranian predecessors. Other Iranian autobiographers have been reluctant to reveal some inner levels of their selves, resorting, for example, to metaphors, allusions, and symbols to camouflage their sexual activities and experiences, if they are mentioned at all (Milani 143–44, 223).[2] In contrast, "Marji"—Satrapi's narrating "I" in both volumes—courageously confides in and shares with her audience the most intimate events of her and her extended family's lives. Such revelations include her pre-marriage relationships and sexual experiences, intimate circumstances regarding her parents and grandmother, her searching for food in trashcans, and her attempts to urinate like a man based on Simone de Beauvoir's advice. Furthermore, as mentioned above, Satrapi is the first Iranian author who has transcended the verbal medium of autobiography and chosen the "image-text" medium of comics for her narrative.

Through the eyes of a Western audience, Satrapi's act is not extraordinary, but in the context of Iranian taboos concerning women's self-unveiling and in light of the fact that her work is addressed to Iranian audiences as well, her act gains remarkable significance. Thus, if autobiographies are in themselves a form of self-disclosure (Milani 201), *Persepolis* and its sequel take self-disclosure to a new level. Arguing that Satrapi's "image-text" is not merely a documentation of her past but a "solo performance" achieved through "the mimetic acts of showing and telling her personal history," Jennifer Worth calls attention to "the personal nature of the narrative" as well as to "the presence of the body and focus on embodiment" (144). As she notes, despite the dominant presence of bodies of all kind in the *Persepolis* volumes, "it is Satrapi's own figure that predominates" (146). Not only does Satrapi's work expose the self through words, it visually depicts this multifaceted unveiling for the first time in the history of Iranian literature, despite the strong cultural, religious, and/or legal bans on any public or published self-disclosure and self-unveiling on the part of Iranian women. Therefore, only on a relative basis do I agree with Worth when she remarks,

> Given the forthrightness of both word and image in Satrapi's works, there is almost nothing that could be considered vulgar or offensive. Nudity, although rarely used, is implied through silhouette; coarse sexual language (terms stronger than "ass") occurs only once or twice; and Marjane's sexual encounters are visually elided and only textually alluded to in the vaguest of terms: "I've had a few experiences" is as explicit as she gets. This type of discretion indicates both Satrapi's Persian modesty and her respect for the power of the body. (153)

Worth's words may ring true for Western audiences, but from the perspective of Iranian culture, Satrapi has actually violated the boundaries of "modesty," an ideal best understood, as Milani explains, through the complex concept of *sharm* and a network of related subconcepts (52–53). I utterly agree with Naghibi and O'Malley, who—having a better understanding of Iranian culture both inside and outside Iran, especially in reference to *Persepolis 2*—deem Satrapi's unprecedented degree of self-disclosure to be "particularly shocking." As they note, "As an adolescent in Vienna and a young woman in Iran, Marji discloses much of her private life, including her sexual experiences. This is particularly shocking in an Iranian cultural context; Satrapi ventures into territory that is still off limits to the growing field of diasporic Iranian women's autobiographies, texts which tend to skirt the issue of sexuality" (241).

As if to provide a counterpoint to self-revelation, Satrapi begins her account with an episode titled "The Veil" (*Persepolis 3*), thereby establishing, from the outset, the theme of veiling—the troublesome concept that still complicates the disclosure of the self in Iranian society and culture (see figure 4.1). One could even argue, as Naghibi and O'Malley propose, that the veil is introduced from the very front cover of the first volume, which features an image of the young Marji wearing a veil (231). "The Veil" is, moreover, the only episode title that appears twice, once in each volume (see Worth 155). Both occurrences anticipate others related to Iran, and both end similarly with Marji leaving Iran. Thus, in a sense, the veil becomes the cultural icon of Iranian society in the text.

Figure 4.1. Panel from p. 3 of *Persepolis*. The image, used to title the opening episode, is repeated in *Persepolis 2* (p. 79)—the only episode title that occurs twice.

Figure 4.2. Panels from p. 132 of *Persepolis*. Here, Marji purchases some illegal music tapes. By depicting both the dealer and Marji as looking furtively in two directions at once, Satrapi suggests how censorship imposed from the outside can be internalized as self-censorship.

Although Satrapi refers frequently to the physical limitations that the veil imposes on women, her complex treatment of the veil transcends this literal sense. For instance, she artfully shows that outer censorship can create an internalized form of censorship and may therefore lead to internal conflict. Milani argues that the cultural features of veiling and censorship will necessarily result in a culture of self-censorship, a deliberate dichotomy between the inside and the outside (210), and that a "certain role playing, a constant watchfulness are the inevitable outcome" (213). As a result, life becomes a complex calculation of when, where, and to what degree the self should or should not be revealed (see *Persepolis 2* 148, sixth panel) and of the possible personal and/or social consequences of a failure to judge a situation accurately. Critically intervening in her own culture, Satrapi repeatedly calls attention to the existence of this dichotomy in contemporary Iranian society, especially after Marji's first return to Iran. In a scene in the first book, for example, Marji ventures out to buy some illegal music tapes (*Persepolis* 132). In two separate panels, Satrapi depicts both the dealer and Marji as necessarily on the alert, looking in two directions simultaneously in order to avoid being arrested (see figure 4.2).

However, much as Milani argues, Satrapi manages to suggest to her readers that in her society, external censorship will eventually lead to a sense of self-censorship, and thus a possible manifestation of internal conflict. This becomes more explicit when, after little Marji purchases the illegal tapes and is arrested by two female guardians of the Revolution, she manages to escape the predicament through a series of lies that build on one another. In the last panel of the incident, through a self-reflexive technique, Satrapi draws our attention to the role Marji has had to play in order to survive: the features of Marji's crying face are exaggeratedly deformed, making her face reminiscent of the tragedy mask of dramatic theatre (see figure 4.3).

Figure 4.3. Panel from p. 134 of *Persepolis*. Caught in the act of her illegal purchase, Marji lies her way out of arrest by a dramatic display of anguish and remorse.

Figure 4.4. Panels from p. 151 of *Persepolis* 2. The juxtaposed images suggest the way in which compulsory veiling extinguishes women's identity in public space. By allowing women to become individuals only in domestic settings, veiling produces a psychological split between the private and the public self.

With the compulsory hijab (veiling) in post-revolutionary Iran as one of her main themes, Satrapi explores the possible psychological implications of such an issue for women. As evidenced throughout her text, different situations in the lives of women living in contemporary Iran require different degrees of self-revelation. At home, a woman possesses the freedom to unveil, as shown by a host of domestic images throughout the text.[3] In public, however, a woman may dare to leave only a few tufts of hair unveiled. Yet, if a woman is about to be interviewed for a job or for admission to university, or to discuss her project with the "mayor's deputy," she must be as veiled as possible to increase her chances of success (see the interview panels in *Persepolis 2* 130, 177). The juxtaposition of two contrasting images in *Persepolis 2* successfully captures such an inside/outside dichotomy (see figure 4.4). The caption, split between the two panels, reads: "Our behavior in public and our behavior in private were polar opposites. This disparity made us schizophrenic" (151).

In fact, one major reason for Marji's second, "much less painful" exit from Iran (*Persepolis 2* 187) is arguably this intolerable cultural schizophrenia (to borrow the title of Dariush Shayegan's book). In other words, the text can be interpreted as Satrapi literally and figuratively choosing "freedom" (187) and unveiling over censorship and veiling. Upon her very arrival in Iran, Marji says, "After four years living in Vienna, here I am back in Tehran. From the moment I arrived at Mehrabad Airport, and caught sight of the first customs agent, I immediately felt the repressive air of my country" (*Persepolis 2* 92). Significantly, Marji's desire to leave Iran for the second time is both provoked and intensified by a series of events that illustrate what she calls "the repressive air of my country," generated mainly by the state's heavy implementation of veiling and censorship and sometimes by her fellow citizens as well. For example, when Marji is about to leave the house for the first time after her return from abroad, out of habit, she neglects to cover her head, at which point her mother warns her, "Don't forget your veil!" In response, Marji says, "Oh shit! I'll have to put it back on!" (96). Marji's hair, which she had the freedom to ignore in her social relations while she was abroad, becomes such a conscious part of her body as a woman in Iran that the cotton head scarf her grandmother gives her is regarded as a very precious gift. "This way," Marji's grandmother says to her, "your head can breathe. Otherwise you'll be bald in no time" (140).

Marji notices signs of the above-mentioned cultural schizophrenia early on, in the attitudes of her Iranian girlfriends. While Marji is spending time with her friends to escape her temporary state of depression (*Persepolis 2* 114–16), they urge her to tell them about her sexual experiences abroad. Accordingly, she informs them of her "few experiences," only to be shocked when one of them retorts: "So, what's the difference between you and a whore?" As Marji thinks to herself in retrospect, "Underneath their outward appearances of being modern women, my friends were real traditionalists" (116). The very incident causes Marji to go back home "even more depressed," after which she has to visit a psychiatrist (117). Later, at university, while Marji is encountering friends with similar attitudes, Satrapi significantly points out a resemblance between those friends' and the Islamic regime's repressive strategies (149).

The regime imposes sexual segregation on the society, including educational environments (*Persepolis 2* 127, 138, 145). The guardians of the Revolution control the relationship between couples of the same and different sex (134–35), as well as people's clothing on the street (147). Yet the people themselves also monitor each other's sexual relationships through self-censorship (141, 149). The atmosphere, Marji complains, is so oppressive that she and her fiancé often do not leave home: "The outside being dangerous, we often found ourselves inside, at his house or at my house. This situation was suffocating me" (136). Even at university, an Islamic style of dress is directly promoted, and women, especially, are advised to abide by that dress code (141–42). When "courageous" Marji objects to the prohibitive situation at her own university (143), not only does she not receive any convincing reply, but she is later summoned to be advised by a cleric that "wearing the veil is synonymous with emancipation" (144). Also, given the strict limitations concerning women's unveiling in institutional settings, Marji and her friends have to repeat their anatomy classes in the privacy of their own homes (150), since their drawing model at the university can only be either a veiled woman (145) or a man (146). Upon increasingly noticing the double lives of Iranian people, Marji remarks, "The more time passed, the more I became conscious of the contrast between the official representation of my country and the real life of the people, the one that went on behind the walls" (150; see also the episode titled "The Socks" 145–57).

The last and perhaps most crushing incident in this series of events, and the one that significantly prompts Marji to leave Iran—appropriately titled "The End"—is the failure of Marji and her fiancé to implement the design project they have worked on for seven months as their shared dissertation project (*Persepolis 2* 176). The project "involves creating a theme park using [Iranian] mythological heroes" (174), and Marji and Reza hope that it will eventually lead to the creation of "the equivalent of Disneyland in Tehran" (175). They earn the highest grade for the project and are advised by their supervisor to propose the project to the mayor of Tehran (176). Both before and during the meeting with the mayor's deputy, however, the issues of veiling and censorship resurface. Twice, Marji is denied the opportunity to meet with the deputy because of her indecent veiling and makeup. When she does finally manage to meet with him, she is disappointed when the long days and nights of serious effort on her and Reza's part are simply ignored and the project rejected because of its images of female mythological characters unveiled (see figure 4.5).

Figure 4.5. Panels from p. 177 of *Persepolis* 2. Marji's meeting with a deputy of the mayor of Tehran marks an epiphanic moment in her life, the end of a series of events that culminate in her decision to leave Iran.

Marji's closing " . . . I understand . . ." is uttered in an obviously depressed state at the end of her short exchange with the mayor's deputy, and the situation proves to be epiphanic and highly ironic in light of her departure from Iran for "freedom" shortly thereafter (187). It also gives richer meaning to the volume's subtitle, "The Story of a Return." Satrapi's desired freedom has now become manifest not only in her physically unveiled appearance abroad but also in her candidly and freely written, illustrated, and published narrative, which, because of the harsh censorship existing in Iran, could not have been published had Marji not left her homeland.

Yet, in addition to Satrapi's critical intervention in the Self through her content, she simultaneously engages with the Other through aspects of her text's form. While Satrapi emphasizes the educational aspect of her work with regard to Western audiences, I focus on somewhat different dimensions of her text. Specifically, I look at how aspects of her style challenge and contribute to the appreciation of the expressive language of comics as a medium still practiced and enjoyed mainly by Western authors and readers.

CHALLENGING THE OTHER: SATRAPI'S DRAWING STYLE AS ARTISTIC DEVICE

In the popular imagination, comics are often assumed to constitute a genre, a misconception that probably reflects the early association of comics with stories about "superheroes" (Wolk 11). In Scott McCloud's definition, however, comics consist of the juxtaposition of "pictorial and other images" (that is, words) so as "to convey information and/or to produce an aesthetic response in the viewer" (9). In other words, the comic format is a medium, not a genre. In *Reading Comics*, Douglas Wolk argues that media are "forms of expression that have few or no rules regarding their content" (11). Accordingly, a definition of comics should never predict or presume anything about the narrative content of comic works (see, for example, Chute, "Comics" 452; Eisner, *Comics* 5; McCloud 6, 9).

Understanding comics as a *form* of expression is, by implication, to underscore the crucial importance of *style*, which Wolk defines as "all the elements that go into a comic's 'look and feel'"—"the things that affect the reading experience irrespective of the story's content." Style is, as Wolk notes, partly a product of non-visual elements, including characteristic uses of language, pacing, and narrative structure, "but the biggest element of it is the idiomatic way a comic is drawn" (24). Style is thus associated above all with the manner of *drawing* itself, which Wolk describes as "the most immediate aspect of comics" (125). Style is thus associated above all with the manner of *drawing* itself, which Wolk describes as "the most immediate aspect of comics" (125).

As W. J. T. Mitchell reminds us, comics demand a "double literacy" (89). For this competence to be actualized on the reader's part, words must be intelligible, but visual images must likewise pass what Wolk calls the "legibility test." As Wolk points out, "In a cartoon, every object's form is subject to interpretive distortion—even when what's being distorted isn't a real image but a distant cousin of something real" (123). This distortion, he argues, "has only one hard limit. It has to be legible—the reader has to be able to recognize everything and everyone in the image very quickly" (124). In Wolk's view, the legibility of images is part of what distinguishes a good cartoonist from a bad one: "Every great cartoonist has a specific, intensely personal style, and so do most decent-to-middling cartoonists. Mediocre cartoonists' work blurs together; bad cartoonists generally either don't have enough control to work up a style of their own or fail the legibility test" (124). Although assessing whether Satrapi is a "great" or merely a "decent-to-middling" artist is beyond the scope of this chapter, the sheer popularity of the two *Persepolis* volumes suggests that Satrapi's style holds appeal for readers.

Hillary Chute remarks that Satrapi's cartooning has been "a subject of debate" to the point that some critics, while praising the content of *Persepolis*, have "devalued its aesthetics" ("Texture" 108n10). Other critics, including Naghibi and O'Malley as well as Chute herself, have tried to justify Satrapi's style. Chute emphasizes that "style as a narrative choice—and not simply a default expression—is fundamental to understanding graphic narrative" (99); she argues that Satrapi's "pared-down techniques of line and perspective" in her "devastatingly truthful and yet stylized" *Persepolis* is "a sophisticated, and historically cognizant, means of doing the work of seeing" (99). Likewise, Naghibi and O'Malley note the usual criticisms of Satrapi's "very 'cartoony'" style and maintain that "Satrapi's style is deliberate and has definite effects. It is part of her effort to make familiar, to universalize, but at the same time to other" (228).[4] While building upon this conversation, I attempt to advance it by suggesting that through successful eclecticism, Satrapi employs a perceptibly personal and creative style in the service of her artistic expression. In fact, as revealed through examples from the two volumes, Satrapi's graphic text fulfills Duncan and Smith's expectation of successful comic book writing, which they describe as "a creative act done with both words and pictures wherein 'the images are employed as a language'" (147, quoting Eisner, *Graphic Storytelling*).[5]

In an interview, Satrapi was asked whether she deploys techniques such as "breaking the frame," as Art Spiegelman does in parts of *Maus*, which serve to remind readers of the authorial presence.[6] She answered:

> No. Because I didn't come from a culture of comics. People like Art, they were kids that read comics, so they have lots of knowledge about the comics. They're aware of what they're doing. I didn't know anything about comics. . . . Now, with the work, I have some ideas about comics, but at the moment I started doing it . . . I didn't know what I was doing. I didn't have the experience and the background and all the theory. I didn't think about the comic; I was just doing it, and that was it. (qtd. in Root 157)

Satrapi's self-professed relative unfamiliarity with the medium of comics might have caused her to opt for eclecticism in developing her own style. As Wolk notes, Satrapi's cartooning method and her special use of intense contrasts of black and white suggests the influence of her mentor, David B. (the pen name of Pierre-François Beauchard), as a glance at his most famous work, *Epileptic*, reveals.[7] Another major influence on Satrapi's drawing style, as she herself acknowledges, is the dominant style of drawing in Persian classic miniature. In response to an interviewer's question, "Is there nonetheless something in your style that is unique to your Persian cultural background?" Satrapi said, "Certainly. The characteristic of including little perspective, and that of characters becoming taller or smaller based on their importance. These devices very much evoke Persian miniatures" (Hill 20). The only significant difference—which could be due to the influence of David B.—is that most Persian miniatures feature extensive use of various colours, whereas Satrapi's images are drawn in a sharply contrasting black and white. Richard Ettinghausen's description of the Iranian miniature is strongly reminiscent of Satrapi's drawing style. One special feature, he writes,

> which must strike anybody who views an exhibition of Persian art especially after having first visited the other sections of a museum containing Western art . . . is that the human figure is usually *highly stylized* or rendered in such a way that its features have aspects of caricatures, while in still other cases painted figures are given in a *disembodied, flat manner, which makes them appear to be without corporeal substance*. (qtd. in Milani 205–06; my emphasis)

Satrapi's cartooning style, with its simplified and sometimes highly stylized features as well as its intense black and white contrast, is also very much reminiscent of the comic strips published in Persian satirical newspapers and journals approximately three decades ago, when Marji was a child (see *Persepolis* 12).[8] This possible source of influence is compatible with Satrapi's sometimes humorous or satirical attitude toward her traumatic memories and the vices and absurdities of her native society. In one example, returning from her war-injured friend's home, Marji remembers: "That day, I learned something essential: we can only feel sorry for ourselves when our misfortunes are still supportable. Once this limit is crossed, the only way to bear the unbearable is to laugh at it" (*Persepolis 2* 112). This tactic—transforming cruel or upsetting realities into the subject of irony or humour—is visible in both volumes.

In *Persepolis*, Satrapi's highly simplified style serves to produce what Hillary Chute calls a "child's-eye rendition of trauma," in which the often horrific political events of Marji's childhood are rendered in a highly simplified manner, as if they had been sifted through the mind of a small child ("Texture" 98). The contrast between the style of depiction—images that suggest "a child's too-tidy conceptualization" of violence and death (100)—and the underlying reality has a defamiliarizing effect, at once distancing us from the trauma and forcing us to remember and acknowledge it.

Figure 4.6. Panel from p. 115 of *Persepolis*. Marji's "child's-eye" perspective on trauma has a defamiliarizing effect, in this case inviting readers to reinterpret post-revolutionary propaganda about the glory of martyrdom.

One example occurs as Marji grapples with ideas about war and martyrdom after the Iranian government refuses to accept Iraq's proposal for settlement and openly declares its intention to continue the war. Her imaginative reaction to government rhetoric is illustrated in a panel depicting a martyr's corpse (see figure 4.6). Post-revolutionary Iranian propaganda habitually sanctified images of martyrs, but the rather horrifying depiction of the corpse from the point of view of an innocent child invites readers to re-evaluate the seductive discourse of the Islamic Republic's mottos such as the one quoted in the panel's caption: "To die a martyr is to inject blood into the veins of society." Marji's reaction to the glorification of bloodshed is also revealed in her manipulation of Michelangelo's *La Pietà* in a drawing done to pass her qualifying exam (see figure 4.7). As Gillian Whitlock argues, through this manipulation, Marji the student acts politically by "subverting the political correctness" expected of her by the examiners (975–76). Later, Marji reaches the same conclusion when pondering the execution of Nilufar (the communist girl arrested in Khosrow's house). Marji remarks: "All night long I thought of that phrase: 'To die a martyr is to inject blood into the veins of society.' Nilufar was a real martyr and her blood certainly did not feed our society's veins" (*Persepolis* 146).

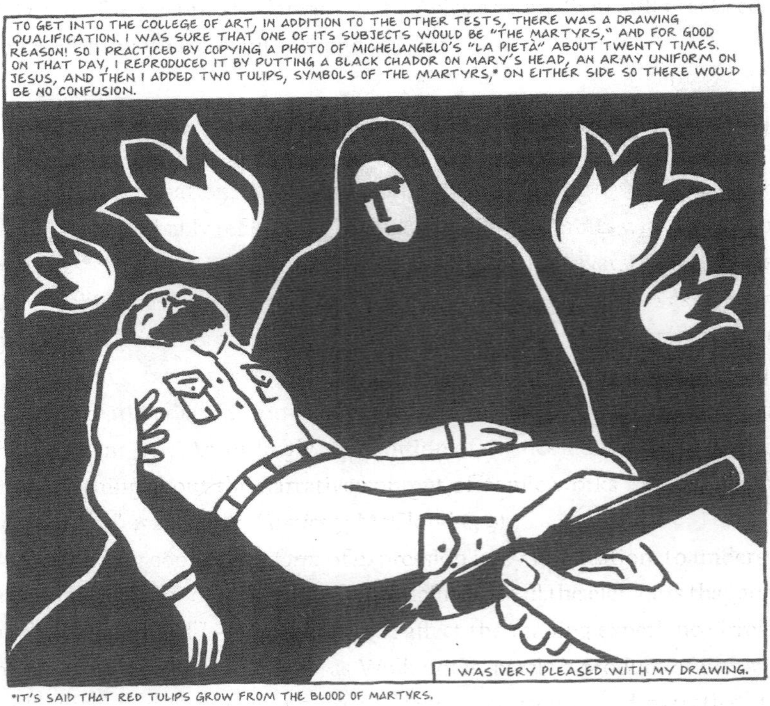

Figure 4.7. Panel from p. 127 of *Persepolis 2*. The panel illustrates Marji's subversive transformation of Michelangelo's *La Pietà* in the context of early post-revolutionary Iran, in a drawing done to pass a qualifying exam.

This "child's-eye rendition" allows Satrapi to present Marji's appalling childhood experiences in a way that enhances their visual power. As McCloud maintains, drawing styles in comics can range from the "extremely cartoony" to the highly realistic or even "near-photographic" (44; see also his second chapter), with each style having its own aesthetic functions. Therefore, adopting a realistic style in itself does not necessarily add to the aesthetic value of a work. As McCloud himself puts it, in reference to Art Spiegelman's *Maus*, "a simple style does not necessitate a simple story" (45). Nor does choosing a simplified mode of drawing signify an artistic flaw. Rather, the artist, according to the content of her work, chooses to develop a certain style. If we accept McCloud's theory that "[i]f an artist wants to portray the beauty and complexity of the *physical world*, realism of *some* sort is going to play a part" (41), then Satrapi's simplified cartooning could be taken to represent Marji's inability to recall clearly (or perhaps even to find at all) the complexity and beauty in her past life. Indeed, parts of Marji's past life are too unpleasant for a realistic style of drawing. Instead, Satrapi draws in a way that engages readers while simultaneously protecting them from trauma that would turn them away. As Amy Malek remarks,

> By using her simple, clean, wood-cut-like images to depict otherwise disturbing scenes of torture, war, or suicide, she ensures that the reader feels sympathy, pain, and anger, but does not experience the gruesomeness that may otherwise turn them off from the book: their imaginations are kept active, their hearts are strained, but their stomachs remain settled. (372)

Similarly, describing Satrapi's drawing style as "expressionistic" and "minimalist," Chute comments, "The stylization of *Persepolis* suggests that the historically traumatic does not have to be visually traumatic" ("Graphic Narrative" 135). Thus, as far as the harsh violence in the text is concerned, Satrapi's drawing style is intended to create some aesthetic distance.

McCloud's theory of cartooning as a form of "amplification through simplification" (30) can also assist us in appreciating aspects of Satrapi's visual idiom. What McCloud means is that by creating more abstract images in comics, the artist's intention is not to eliminate details but to foreground specific details. "By stripping down an image to essential 'meaning,'" explains McCloud, "an artist can amplify that meaning" (30). In many of the panels, Satrapi's characters—who are simplified to the point of "legibility"—"focus our attention on an idea" (31; see also Worth 154) by having been reduced to their most noticeable features or expressions. For example, in the first two panels on page 3 of *Persepolis*, we see Marji and four of her friends one year after the Revolution, when girls are segregated from boys and made to wear veils at school (see figure 4.8). The most noticeable expression conveyed to the audience, mostly through the simple shapes of lips, eyes, and eyebrows, is a sense of distraction and unhappiness, which is expressed by sacrificing all the complexities of the countenances. By contrast, the second panel on the following page shows an integrated class of boys and unveiled girls, and the expressions on faces (again conveyed through the shapes of lips, eyes, and eyebrows) are more varied. However, none of the pictures represent any expected childish enthusiasm, since even the picture of the integrated class belongs to the extremely chaotic year of 1979, when most streets in Iran were sites of demonstrations against the Shah.

Figure 4.8. The first two panels from p. 3 and the second panel from p. 4 of *Persepolis*. Using the technique of "amplification through simplification," Satrapi concentrates our attention on the contrast in facial expressions.

Satrapi's "simplification" sometimes takes a deliberately metonymic form, which, as I explain below, may be related to problems of memory and representation. One early example of this occurs in the episode titled "The Bicycle" in *Persepolis*, when the issue of the causes of the famous Cinema Rex fire is raised. This event, which occurred on 18 August 1978 and in which nearly 410 people were burned to death (Hiro 74), was one of the most painful, and still unresolved, events in the recent history of Iran: "The government blamed religious fanatics; the public accused Savak" (Hiro 74). In "The Bicycle," Marji's parents are in bed late at night, talking, as Marji eavesdrops (*Persepolis* 14, third panel). Marji's father is explaining to her mother the *real* reason behind the fire, that is, the reason alleged by the public rather than the one proposed by the government. Interestingly, after this panel, which introduces the source of the conversation, the voice of Marji's father merges into Satrapi's autobiographical narrator's voice. Satrapi's drawings illustrate her narrator's words, serving to supplement them, until we reach the final large panel on page 15 (see figure 4.9), in which the visual parts with the verbal, the image referring not to the words but assuming the task of narration. The drawing depicts the victims of the fire in the interior auditorium of Cinema Rex—not in any familiar human-like shape but in the shape of flame-like, ghostly bodied, open-mouthed, screaming skulls burning up—with most figures being reminiscent of Edvard Munch's *The Scream*. Using metonymy to powerful effect, Satrapit distills the scene down to its most essential and significant elements: flames and death skulls.

Figure 4.9. Panel from p. 15 of *Persepolis*. The panel demonstrates Satrapi's use of metonymic drawing in the service of narration.

Another equally thought-provoking example of Satrapi's use of metonymy in *Persepolis* occurs in the panel depicting the days during the Iraq-Iran war when many people in western and southern Iran were retreating to the safer parts of the country (89; see figure 4.10). The caption over the panel reads: "After Abadan, every border town was targeted by bombers. Most of the people living in those areas had to flee northward, far from the Iraqi missiles." In the image accompanying these words, Satrapi reduces the whole situation to an extremely simple, yet powerful, metonymy: cars being drawn upward by rising flames. The cars represent the people living in the border towns, fleeing north at full speed, while the flames pressing on the cars from three sides and funnelling them upward suggest the rapidly spreading annihilation of war.

Figure 4.10. Panel from p. 89 of *Persepolis*. In another noteworthy example of Satrapi's use of metonymic pictorial representation, cars squeezed by flames illustrate the flight of Iranians from Iraqi missiles.

In both examples, by preferring highly simplified, metonymic images to literal depictions of traumatic events, Satrapi seems to have been dealing with the problems of collective memory and the difficulties of historical representation. While such images illustrate Chute's "child's-eye rendition" of trauma, they may also be interpreted as attesting to a failure of memory on Satrapi's own part, which leaves her unable to reconstruct and/or represent such traumatic events literally. They might even be understood as Satrapi's subjective interpretation of her narrator's "postmemories,"—her depiction, long after the fact, of events that were originally related to Marji by others. In Marianne Hirsch's definition, the term *postmemory*

> describes the relationship that the generation after those who witnessed cultural or collective trauma bears to the experiences of those who came before, experiences that they "remember" only by means of the stories, images, and behaviors among which they grew up. But these experiences were transmitted to them so deeply and affectively as to seem to constitute memories in their own right. ("The Generation" 106–07)

However, even "memories in their own right," that is, personal memories, are narrations—subjective reconstructions, rather than objective descriptions, of past events. Sidonie Smith and Julia Watson warn of the problem of "assuming a transparent or 'mirror' relationship between the life and the visual and/or verbal text" (11). They point out that

> narrated memory is an interpretation of a past that can never be fully recovered. As psychologist Daniel Schachter has suggested, "Memories are records of how we have experienced events, not replicas of the events themselves." He goes on to explore how "we construct our autobiographies from fragments of experience that change over time." That is, we inevitably organize or form fragments of memory into complex constructions that become the stories of our life. (9)

Rather than actual representations of what the young Marji experienced (either herself or through postmemory), the above examples can thus be considered personal readings of these collective traumas as they are later remembered.

At the same time, such scenes are also descriptions of events reconstructed through the memory processes of the adult Satrapi, the artist, who has obviously manipulated and altered such visual memories using her repertoire of artistic skills. This distortion is, in effect, proclaimed by the cartoon medium itself, which is, in its very nature, "cartoony." As Wolk argues, in contrast to drawing, cartooning generally demands that the audience view the characters depicted as fictional ones, even if they are based on real historical persons. Using Joe Sacco's *Palestine* as an example, Wolk observes that "his drawing relies on careful observation, but its style indicates that his stories are subjective interpretations of those observations" (121). The same can be said of Satrapi's work, especially with regard to her rendering of historical events. While clearly referencing well-documented events, they are nonetheless imaginative revisions—stories about history.

In this respect, Satrapi's use of the word *story* in the subtitles of both *Persepolis* and *Persepolis 2* is noteworthy. When asked in an interview about the degree of truthfulness in her work, Satrapi answered: "As soon as you write your story, it is a story; this is not a documentary. Of course you have to make fiction, you have to cheat, you have to make some angle around there, because the story has to turn, so that is the reconstruction of what we do" (Root 150). Satrapi's declaration that any retelling of one's past results in a fictional account may be an indirect admission that memory is not capable of fully and objectively reconstructing the past. While listening to her Uncle Anoosh vehemently relating his memories, little Marji, who is concerned that she has no family heroes to boast about, thinks to herself: "What a story!" (*Persepolis* 56). Like Satrapi herself, Marji suggests here that any lived experience, once recounted, becomes a story, told from a specific viewpoint. Even the most "photographic" memory is inevitably a subjective reworking. Yet Satrapi's awareness of the limits of memory is revealed, perhaps more than anything else, by the episodic nature of the *Persepolis*, in which specific events in Satrapi's past provide the starting point for separate stories in her text. As Michael Sheringham points out, it is often assumed that "the office of memory is to gather, preserve, and unify." In this view, "Memory is redemptive: its miracle is to remedy apparent disparateness and loss by restoring a living continuity" (597). The episodic structure of the *Persepolis* volumes suggests instead what Sheringham describes as "the problematic, troublesome aspect of memory" (597)—its discontinuous nature, its blank spaces, its apparently arbitrary privileging of one event over another. Like the metonymic nature of some of her image-texts, Satrapi's episode titles seem to have served as personal mnemonic codes, as triggers for memory, through which she has tried her best not to forget.

CONCLUSION

Considered in the context of Iranian literature in general and Iranian autobiography in particular, Satrapi's two *Persepolis* volumes have successfully opened previously unexplored paths to self-revelation. As Farzaneh Milani argues in *Veils and Words*, the fact that autobiography has been slow to emerge in Iran has roots in the serious issue of self-disclosure in Iranian culture. As she notes, "This reluctance to talk publicly and freely about the self, however, is not confined to women. Iranian men have also shunned self-representation. Even in the few published autobiographies available, authors often suppress their uninhibited, unformulaic public self-disclosure" (201). In *Persepolis* and again in *Persepolis 2*, Marjane Satrapi breaks with this tradition, exhibiting a degree of self-disclosure that, as Naghibi and O'Malley remind us, is "particularly shocking in an Iranian cultural context" (241). Efforts to ban her work notwithstanding, her achievement in overcoming her "internal ancestral censor" (Milani 47) must be cherished. She engages in self-revelation in the face of strong cultural taboos concerning self-unveiling that exist not only inside but outside Iran. As is rightly noted by Naghibi and O'Malley, Satrapi risks travelling into a territory that is still out of bounds even to the diasporic Iranian female autobiographer (241).

As my analysis of the concept of "veil" in the *Persepolis* volumes suggests, Satrapi's innovative autobiographical self-revelation is further supported by her critical attitude toward that concept, not only as a physical impediment to self-revelation but also as a cause of possible psychological and cultural disorders. In considering this issue, Satrapi shows awareness of the intricacies of the concept, including not only the problem of external censorship as manifested in the mandating of women's veiling but also the problem of self-censorship as one of its major psychological implications. Evidently, Satrapi's self-unveiling has already served to inspire others. In 2012, Mana Neyestani—an Iranian cartoonist and illustrator now based in France—became the first Iranian male author to recount his life story using the medium of comics. His *Une métamorphose iranienne* was soon translated into several languages, including English. Neyestani's drawing style is very different from Satrapi's; however, particularly in depicting aspects of his relationship to his wife, he shares her willingness to shatter Iranian cultural taboos surrounding self-revelation.

While challenging and contributing to Iranian culture and literature via aspects of its content, Satrapi's text, through the specific drawing style she adopts, also intervenes in, and helps advance, the medium of comics as a form still mostly practiced and enjoyed by Western artists and readers. Whereas Satrapi has often expressed her hope that her books will help to educate Western readers about Iran, I would instead emphasize how certain formal and stylistic aspects of her work engage with, and contribute to, the aesthetics of comics in the West. As I have argued, different degrees of realism in drawing, far from necessarily signifying the artist's skill or lack thereof, may be adopted by artists for different expressive needs and purposes. Thus, Satrapi's "cartoony" drawing should be regarded as a deliberate stylistic attempt to create special aesthetic effects. As I have demonstrated through analyzing a number of examples, Satrapi's simplified style is effectively employed to deal with important themes and to convey to readers the general feel of particular events despite problems of memory and historical representation. Among other things, Satrapi's "stylized" approach to drawing allows her to mitigate the effects of scenes of graphic violence, to amplify meaning through (metonymic) simplification, to focus on the fictionality of her narrative, and to disclose the imperfections of memory. In this respect, Satrapi's unfamiliarity with the medium of comics may thus have worked to her advantage. Integrating eclectic sources of influence, she has created a visually dramatic style entirely her own, through which she constructs dialogues of Self and Other that unveil both herself and her country.

I would like to thank Jerry Varsava, and especially the editors of the volume, Manijeh Mannani and Veronica Thompson, for their helpful comments on earlier drafts of this chapter. I am also grateful to Joyce Hildebrand for her thoughtful and attentive copy-editing of the text and to Pamela Holway, of Athabasca University Press, for her close and perceptive reading of my argument.

NOTES

1 The first known Iranian autobiography by a woman is Taj al-Saltana's memoir, which was written in 1924. It was, however, not published until 1982 (Milani 220), with an English translation, *Crowning Anguish: Memoirs of a Persian Princess from the Harem to Modernity*, appearing in 1993. In Jolly's two-volume *Encyclopedia of Life Writing*, the only material on Iran and the Persian language is a short passage under the entry "Islam and Life Writing" (2:475).

2 The only apparent exception in this regard is Jalal Al-e Ahmad's *A Stone on a Grave* (written in 1963 but published only in 1981), a memoir of infertility, in which Al-e Ahmad reveals some of the most private aspects of his and his wife's relationship and of his extended family. Yet even Al-e Ahmad is bound by the concept of "veil," referring his wife, a respected and well-known writer, by her name only once in the entire book (see Milani 47).

3 According to mainstream Islamic jurisprudence, even in their own homes Muslim women cannot appear unveiled if any *na-mahram* people (those outside the circle of their close kin, or *maharem*) are present. This rule is not observed in Satrapi's family (for instance, see *Persepolis* 49–50) because they are not religious.

4 For other attempts to explain possible special effects of Satrapi's style, see Davis; Malek (372); and Whitlock (974, 976–77).

5 Employment of images as language is also quite discernible in many of the examples I mention in the first part of the essay. See figures 4.2, 4.3, and 4.4.

6 The term *breaking the frame* refers to the visual device of moving the action of a comic beyond the edges of the frame, so that images transgress the established boundaries. In posing his question to Satrapi, Root states that, by breaking the frame, Spiegelman is "coming out of the book and saying, this is a comic book, in case we didn't know." Here, Root appears to be using the example of breaking the frame to refer more broadly to what theorists of postmodernist fiction call self-reflexivity. Patricia Waugh considers self-reflexivity to be the pivotal element in "metafiction," which she defines as "fictional writing which self-consciously and systematically draws attention to its status as an artefact in order to pose questions about the relationship between fiction and reality" (2; see also Lodge 220–45). Despite Satrapi's denial of using such metafictional techniques, she does, in effect, "break the frame" at least a few times in *Persepolis* (4, last panel; 114, panels 4–7; 115, panels 2 and 4; 116; 117) and once in *Persepolis 2* (32), collapsing the boundary between Satrapi the narrator and Marji the character by blurring their narrative voices. In fact, Gillian Whitlock refers to both Satrapi and Spiegelman as "self-reflexive practitioners in their use of cartoon drawing" (971). My thanks to Brad Bucknell for alerting me to the self-reflexive aspects of Satrapi's work.

7 Satrapi recognizes the influential role of David B. as a former instructor who "helped me for the first two, three chapters of *Persepolis*. He taught me a lot of things" (Chute, "Graphic Narrative" 242–43n4). As Wolk remarks, Satrapi's success in attracting an audience has overshadowed that of her mentor to the point that people sometimes confuse the direction of influence: "When I show people *Epileptic*," he comments, "they often note that it takes after *Persepolis* a bit" (145).

8 For examples of strips from different journals that, to different degrees, evoke Satrapi's drawing style, see Javadi (174, 285, 297, 298, 302, 303).

WORKS CITED

Al-e Ahmad, Jalal. *A Stone on a Grave*. Costa Mesa, CA: Mazda, 2008.

Al-Saltana, Taj. *Crowning Anguish: Memoirs of a Persian Princess from the Harem to Modernity*. Ed. Abbas Amanat. Trans. Anna Vanzan and Amin Neshati. Washington, DC: Mage, 1993.

Buss, Helen M. "Memoirs." Jolly 2:595–97.

Chute, Hillary. "Comics as Literature? Reading Graphic Narrative." *Publications of the Modern Languages Association of America* 123.2 (2008): 452–65.

——. "Graphic Narrative as Witness: Marjane Satrapi and the Texture of Retracing." *Graphic Women: Life Narratives and Contemporary Comics*. Hillary Chute. New York: Columbia UP, 2010. 135–73.

———. “The Texture of Retracing in Marjane Satrapi’s *Persepolis*.” *Women’s Study Quarterly* 36.1–2 (2008): 92–110.
Davis, Rocío G. “A Graphic Self: Comics as Autobiography in Marjane Satrapi’s *Persepolis*.” *Prose Studies* 27.3 (2005): 264–79.
Duncan, Randy, and Matthew J. Smith. *The Power of Comics: History, Form, and Culture*. New York: Continuum, 2009.
Eisner, Will. *Comics and Sequential Art*. Tamarac, FL: Poorhouse, 1985.
———. *Graphic Storytelling and Visual Narrative*. 1996. New York: W. W. Norton, 2008.
Gunzenhauser, Bonnie J. “Autobiography: General Survey.” Jolly 1:75–77.
Hill, C. “Marjane Satrapi Interviewed, August 24, 2003.” *International Journal of Comic Art* 8.2 (2006): 6–33.
Hiro, Dilip. *Iran Under the Ayatollahs*. London: Routledge, 1987.
Hirsch, Marianne. “The Generation of Postmemory.” *Poetics Today* 29.1 (2008): 103–28.
Javadi, Hasan. *Satire in Persian Literature*. Rutherford, NJ: Fairleigh Dickinson UP, 1988.
Jolly, Margaretta, ed. *Encyclopedia of Life Writing: Autobiographical and Biographical Forms*. 2 vols. London: Fitzroy Dearborn, 2011.
Lodge, David. *The Modes of Modern Writing: Metaphor, Metonomy, and the Typology of Modern Literature*. London: Edward Arnold, 1977.
Malek, Amy. “Memoir as Iranian Exile Cultural Production: A Case Study of Marjane Satrapi’s *Persepolis* Series.” *Iranian Studies* 39.3 (2006): 353–80.
McCloud, Scott. *Understanding Comics: The Invisible Art*. New York: Harper, 2004.
Milani, Farzaneh. *Veils and Words: The Emerging Voices of Iranian Women Writers*. Syracuse, NY: Syracuse UP, 1992.
Mitchell, W. J. Thomas. *Picture Theory: Essays on Verbal and Visual Representation*. Chicago: U of Chicago P, 1994.
Naghibi, Nima, and Andrew O’Malley. “Estranging the Familiar: ‘East’ and ‘West’ in Satrapi’s *Persepolis*.” *English Studies in Canada* 31.2–3 (2005): 22–48.
Neyestani, Mana. *An Iranian Metamorphosis*. Minneapolis: Uncivilized Books, 2014.
Root, Robert. “Interview with Marjane Satrapi.” *Fourth Genre: Explorations in Nonfiction* 9.2 (2007): 147–57.
Satrapi, Marjane. *Persepolis: The Story of a Childhood*. Trans. Mattias Ripa and Blake Ferris. New York: Pantheon, 2003.
———. *Persepolis 2: The Story of a Return*. Trans. Anjali Singh. New York: Pantheon, 2004.
Shaikh, Nermeen. “Marjane Satrapi: ‘I Will Always Be Iranian.’” Asia Society, 9 May 2005. 3 Apr. 2009. http://www.asiasociety.org/arts-culture/literature/marjane-satrapi-i-will-always-be-iranian.
Shayegan, Dariush. 1992. *Cultural Schizophrenia: Islamic Societies Confronting the West*. Syracuse, NY: Syracuse UP, 1997.
Sheringham, Michael. “Memory.” Jolly 2:597–98.
Smith, Sidonie, and Julia Watson. “Introduction: Mapping Women’s Self-Representation as Visual/Texual Interfaces.” *Interfaces: Women, Autobiography, Image, Performance*. Ed. Sidonie Smith and Julia Watson. Ann Arbor: U of Michigan P, 2005. 1–46.

Tully, Annie. "An Interview with Marjane Satrapi." *Bookslut*, Oct. 2004. 3 Apr. 2009. http://www.bookslut.com/features/2004_10_003261.php.

Waugh, Patricia. *Metafiction: The Theory and Practice of Self-Conscious Fiction*. London: Methuen, 1984.

Whitlock, Gillian. "Autobiographics: The Seeing 'I' of the Comics." *Modern Fiction Studies* 52.4 (2006): 965–79.

Wolk, Douglas. *Reading Comics: How Graphic Novels Work and What They Mean*. Cambridge, MA: Da Capo, 2007.

Worth, Jennifer. "Unveiling: *Persepolis* as Embodied Performance." *Theatre Research International* 32.2 (2007): 143–60.

Zahedi, Ashraf. "Concealing and Revealing Female Hair: Veiling Dynamics in Contemporary Iran." *The Veil: Women Writers on Its History, Lore, and Politics*. Ed. Jennifer Heath. Berkeley: U of California P, 2008. 250–65.

CHAPTER FIVE

Mr. and Mrs. F and the Woman

Personal Identities in Zoya Pirzad's *Like All the Afternoons*

Madeleine Voegeli

Despite their brevity, the short stories in Zoya Pirzad's collection *Like All the Afternoons* (*Mesl-e hameh-ye asr-ha*, 1991) offer telling pictures of the life circumstances of their protagonists.[1] How they live their lives, respond to their circumstances, and relate to themselves and others are the questions to be explored in this chapter. But before we enter into this discussion, I will locate Zoya Pirzad's short stories in the Persian literary landscape.

The literary historian Hasan Mir-Abedini opens one part of his annals on Persian prose fiction with observations on a type of neo-realism that came to the fore in the 1990s. He characterizes this neo-realism, which he notices especially in the works of women authors, as a realism that—unlike the magic realism of the 1980s and the earlier socialist realism—does not seek social struggle or the exalted and removed but rather devotes itself to the ordinary lives and experiences of the urban middle class ("Dastan-nevisi-e Iran," 64). This neo-realism, he explains, "shows signs of a change in the way of looking at life. It rejects the conventional way of looking at the facts of reality. Whatever there is, it is worth looking at, since it is based on experience that has been lived and felt" (65). This neo-realism has, in other words, elevated the ordinary and banal to the rank of literariness.

One of the authors whom Mir-Abedini presents under the heading of neo-realism is Zoya Pirzad, albeit with her third, not her first, collection of stories titled *Yek ruz mandeh be eyd-e pak* (*One Day Before Easter*, 1998). While he praises this third collection for its persuasive power ("Dastan-nevisi-e Iran," 66), he is less positive about Pirzad's first collection, *Like All the Afternoons*, which he characterizes as sketchy and aloof ("Adabyat-e dastani," 214). Other, less content-oriented critics have judged *Like All the Afternoons* differently. After a second, expanded edition appeared in 1996, Zhinus Azadegan published a subtle review, stating that Pirzad "writes from the depths of the ordinary Iranian city-dwelling woman." She adds, "What distinguishes these stories is the author's intelligent expedition into the lives of ordinary people, which induces the readers to appraise themselves and their society" (16).[2] Thus, even if some of the stories do not adhere to realism exclusively in their narrative mode, *Like All the Afternoons* falls under Mir-Abedini's definition of neo-realism and should, following Azadegan, allow us to sound out ordinary attitudes toward ordinary urban, middle-class lives in convincing literary reflections.

Having situated the literary material on which this study is based, I now turn to the questions of identity, Pirzad's protagonists, and our approach to them. When discussing identity in the works of Pirzad, scholars have focused on national and cultural identities.[3] But while these issues are inherent in Pirzad's later works, they have little impact on her first collection. The short stories of *Like All the Afternoons* are not located precisely either in space or in time.[4] They are set in surroundings that are recognizably urban middle class, with neighbouring houses, lanes, streets, crossroads and park benches, with nuclear families, housewives, and wage earners. Some disparate hints at clothing suggest one location more than another—a tie, for instance; stockings or a headscarf—and some personal names and references to food indicate linguistic and cultural surroundings, as does, in one instance, the mention of exile and Oriental carpets. But the settings are generally pinpointed more by the reader's associations than by explicit designation. Rather than promoting national or cultural issues, the short stories in *Like All the Afternoons* seem preoccupied with the human condition in a specific social setting, and our focus here rests, therefore, not on national nor cultural identities but on personal identities in a sociopsychological sense. Within the limits imposed by the looking-glass of fiction, I will examine selected protagonists of *Like All the Afternoons* as sociological subjects in order to reveal the identities they construe for themselves.

Like All the Afternoons comprises fifteen short stories (seventeen and eighteen in the second and third editions, respectively), the settings of which are mostly domestic, either indoors or in the vicinity of private homes. They revolve around the daily routines of the protagonists, most of whom are single, and rather than relating specific events, many of them resemble still lives of the protagonists in their domestic habitats. Several of the stories embrace diachronic themes of individuals and their roles in the succession of generations, but since personal identity is here understood as the temporary result of a continuing process, I have disregarded generational themes in the following discussion. For our purpose, I have selected three short stories in which single protagonists are displayed at a certain stage of their lives. "The Stain," "Mrs. F Is a Fortunate Woman," and "The Desired Life of Mr. F" share enough features to allow for comparison and differ enough to make such comparisons profitable.[5] The three stories will be explored with regard to the life circumstances, responses, and individual characteristics of the protagonists, and the cornerstones of their personal identities.

"THE STAIN"

"The Stain" ("Lakkeh," Pirzad, *Mesl-e* 19–22) relates a housewife's late afternoon hours. The story begins with a woman sitting beside a window and listening to the sounds of the children playing outside in the lane. The woman eventually dozes off. At the end of the story, she wakes up, sees her husband coming home, and gets up to complete her dinner preparations.

In the few paragraphs of her late afternoon nap, on one diegetic level, we learn more about the main protagonist, referred to as "the woman" (*zan*) throughout the story. The woman moved into the present location with her husband when they were married thirty years ago. They have no children. Over all these years, she has followed an unvarying household routine, and nothing has changed except that she has decorated the house with some additional vases and porcelain figures. In the afternoons, she sometimes visits her neighbours, and in the evenings, toward seven o'clock, she awaits her husband's return. While waiting for her husband, she sits beside the window overlooking the lane, her gaze reaching to the point where the lane opens into a street. At that time of the day, the lane is normally dark and quiet—quite to the contrary of the street. From her point of view, the general hustle of that distant street, its lights and sounds, melts into one luminous and humming stain, and she is afraid of it. When she sees it, she is so discomposed that she starts hallucinating: sometimes she sees the stain change shape or approach her as if to swallow her; sometimes she hears its terrible laughter. Although terrified by it, she is forced to look at the stain, because sooner or later her husband's silhouette would detach itself from the stain in the shape of a blurred black dot, would grow bigger and distinct until he is home in person. With the return of the husband, her fears disappear. The moment of his return is described thus: "This would be the best moment of her day, the moment when the small black dot brings the intimately familiar assembly of her small world to perfection" (22).

What is the woman's situation and how does she respond to it? The woman has been living her life in her domestic world unchangingly for thirty years. Apart from contact with the neighbours, she has no connections with the outside world. This outside world, condensed in the image of the stain, terrifies the woman, but her husband, a regular wanderer between the outside and domestic worlds, establishes her indirect contact with it and soothes her fears. The husband's role of the material provider is only implied. In addition to her material dependency as a result of the role allocations of housewife and provider, the woman is also shown as depending on her husband emotionally: her peace of mind is restored daily by his return, the climax in her twenty-four-hour cycle.

The extradiegetic narrator, with his or her limited insight into the woman's consciousness, offers a picture of the woman's response to her situation and the workings of her mind. The fact that the narrator enjoys or pretends only limited insight becomes manifest when he or she resorts to speculation, as the word "perhaps" in the quotation below will show. According to this narrator, the woman has a clear preference in life: what she appreciates more than anything is calmness (*aramesh*). She dislikes unexpected events (*ettefaq*) and likes to know exactly what to do and what to expect at any time of the day. Such calmness is endangered by any change in her routine: for example, changes caused by illness or the acquisition of new household appliances, the handling of which needs some getting used to. This calmness of hers would also be at risk on an emotional level by having children. Upon learning that she has no children, we read: "She did not complain about this. Perhaps she was even pleased. It was difficult for her to imagine a new living creature in the house. For a child's sake, one would have to be sad, or one would have to be happy. And she did not like to be sad or happy. Children disrupt one's calmness of life, and the woman loved this calmness above everything" (21).

So, as long as no emotions are stirred and her calmness is undisturbed or—as in connection with the stain—is restored regularly, the woman lives a life of strict routines and does so uncomplainingly, perhaps even contentedly.

Who is the character underlying such a response to the circumstances described? There are two distinctive features of the protagonist's makeup. First, she is stripped of individuality by denomination.[6] While peripheral figures such as the children playing in the lane are mentioned one by one by their personal names and momentary actions, the main figure, "the woman," has no name, nor, for that matter, does her husband, who is referred to throughout the story simply as "her husband" (*shohar-ash*).[7] Renouncing a personal name in favour of a generic denomination affects the tangibility of the protagonist. The term zan, "the woman," denotes not only her femaleness but also—as opposed to *dokhtar* (a girl or unmarried female)—her marital status. Yet, without a personal name, the protagonist could be any married woman. The denomination emphasizes what she has in common with other individuals of the same type rather than what distinguishes her from them.

Second, the story deprives the protagonist of her personal history. The woman's wedded life is condensed into a twenty-four-hour cycle: since, as the narrator tells us (20), every year, every month, and every day has been exactly like the one before, the description of one single day is sufficient to describe thirty years of married life. As for her life before marriage, the woman hardly recollects anything apart from some faded memories of her deceased parents, and when looking at old pictures of herself, she cannot relate the young woman in the picture to her own present self. According to the narrator, the woman sees her life thus: "To her, life had started on the first day of her marriage; but even that day she could hardly remember. As if she had married on the day of her birth or had been born on her wedding day" (20). The woman's lack of recollections is in agreement with the typifying denomination: married women "come into existence" through marriage. Marriage here is equated with the woman's birth, and not even a physical continuum, the body, has had the power to bridge the gap between the different identities before and after the caesura of marriage. If there was a notion of a self in the woman before marriage, then it was not linked to the body and it disappeared with marriage, while the body was handed over to some other occupant. This other occupant, as it is described by the narrator, seems a zero-realization of a self: deindividualized, with limited emotionality, without history or personal interests beyond an inclination toward calmness. As such, the body's occupant appears more like a dummy than a "real" human being. Nevertheless, with this makeup, the woman seems fit to persevere uncomplainingly in her circumstances.

For interpretations of this story, it does not suffice to rely only on the narrator's account; to penetrate the workings of the main protagonist's character more deeply, the possible meanings of the stain and the woman's fear of it must be taken into consideration.[8] Viewing matters from the angle of personal identity, a reading of the stain as a metaphor for the woman's displaced self seems promising: the alienated self, relegated to the stain, still has the power to stir a memory of her (former) self in the deindividualized dummy. When the dummy is confronted with the stain, it faces a dilemma of longing for its lost individual self, including history and emotionality, and an equally strong longing for calmness. Since the woman faces this dilemma daily, she obviously is—for whatever intrinsic or extrinsic reason—unable to find a way of either resolving this dilemma or resigning herself to the present situation completely. Her daily discomposure is both the consequence of her daily confrontation with the dilemma and—together with the abandonment of her individuality—the price she pays for living in relative peace. In terms of personal identity, the situation of the woman is that of a subject whose balance between the individual and social sides of her identity has been overthrown totally in favour of the latter.

In summary, "The Stain" presents the empty shell of a general type fulfilling its social tasks (with the exception of reproduction) perfunctorily, and the general type appears in the guise of an individual heroine—as suggested by the conventions of this literary genre. Hints at an individual identity of the protagonist can be gathered from the narrative (and are highlighted by the title) and have the potential to make the reader distrust the narrator and his or her picture of uncomplaining perseverance.

The next of Pirzad's protagonists to be examined here is more palpable, more a creature of flesh and blood, than "the woman" and, unlike her, is not just uncomplaining but—as announced in the story's title—positively fortunate.

"MRS. F IS A FORTUNATE WOMAN"

"Mrs. F Is a Fortunate Woman" ("Khanum-e F zan-e khoshbakht-i ast," Pirzad *Mesl-e*, 51–57) describes the monthly payday events in the private home of Mr. and Mrs. F. Mr. F is an accountant in the wages department of the Ministry of Education, and Mrs. F is a housewife; they have been married for twenty-five years and have two children, a son called Bardya and a daughter called Yasaman. Every month, Mr. F delivers his salary directly to his wife. While the husband then relates insider news from the ministry, Mrs. F serves him tea, counts the notes, puts the money away, and prepares dinner. At night, when the husband and children have retired, Mrs. F prepares the budget for the coming month and balances accounts for the month past. Three scenarios are shown: (1) if Mrs. F has just about managed to make ends meet, her reaction is neutrally listless; (2) if the expenses have exceeded the income, she is despondent for some days and tries to economize in her housekeeping; and (3) in the rare case of having managed so well that some money is left over, she smiles happily. In this happy third scenario, Mrs. F takes the remaining money to the bank the next day and pays it into the accounts of her children—saving what she can for Bardya's later education abroad and for a respectable dowry for Yasaman. Very occasionally when profits exceed expenses—after much hesitation and many pangs of conscience and justifications to her husband, her mother, and even her children—she keeps some of the remaining money and buys something for herself: a pair of nylon stockings or a headscarf, for example. She has these items gift-wrapped in the shop and stores them at home in their original wrappings. In moments of leisure, when she has seen to all her duties and is sure that no one is around to disturb or watch her, she sits down solemnly, unwraps the purchases with the utmost care and gazes at them, pondering what a fortunate woman she is. This is the sum of the story.

The monthly events, which recur year in and year out, are related in the present tense. The story is told by an extradiegetic third-person narrator with full insight into Mrs. F's consciousness and emotions, the pivotal point of which seems to be her financial circumstances. Yet Mrs. F is stirred by more than pecuniary issues.

One such issue concerns a possible alternative lifestyle. When Mrs. F visits the bank, she is always received by Mrs. Taqizadegan. The two women have known each other for many years—since the day Mrs. F first entered the bank to open an account for Bardya. Mrs. Taqizadegan, now director of the bank, was a mere petty employee at that time. She, too, has a son and a daughter, though they are somewhat younger than those of Mrs. F. While the two women sit and chat about their children, Mrs. Taqizadegan answers phone calls and deals out signatures and orders. On her way home, Mrs. F routinely wonders how Mrs. Taqizadegan manages the tasks of a mother as well as those of a bank manager—whether, perhaps, it is not all that difficult and whether she herself might have reached a position with responsibilities if she had not quit work when she got married. But just as routinely, she acknowledges to herself that she was never fond of work and studying and that she had gladly submitted to Mr. F's insistence on her becoming a housewife. Yet acknowledging this does not prevent her from feeling jealous of Mrs. Taqizadegan, a resentment she regularly silences with the belief that "a woman who works outside can never meet the requirements of her husband and children" (55). Thus blocking unsettling thoughts, she unlocks the front door and re-enters her domestic realm.

In spite of these repeatedly arising doubts as to her own lack of career, Mrs. F declares herself a fortunate woman, as we read at the end of the story. Her thought is followed by a list of reasons why she is fortunate:

> She has a husband who does not squander money as some men do and who does not take offence at his wife's extravagance. She has two healthy children, Yasaman, who—as everybody says—is beautiful, composed, and brought up excellently, and Bardya, who is taller than all his coevals in the family, studies eagerly, and wants to become a structural engineer. They have a house that despite its smallness spares them living as tenants and endearing themselves to the owner of the house. What else should a woman want from life? (57)

Her reference to her "extravagance" is revealing. Although the F family live in their own home and lack no essentials, there is no room for extravagance, as can be deduced not only from the "smallness" of the house but also from the holes in Mrs. F's shoes (53). Indeed, the entire story shows how little material (and temporal) extravagance Mrs. F allows herself—and then, only after the needs of all the others have been met.

Mrs. F's assessment of her good fortune is no original product of her own deliberation but an extrinsic concept that she has appropriated. The declaration that she is fortunate, made in the title and in the opening sentence of the story, is followed by "everybody says so" (*in ra hameh miguyand*, 51). The title and first sentence thus express a general opinion. One proponent of this opinion is Mrs. F's mother, who considers her daughter's situation so enviable that she burns rue seeds every Saturday morning in order to avert the evil eye, as stated in the opening paragraph. The question of whether Mrs. F actually thinks of herself as fortunate, as is suggested at the end of the story, or simply mimics the general opinion, trying to convince herself, remains open. The story does provide evidence that the latter might be the case. As we have seen, Mrs. F raises the question of what else a woman might want from life, and although she pretends to herself that her own answer is "nothing," her doubts after the meetings with Mrs. Taqizadegan tell a different tale. These doubts would not recur regularly if Mrs. F was really convinced by her own self-persuasion. It is more likely that her doubts are merely subdued, her question swept under the carpet rather than answered convincingly. In this story, being fortunate is a concept defined and attributed by a nondescript public and handed down from mother to daughter. Considering Mrs. F's list of reasons why she must be fortunate, it is evident that good fortune is a concept based on circumstantial factors without reference to a person's psychological constitution.

How does the fortunate Mrs. F feel in or about her situation? She has a range of feelings connected with the family's financial circumstances, but the strongest emotions described in the story arise in Mrs. F when she buys something for herself: "When she buys something she wants, she inevitably gets into a state which she does not want anyone to witness" (56). In what follows, I will refer to this state of hers as ecstasy. There are two follow-up effects of these items and the ecstasy that accompanies their purchase: first, merely thinking of these private possessions revitalizes her during her daily chores and helps her to continue with renewed energy regardless of pain and fatigue; and second, she experiences a mix of emotions when she sits down on occasion to unwrap her unused possessions and gaze at them.

When Mrs. F gazes at her purchases, it becomes clear that she does not necessarily want to use them for herself; the stockings, for instance, she might eventually give to Yasaman. The attraction of these moments must therefore lie in something other than the goods themselves or any pride of possession. Although the narration does not make an explicit causal connection, it suggests by juxtaposition that the importance of these moments lies in something immaterial: "These rare moments are the only private moments in her life" (56). The common denominator of this threefold pleasure—the ecstasy at the purchase, the elation while remembering, and the moments of contemplation (rather than consumption)—is privacy, the fact that she is tending to herself rather than to others. But tending to herself has its cost, as we read immediately afterwards: "She feels guilty (*ehsas-e gonah mikonad*) about the privacy of these moments and about the fact that neither her husband nor her mother or children partake in or benefit from them, but she cannot resist these occasional temptations" (56). Out of this sense of guilt, Mrs. F compensates for her privacy in advance by accomplishing her household chores even more assiduously than usual.

The moments of privacy facilitate Mrs. F's accomplishment of her tasks as a housewife, mother, and daughter, and there is no hint in the story that the husband, mother, or children resent her personal purchases. But still, tending to herself instead of to others makes Mrs. F feel guilty. Mrs. F is shown as a character with self-awareness and a desire for self-fulfillment. Her sense of guilt derives from her assumption that the roles of devoted wife and, especially, mother are irreconcilable with any kind of self-interest—the same assumption she uses to dispel her doubts about having a professional career of her own. Nurturing the self, in her view (and probably in the view of others, given the nature of the reasons for her good fortune), is morally questionable: it is a transgression that calls for compensation. Though well accomplished in balancing the budget in a pecuniary sense, she does not regard balancing the care of others with care of her own self as a blameless act of give and take. For Mrs. F, not only is the display of a self in public taboo, but even privacy—that is, the rare moments when this self is nurtured in the absence of others—is objectionable.

In short, Mrs. F is a dutiful mother and housewife who subdues disturbing questions and procures some rare occasions to see to her personal needs. Her seeing to personal needs and individual pleasures is regularly accompanied by feelings of guilt and compensational acts. Contrary to the woman of "The Stain," whose commitment to wedlock is a deadlock in terms of her individual identity, Mrs. F finds a way to balance her individual and social identities, even if she has to bridge the gap between her ideal view of the social performance and her self-centred deviations from this ideal by a succession of guilt and atonement.

With regard to Pirzad's novel *'Adat mikonim* (*We Will Get Used to It*, 2004), Ma'sumeh Aliakbari proposes that "the female identity . . . is still struggling with her own traditional mindset. She is still stuck looking for a significant other instead of pushing to discover her independent self" (11). Although I do not see the search for the self and for the other as mutually exclusive alternatives—like Keupp (and his predecessors), I perceive individuality and social orientation as inevitably referring to each other (37)—it is worth examining the stories discussed here in the light of Aliakhari's proposition. On the one hand, the woman in "The Stain" cannot aspire to emancipation because she lacks a self; she perseveres in her isolated world provided for by the husband—her "other," not unlike an unborn child connected to its mother by the umbilical cord. In her case, Aliakbari's proposition applies—except that the woman does not seem to struggle (unless when facing the stain). Mrs. F, on the other hand, has an independent self but is reluctant to show or admit it. The image Mrs. F chooses to display in public is that of a woman exclusively devoted to others. In her case, Aliakbari's proposition applies with regard to the "significant other," but the issue in connection with her independent self is that of public disclosure rather than private discovery of self.

If, in Pirzad's fiction, "the other" is a more prominent concern in female personal identities than is "the self," one wonders about the concepts or concerns of male personal identity and whether and how this concern correlates with gender issues. Another of Pirzad's stories offers the chance to look into one of her male protagonists.

"THE DESIRED LIFE OF MR. F"

"The Desired Life of Mr. F" ("Zendegi-e delkhah-e Aqa-ye F," Pirzad *Mesl-e*, 41–45) narrates the story of Mr. F's retirement, which is depicted in six episodes.[9] In the first episode, the omniscient extradiegetic narrator relates the events of the very day of Mr. F's retirement: a celebration at the office, a wristwatch as a gift from his daughter Fataneh, another watch with fluorescent hands from his daughter Farzaneh, and sweet rice as a special treat for dinner, cooked by his wife. His daughters comment on his new leisure to get up as late and sleep as much as he wants to, his wife notices his white hair, and everybody smiles while they are listening to Mr. F's account of the farewell celebration in the office. The next morning Mr. F wakes up late, listens to the sounds of the already busy household, and imagines what his former colleagues are doing at that moment. Declaring, "From today I will do the things I like" (42), he decides to refurbish the garden.

The next four episodes, spanning almost one (gardening) year, show how Mr. F fares in his new life. When he has finished refurbishing the garden, the family reacts enthusiastically; the completion of his next project, repainting the house, however, is not celebrated with the same enthusiasm but is drowned in the family routine. While his wife and both grown-up daughters pursue their professions and various outside obligations, all Mr. F finds to do until spring calls for renewed activities in the garden is minor servicing of door hinges and taps.

The last episode shows Mr. F dressing smartly and going out to visit his former workspace. He finds the building unchanged; employees bustle in corridors and joke with each other as they did in his time. When he is about to enter his former office, he remembers, just in time, to knock on the door and is invited in. Mr. F enters and perceives the office unchanged. Intriguingly, not even the occupant of the office seems to have changed: the visiting Mr. F takes a seat in front of the desk, behind which Mr. F is busy perusing some documents. The working Mr. F smiles at the visitor, saying that the work never ends, and compliments him on his blessed repose. After a few moments of sitting, smiling, looking round, and feeling that he is being a nuisance, the visiting Mr. F takes his leave and returns to his empty home.

This is the story of Mr. F's desired life, the title of which points in two directions: the life before retirement, which is an object of desire after retirement, and the life after retirement, which is an object of desire to those still actively engaged in working life, including Mr. F himself before retirement, as suggested in the final scene in the office.

Two major issues are affected by Mr. F's retirement: time and a sense of belonging. Being in control of one's own time is a recurring topic in the story, materialized in the daughters' gifts of watches. With his retirement, Mr. F has gained control over his time: it is no longer in thrall to his employer. Now, facing the challenge of structuring time himself, he decides to explore some personal interests, such as gardening. But gardening is a seasonal activity and does not fulfill his year-round need for temporal structure, so he resorts to minor home maintenance tasks to keep himself busy throughout the year. While the structuring of time is a challenge that Mr. F appears to take on successfully, the problem of his sense of belonging remains unresolved. On the one hand, his retirement has excluded him from the group of his fellow workers, whom he recalls affectionately as "the children" (*bacheh-ha*). They are no longer his teammates, as is illustrated by the return to his former workspace in the last episode: the employees joking in the corridors no longer joke with him, only with one another. He has become an outsider. On the other hand, he has not managed to find a new role at home. In the family setting, the pre-retirement Mr. F was the provider and breadwinner with obligations outside of the domestic sphere and was apparently marginal to the immediate running of the household. Now that he is retired, he has forfeited his role in the family setting. Although he probably still contributes to the family's livelihood with a pension, he is a largely superfluous figure in the home setting. The grown-up daughters need no fathering; the wife perceives him as an old man. While the family welcomes the retiree in a general way, they do not support him in finding a new role among them. The desire for a discernible social identity and corresponding acceptance is therefore, we assume, the incentive for his reminiscences about and eventual return to the office.

Yet Mr. F's return to the office proves devastating. Let us examine two variant readings of the puzzle presented in the final scene with the two men called Mr. F: the first is that Mr. F meets another man called Mr. F, and the second, that Mr. F meets himself. In the first reading, the retiree Mr. F, already severely shaken in his personal identity, not only discovers that he is no longer treated as a colleague but he is also confronted with missing singularity. There is nothing that marks him as different from his successor; on the contrary, the identical naming of the two men, without any further comment, suggests that there are no features that distinguish them. If personal identity depends on a sense of belonging and identification, then it also requires demarcation, a sense of difference and uniqueness. In facing the working Mr. F, the retiree is deprived of any sense of uniqueness that he may have derived from his former working position. He returns to the office to discover that he was totally replaceable, an insight that, instead of reinstating his identity, is likely to aggravate his crisis.

Now to the second reading, in which the protagonist is doubled in the final episode: that is, the Mr. F behind the desk is the very retiree Mr. F. If Mr. F returns to the office and discovers that he is already there—or rather, that he actually never left—then one is led to assume that he—unknowingly—left his self behind when he retired. His notion of self has been based entirely on the role he played in the office, as an employee in a certain position with co-workers and corresponding social exchanges, and on his concomitant role at home, as the family provider. In this case, Mr. F is, like the protagonist of "The Stain," another self-less dummy, his alienated self dislocated to his former working position as its only stronghold, while the retiree just mimics life perfunctorily.

Both readings show Mr. F in a state of crisis, needing to redefine himself after a change of his social position and functions. After retirement, he is looking for new cornerstones for his identity. In the first reading, there seems to be room for hope: given that the retiree has already managed to solve the problem of structuring time and found new occupation at home, why should he—once confronted with the fact of his replaceability in the office—be unable eventually to satisfy his sense of belonging and craft new social bonds? The second reading, with Mr. F facing his left-behind self, seems indicative of an insurmountable crisis. The surprising confrontation with his self (or himself) is only surprising to the reader; Mr. F has no perceptible reaction to his double and the narration does not, at that instant, intrude into his consciousness. Viewed from the outside, the zero reaction of Mr. F to facing his self in the office does not encourage the reader's hopes that Mr. F will soon reintegrate his alienated and left-behind self.

Returning to Aliakbari's proposition about the concern with the "significant other" in Pirzad's stories, I conclude that it can also be applied in the case of Mr. F and is thus not restricted to female identities. Mr. F does not depend on "the other" for sustenance as do "the woman" and Mrs. F, but he does so in terms of a necessary constituent for his personal identity: with the women of his household economically emancipated (to some degree) and used to his absence from the house, and his work colleagues lost through retirement, he is shaken because he has lost those with whom he can identify and against whom he can set himself off as individual. The self-fulfillment he is supposed to find in being in control of his time and his choice of occupations does not satisfy all his personal needs. Although he is free to indulge his passions, his sense of belonging is frustrated, and this frustration motivates the pivotal action in the story. As with the female protagonists of the other two stories, with Pirzad's male protagonist Mr. F, the discovery of the "independent self" is disregarded in favour of the search for "the other."[10]

CONCLUSION

The personal identities we have met in these three stories are predominantly informed by the social positions and functions of the protagonists, on which their self-esteem depends; these social functions and positions are so vital to the protagonists that they serve as a base not only for their social but also for their individual identification. Yet the social positions and functions portrayed are not homogeneous. The society sketched in these stories has modern as well as traditional traits: on the one hand, the traditional division between the private and public domains and the corresponding role allocation for men and women are clearly depicted; on the other hand, they are juxtaposed with characters and events transgressing this division. Mrs. F's considerations of an alternative lifestyle for herself are inspired by Mrs. Taqizadegan, who has abandoned the traditional role for women: she not only earns her own wages but has moved to a position of responsibility and prestige.

It seems that the modern choices open to Mrs. Taqizadegan would also have been available to Mrs. F, whose reasons for choosing the traditional role instead are compliance with her husband and her own disinclination toward serious study. Nevertheless, she seems to have had a choice and made it. The story does not inform us to what extent the husband would have accepted it had her choice been a different one. It does, however, inform us that additional factors are likely to have been involved in Mrs. F's choice. As we have seen, Mrs. F is reluctant to admit to her individual needs and interests in public. The arguments she brings forth to end her considerations regarding mothers who work outside their homes indicate that her moral assessments are rooted in a traditional value system and that she has not (yet) absorbed the diversity of role models for women. As a consequence, being a modern woman is an option that would be contrary to Mrs. F's (self-)respect.

However, if the entering of women into the public domain is presented in Pirzad's stories as problematic, a man's entering the private domain is no less so. When retirement forces Mr. F into new life circumstances, this is neither a modern nor a traditional choice but a normal and forseeable event in the career of an employee. Neither is his transgressing the boundary from public to private a matter of shame or pride, as the opposite movement of women seems to be. If there is a gender division to be observed in Pirzad's presentation of personal identity, then it is the line that divides shame from pride with regard to individual identity and self-esteem. While Mrs. F's clandestine dedication to herself is accompanied by concealment, guilt, and atonement, Mr. F is publicly congratulated on his retirement, and his dedication to himself is the ensuing social imperative. The gender-specific difference consists in the moral evaluation of the coveting of an "independent self," not in the way it is conducted. A woman's self-esteem seems endangered by coveting individual distinction, while a man's would probably gain by it.

The identity crisis faced by Mr. F is rooted in his personal identity being construed predominantly on social relations. Individual identity comes across as a blind spot in these short stories. Mr. F is mostly absorbed with the loss of his social identity; if we put Mrs. F's individual identity to the test, we find that it, too, is problematic, since it is presented as nothing but the absence of others: either physically or as the object of her care. The life circumstances presented in these stories are those of subjects who seem to be given chances to develop individual identities but who struggle with various obstacles and find a real hold only in their social identities. Viewed from this perspective, the woman of "The Stain" enjoys a privileged position: if individuality is abandoned, then the struggle is at its end.

Recalling the introductory thoughts on neo-realism on which *Like All the Afternoons* has been predicated, I conclude that the life circumstances presented in these short stories are not eclectic or singular; rather, they show ordinary experiences of ordinary people. But this neo-realism only refers to the sociological content matter. For an evaluation of such ordinary lives as they are depicted, their literary presentations have to be consulted. What are we to make of the dummy that the woman in "The Stain" is seen to be? Whether one choses to commiserate or condemn her, she cannot possibly be a prototype for a hoped-for society of any sort. If she were, then the social experiment would come to an end after one generation. The narrative means by which these ordinary urban realities have been put forward is beguiling. On the surface, the protagonists are presented either as contented and fortunate or simply as resigning themselves to their circumstances, but the narratives offer reasons enough to believe that in Pirzad's urban habitat, hidden currents of doubt and discontent swirl beneath this stoic acceptance.

NOTES

1 Unless otherwise indicated, the translations from Persian are my own.

2 In Azadegan's Persian original, "the readers" is singular; I have chosen the plural to maintain the gender ambiguity of the original. The second edition of *Like All the Afternoons* includes two additional stories, "Malakh-ha" ("The Locusts") and "Yek joft jurab" ("A Pair of Stockings"), as is indicated in an editorial note opposite the table of contents. The latest edition, incorporated in the collection *Seh ketab* (Three Books, 2002), adds a third story, "Lengeh bi-lengeh-ha" ("The Unpaired to the Unpaired Ones"), but without editorial comment.

3 In exploring Pirzad's first novel, *Cheragh-ha ra man khamush mikonam* (*I Will Turn Off the Lights*, 2001), Nasrin Rahimieh argues that Pirzad's understanding of Iranian identity is directly opposed to the concepts of purification (from the non-Persian) and unification (in language and religion) promoted in the works of Jamalzadeh and Al-e Ahmad: "Pirzad's novel makes it possible to imagine reading and conversing across Iran's multiple languages, religions, and ethnicities not in an attempt to construct a unified national identity but rather to abandon the project of purification and unification of the nation" ("Manifestations of Diversity" 31). A study by Elham Gheytanchi offers a sociological reading of the same novel with regard to Armenians as the "eternal Other (*gheir-e khodi*) in Iranian society" (174).

4 Haqshenas, in his analysis of Pirzad's style and its development over the course of her three collections, criticizes this feature as a failure to meet with the generic requirements of prose fiction (33).

5 All three short stories are available in English translation: "The Stain" in Basmenji (194–97) and "Mrs. F Is a Fortunate Woman" and "The Desirable Life of Mr. F," translated by Assurbanipal Babilla, in Aslan (550–58). The translations used here are, however, my own. The page numbers cited in the following discussion refer to the Persian texts.

6 Haqshenas finds fault with this aspect of Pirzad's story, too (see note 5). He argues that she does not meet the requirement of prose fiction to display individualized protagonists with personal names (33). I argue, however, that the deviation from the generic convention is no shortcoming but a meaningful narratological act.

7 The namelessness of the husband is congeneric. In this way, the woman and her husband are two dependent parts—"the one" and "the other"—of a single social unit. I thank Pamela Holway for pointing this out to me.

8 In "Quiet Lives and Looming Horrors: Subversive Narrative Strategies in the Earliest Short Stories of Zoya Pirzad," I present an interpretation based on my reading of "The Stain" in the light of Plato's *Allegory of the Cave*. The paper, delivered at the Seventh European Conference of Iranian Studies, Krakow, 7–10 September 2011, will appear in the forthcoming proceedings of the conference.

9 According to Green and Yazdanfar (202), this short story was first published in *Chashmandaz* 5 (Fall 1988): 126–29, albeit not under the name Zoya Pirzad but Giti Nikzad.

10 Mr. F is not the only male character in Pirzad's work whose gender role is scrutinized. Nasrin Rahimieh, writing about Pirzad's *Ta'm-e gas-e khormalu* (*The Acrid Taste of Persimmons*, 1997) notes that the instability of gender roles captured in those stories applies not only to the roles of women, whose image as sacrificing wives and responsible mothers is questioned, but also to the roles traditionally prescribed for men ("Women and Domesticity," 11–12).

WORKS CITED

Aliakbari, Ma'sumeh. "Dar jedal ba zehniyat-e sonnati-e khish" ["Confronting Our Traditional Mindset"]. *Jahan-e ketab* [*The World of Books*] 187 (Aban 1383 [2004]): 10–11. Trans. Yousef Tehrani. Jan. 2005. 26 Mar. 2008. http://www.tehranavenue.com/print.php?ln=en&id=306.

Aslan, Reza. *Tablet and Pen: Literary Landscapes from the Modern Middle East*. New York: W. W. Norton, 2011.

Azadegan, Zhinus. "Hichkas hichvaqt nafahmid chi shod" ["Nobody Ever Understood What Happened"]. *Jahan-e ketab* [*The World of Books*] 4/5 (Bahman 1375 [1996–97]): 16.

Basmenji, Kaveh, ed. *Afsaneh: Short Stories by Iranian Women*. London: Saqi, 2005.

Gheytanchi, Elham. "*I Will Turn Off the Lights*: The Allure of Marginality in Postrevolutionary Iran." *Comparative Studies of South Asia, Africa, and the Middle East* 27.1 (2007): 173–85.

Green, John, and Farzin Yazdanfar, eds. *A Walnut Sapling on Masih's Grave and Other Stories by Iranian Women*. Portsmouth, NH: Heinemann, 1993.

Haqshenas, Ali Mohammad. "Yek gam mandeh beh yek roman" ["One Step Left to a Novel"]. *Zanan* [*The Women*] 47 (1377 [1998]): 30–33.

Keupp, Heiner, et al. *Identitätskonstruktionen: Das Patchwork der Identitäten in der Spätmoderne* [*The Patchwork of Identities in Late Modernity*]. Reinbek bei Hamburg: Rowohlt, 1999.

Mir-Abedini, Hasan. "Adabyat-e dastani dar sal-e 1376" ["Prose Literature in the Year 1376 (1997–98)"]. *Bokhara* 7 (1378 [1999]): 211–15.

———. “Dastan-nevisi-e Iran dar sal-e 1377 (Bakhsh-e Sevvom)” [“The Prose Fiction of Iran in the Year 1377 (1998–99)”]. *Bokhara* 16 (1379 [2001]): 64–75.

Pirzad, Zoya. *‘Adat mikonim* [*We Will Get Used to It*]. Tehran: Nashr-e Markaz, 1383 (2004).

———. *Cheragh-ha ra man khamush mikonam* [*I Will Turn Off the Lights*]. Tehran: Nashr-e Markaz, 1380 (2001).

———. *Mesl-e hameh-ye asr-ha* [*Like All the Afternoons*]. 1370 (1991). Tehran: Nashr-e Markaz, 1375 (1996).

———. *Seh ketab: Mesl-e hameh-ye asr-ha, ta’m-e gas-e khormalu, yek ruz mandeh be eyd-e pak* [*Three Books: Like All the Afternoons, The Acrid Taste of Persimmons, One Day Before Easter*]. Tehran: Nashr-e Markaz, 1381 (2002).

———. *Ta’m-e gas-e khormalu* [*The Acrid Taste of Persimmons*]. Tehran: Nashr-e Markaz, 1376 (1997).

———. *Yek ruz mandeh be eyd-e pak* [*One Day Before Easter*]. Tehran: Nashr-e Markaz, 1377 (1998).

Rahimieh, Nasrin. “Manifestations of Diversity and Alterity in the Persian Literary Idiom.” *Critical Encounters: Essays on Persian Literature and Culture in Honor of Peter J. Chelkowski*. Ed. Mohammad Mehdi Khorrami and M. R. Ghanoonparvar. Costa Mesa, CA: Mazda, 2007. 21–35.

———. “Women and Domesticity in Modern Persian Literature.” *New Horizons: Commentaries on Modern Iran*. 4 Mar. 2010. 2 May 2010. http://www.sas.upenn.edu/mec/resources/workingpapers/domesticity.

CHAPTER SIX

Anxious Men

Sexuality and Systems of Disavowal in Contemporary Iranian Literature

Blake Atwood

On 24 September 2007, during a question-and-answer session at Columbia University, Iranian president Mahmoud Ahmadinejad memorably declared, "In Iran we don't have homosexuals like your country." His statement prompted immediate outrage among activists and scholars, who saw this assertion as a resolute denial of the existence of homosexual (and queer) activity in the country. However, such a powerful announcement demands further consideration. Without devaluing the severity of the statement, might we suggest that Ahmadinejad's evaluation represents—in a sense—an accurate account of the situation in Iran? He established at once a critical dichotomy between Iran and "your country" (the United States) and thus generated a sense of dissimilarity between the two cultures. This rhetorical strategy may have served to intimate that the systems of homosexuality and homoeroticism function differently in Iran than in the United States and other Western countries. He further stressed his point about homosexuality by indicating that "in Iran this has no basis in reality." Difference, then, and not negation rests at the centre of his message.

David Halperin classifies the Western notion of homosexuality as "part of a new system of *sexuality*, which functions as a means of personal individualization: it assigns to each individual a sexual orientation and a sexual identity" (134). Certainly, such a system of open identification does not exist in Iran, and its society discourages this kind of public self-representation. Indeed, Ahmadinejad closed his discussion of homosexuality by saying, "[W]e don't allow people to say such things." His particular stress on words and speech, rather than acts or performance, suggests that the problem emerges from a vocalization of sexual identification. Certainly, it is worth remembering British Home Secretary Jacqui Smith's 2008 statement that the Islamic Republic represents no threat to gay and lesbian citizens as long as they keep their behavior "discreet" (Verkaik 1). This statement, though severely misguided, is telling here because it attests to the cultural limitations of sexual identification in Iran. It also raises several questions: How does one identify or fail to identify sexuality outside of the "system of sexuality" that Halperin describes and within a society that promotes rigid homosociality? In what ways do various sexualities manifest themselves, and how do these signs permeate literary texts? In this chapter, I address these questions by examining the representation of men in one short story by author Ghazaleh 'Alizadeh (1947–96). I consider the system of homosociality in Iran and the story's representation of alternative sexualities within the context of male bonds. More specifically, I will demonstrate that while Eve Sedgwick's notion of "homosexual panic" proves instructive to interpretations of Iranian society, so too 'Alizadeh's text can contribute to a restructuring of Sedgwick's theory to account for non-Western modes of expression.

When asked to comment on the process of writing, 'Alizadeh once said, "I took a dive into the depths of human nature. Everyone had a pearl and that's what was important to me" ('Alizadeh, "Dar har roman" 50).[1] The quest to understand the human condition beats like a pulse in much of her fiction, and in this chapter, I seek to uncover one such pearl by locating within "Such," the fourth and final story in the collection *Chahar-rah* (*Intersection*, 1995), a provocative and personal corollary of the male-based homosocial system in Iran. Eve Sedgwick's concept of "homosexual panic" flows as an undercurrent in this text, gushing not explicitly, like it might in American or European literature, but rather under the surface and behind the scenes, dictating actions and determining behaviour in a bizarre way. Indeed, I attempt in this study both to establish the existence of homosexual panic in "Such" and to demonstrate that the two male protagonists in the story literally objectify two female characters and use them to relieve this anxiety.

MOVING IN AND STRETCHING OUT

In her now famous study *Epistemology of the Closet* (1990), Eve Sedgwick boldly asserts that any study of Western culture devoid of a "critical analysis of modern homo/heterosexual definition" is necessarily "incomplete" and "damaged in its central substance" (1). Ghazaleh 'Alizadeh's "Such" enables us to stage an encounter between Sedgwick and Iran that might not otherwise be possible, and such a philosophical juncture is significant insofar as it shows the centrality of the construction of this homo/heterosexual distinction to studies of Iranian culture as well. Nevertheless, it is important to bear in mind that Sedgwick built her theories based on a centuries-long Western narrative. While her ideas remain pertinent to the present discussion of Iran, they require a certain amount of contextualization. By comparing Sedgwick's observations to similar Iranian phenomena, I hope to make a case for the application of her theories. At the same time, this comparative approach will underscore differences in systems of sexuality in Iran and the West. It is a central argument of this chapter that a universalist approach to queer theory ultimately denies some of the complexity of the formation of sociality and sexuality in Iran.

Of the homosocial system in the Anglo-American tradition, Sedgwick argues that "because the paths of male entitlement . . . required certain intense male bonds that were not readily distinguishable from the most reprobated bonds, an endemic and ineradicable state of . . . homosexual panic became the normal condition of male heterosexual entitlement" (*Epistemology* 185). She contends that male homosocial desires—or more simply, relationships between men—maintain a "potentially erotic" element (*Between Men* 3). As a means of disavowing such a possibility, the code of masculinity demands a rigid submission to heterosexuality and equally rigid subscription to homophobia. Men's pervasive fear of homosexuality—enacted by "the permanent threat that the small space they have cleared for themselves on this terrain may always . . . be foreclosed"—explodes from this homophobic arrangement (*Epistemology* 186). Potential threats to normative heterosexuality—including the fear that one might be homosexual—give rise to an enduring abjuration of same-sex desire. Importantly, then, "homosexual panic is . . . a problem only . . . of nonhomosexual-identified men" (201).

Accordingly, homosexual panic both emerges from and contributes to the delineation between hetero/homosexual definitions. The closet, as "the defining structure for gay oppression in this century," represents a space that compounds clean distinctions and thereby raises anxiety (Sedgwick, *Epistemology* 71). Homosexual panic, for Sedgwick, is tied to the closet, a closet that presupposes an epistemology of sexual self-revelation. Although this kind of revelation and disclosure may not be available in Iran, by considering Sedgwick's theory in terms of *movement* rather than *structure*, we can broaden the applicability of her ideas to accommodate contemporary Iranian society. That this moment of self-revelation marks the act of "coming out" is telling insofar as it signals the kind of movement of which I write. The closet—unlike a box, for example—has a door that permits passage in and out. Sexual self-revelation, which is at the core of Sedgwick's analysis, represents travel from the closet's interior to its exterior. "Coming out," though technically possible in Iranian society, does not exist in the same way that it is understood in a Western context. However, the basic movement between the closet and "out" did occur in Iranian society, though the directionality of that movement was markedly different.

Recent historiographies, like Afsaneh Najmabadi's *Women with Mustaches and Men Without Beards* (2005) and Willem Floor's *A Social History of Sexual Relations in Iran* (2008), have successfully demonstrated the existence of a "pre-modern and early modern Persian homoerotic culture" (Najmabadi 15). This culture, based on *amradparasti*, or love for young men, positioned adolescent males who were not yet showing all of the signs of manhood (e.g., a beard) as the objects of older men's desires.[2] Najmabadi's work proves especially useful as we attempt to explain the shift from a homoerotic culture to a rigid homophobic society. She contends that increased relations between Iran and Europe in the late nineteenth century inadvertently triggered this change. Sedgwick covers approximately the same period in her examination of the centrality of the Romantic Gothic in the rise of homophobia in Britain (*Epistemology* 186–87). The implication of Najmabadi's argument is an incisive and unilateral exchange of homophobic idea. Najmabadi maintains that Iranians, obsessed with evading the European scorn directed at their social and sexual practices, "began to reconfigure structures of desire by introducing a demarcation to distinguish homosociality from homosexuality" (38).[3]

An alternative and queer structure for sexual desire thereby existed openly (and poetically) in Iran, albeit in a form radically different from our modern conceptions of homosexuality. Ultimately, this system of sexuality was packed away and hidden. Najamabadi's suggestion that this sexual restructuring occurred because of contact with the West implies that this homoerotic culture was placed in the closet and that an oppressing structure was imposed over Iran's queer culture through scorn and evasion. Sedgwick's discussion underscores movement out of the closet; meanwhile, the Iranian case demonstrates a movement into the closet. Without a doubt, the directionality of these movements is different, even opposite, and the contents of the closet are not necessarily the same. But the similarity of the movement alone clears the way conceptually for the application of Sedgwick's "homosexual panic" to the present study. After all, these parallel motions are responsible for carving forcefully the distinction between homosexuality and heterosexuality. In what follows, I consider what has happened to the homoerotic culture that was so carefully locked away and interrogate its manifestation in contemporary Iranian literature.

TOWARD A THEORY OF IRANIAN HOMOSOCIAL BEHAVIOUR

Central to Sedgwick's discussion of homosexual panic are the social bonds among men. The contextualization of these social relations in the Iranian field marks an important hurdle to understanding male sexual identity in contemporary Iran. Therefore, before continuing, it is worth considering one of the most compelling literary representations of male homosociality in Iran. Goli Taraqqi's *Khab-e zemestani* (*Winter Sleep*, 1973) illustrates effectively the powerful pull of Iranian male homosocial bonds. This novella examines a group of seven men trapped in the crux of significant change. It demonstrates the dynamics of homosocial exchange and the effects of those bonds. It significantly positions masculinity—which informs and benefits from homosociality—as a limiting rather than freeing agent in the lives of the male characters.

Caught in the tension between tradition and modernization, the men in *Khab-e zemestani* are left dazed and emotionally stagnant but find comfort in the group and protection under their undisputed leader, Mr. Heydari. As one character, Ahmadi, puts it, "under Mr. Heydari's umbrella the world is safe and sound," going on to declare that the men in the group "are my friends; they'll become my shield and protect me" (24–25). However, by subscribing to this group mentality, the characters forsake their individuality. Early in the novel, the narrator comments on the group by asking, "What did we ever say? Actually, who were we? Whatever Heydari said, Mr. Heydari" (6). Taraqqi further denies her characters' individuality in her naming of them. The narrator introduces the group: "In the winter we were always together: Hashemi, Anvarii, 'Azizi, Ahmadi, Mahdavi, me, and of course Mr. Heydari" (1). It is no coincidence that these six names rhyme, each consisting of three syllables and ending in the long *ī* sound. Only the leader, Heydari, carries "aqa" (Mister/Sir) as a mark of distinction. Taraqqi shifts her narrative repeatedly, switching the character of focus often. She only sporadically gives the characters depth, providing the reader with a robust depiction of the group as a whole but giving the individual characters importance only vis-à-vis their particular role in the group.

Set in the mid-twentieth century during the reign of Mohammad Reza Pahlavi, the book's historical context holds great importance. During the 1950s and 1960s, Iran's uneven development had immediate and direct ramifications for all branches of Iranian society (Abrahamian). It created an overwhelming sense of confusion as power was repeatedly shifted and artificially created and as the Shah tried to modernize and industrialize the country from the seat of an ancient ruling system. The men's resulting stagnation is represented in Taraqqi's writing—more specifically, through a languid style unique to *Khab-e zemestani*, which is at times painfully slow. The writing in Taraqqi's other stories is typically more lively.[4] This particular writing style appears to be an extension of Taraqqi's hibernation theme. One way in which the author confuses both her characters and readers is by disrupting their sense of time. On one hand, time progresses incredibly fast: "How fast it passed. Seventy-five years or seventy-seven, or more. I don't know. I have lost track of days and years. Two years less, two years more, what difference does it make? When did old age begin?" (1). On the other hand, time also seems to be slowing to a standstill: "It's twenty minutes to eight. It's nineteen minutes to eight. Sixteen minutes, fifteen minutes, ten minutes, nine minutes, five minutes. It is exactly eight o'clock" (5). The contradicting representation of time muddles one's temporal perceptions and adds to the book's overall disorienting feel.

In many ways, *Khab-e zemestani* is the antithesis of the travel narrative genre. Modern Persian fiction grew partially out of a tradition of travelogues (Ghanoonparvar 156), but this novella is a book of failed journeys. Although men in Iran have the freedom to travel, the men of *Khab-e zemestani* go nowhere. They never leave the comfortable confines of their group, and the characters' stagnation is the direct result of their aforementioned intermediate position between tradition and modernity. Significantly, their inability to travel extends beyond physical—their journeys fail on three levels: the physical, the mental, and the emotional.

At the heart of *Khab-e zemestani*, in the fifth of ten chapters, lies the depiction of Taraqqi's quintessential failed journey, as Anvari attempts to take the train to Gorgan to visit his best friend, Mahdavi. His decision to depart represents no small feat. After Mahdavi's departure, Anvari's friends tell him he should visit anytime he wants. However, it takes him a full seven years to work up the courage to go. Wrapped up in Taraqqi's theme of stagnation rests the notion that tasks are started but never completed, attempted but never successful. Ultimately, Anvari's inability to progress emotionally blocks his ability to progress physically. Embarking on this journey, a process seven years in the making, marks a significant psychological development. At the same time, the fact that he does not complete the trip is no less significant. Along the way, Anvari encounters a series of obstacles. First, his fellow travellers are exceptionally rude, seemingly only toward him. He is also weighed down by a potted flower and a bird that Shirin, the group's motherly figure, sent with him. Then his letters are confiscated and an old woman takes his seat, while the other passengers in his car do not even protest on his behalf. The final straw, however, is the train's unexpected stop. No one knows how long the delay will last and the only explanation offered is, "It's orders" (67).

Frustrated, confused, and feeling the effects of an irritated ulcer, Anvari unsuccessfully tries to find solace by thinking of his friends, by "walking and trying to remember all Mr. Heydari's advice" (69). Ultimately, though, he is struck by "something heavy" that "floated in the air, like a bad omen, like a disaster that was gently approaching" (69). His attempts are quickly thwarted by fears of an ominous and immediate future. In the context of obstacle and delay, the train—and by extension, the freedom of mobility—seems "ugly and frightening." Confronted only with himself, Anvari has no idea how to deal with the pressures of reality.. Finally pushed to his limit, he concedes defeat and hails a nearby cab returning to Tehran. He "got into the car, and curled up next to the door. He closed his eyes and rested his head on the back of the seat. He thought of Shirin-khanum, who had said 'Don't listen to them. Get up and go'" (70). Anvari is ultimately not prepared to complete this journey. He is like a small child when he describes himself as "happy,""excited,"and "giddy" (61). Ill-equipped to deal with the hostile environment that he encounters on the train, he begins the return home to the company of his friends. Significantly, in this moment of defeat, Anvari assumes a fetal position, regressing to a comfortable, childlike state.

It is interesting to note that Shirin, a woman, encourages Anvari to take the trip and that throughout the book, it is the women who challenge the men to look past the group. In a book about men, the rare presence of women automatically assumes an important role. While Taraqqi nominally mentions several women, only two of them function as significant—though marginal—characters. Both women are married to men in the group and are, therefore, perceived as an extension of it.

As translator Francine Mahak notes, "Taraqqi's psychological portrayal is unique in Persian literature in that it is Jungian rather than Freudian" (viii). The notion of archetypes functions as a keystone in Jungian theory, and the two women of *Khab-e zemestani* exemplify Taraqqi's archetypical system. Shirin and Tal'at jointly represent the mother figure, each taking on a particular set of characteristics central to that figure. Shirin is the warm and nurturing side of motherhood, with "pockets [. . .] always full of chickpeas and candy, coloured string and jasmine flowers" (7). Although she is only married to Hashemi, she acts as a mother to all of the men. She looks out for the accident-prone Ahmadi, expresses dismay at their behaviour toward Jalili, and gently encourages Anvari to visit Mahdavi.

In contrast, Tal'at exhibits cold and rigid behaviour. She wears manly shoes, curses while driving, and punches men. She is a firm disciplinarian. But in a bizarre way, her actions are just as motherly. At one point in the narrative, her husband, Mahdavi, who is sick, finds comfort "in the middle of her bosom" and is able to "forget everything else" (89). Additionally, Tal'at undertakes the responsibility of nursing Anvari back to health after the death of Mahdavi. The women, therefore, represent two sides of the same figure, which is precisely why the men love Shirin and despise Tal'at. The former exudes warm maternal love while the latter represents the strict and demanding side of mothers. The significance of this dual system rests in the fact that the men are unable to see women outside of the context of mothers. This inability signals a failure to complete the journey from childhood to manhood. The reconfiguration of the female figure away from a strictly motherly role constitutes an important feature in the development to manhood.

One frequently finds this dual maternal paradigm in fairytales, which often feature an evil stepmother and her counterpart, the fairy godmother. Taraqqi is undoubtedly aware of this existing model and constructs her own system upon it. She mythologizes elements of both female characters. Shirin, for example, appears mysteriously from a fountain and later returns to the powers of water when her body vanishes in the Caspian Sea. Likewise, the first time Mahdavi sees Tal'at, he senses that "something invisible, and yet tangible, floated through the air. He sat up and, spellbound, looked around" (77). And Tal'at maintains this air of fantasy at her wedding: "With splendour and magnificence, she stood in the middle of the room like a mythological woman, who had emerged from the depths of the farthest dreams" (75). These fabled elements function as more than just allusions to the maternal archetype; they also serve to enhance Taraqqi's commentary on the men's relationship with women and their dependence on them.

Like children, the men of *Khab-e zemestani* view woman as a part of some larger mythological narrative. Women are, therefore, limited to either the realm of mothers or of myth and magic. Taraqqi uses the word "farthest" to suggest the extremity of their "otherness." The men pursue their relationships with each other and with women like children, markers of a failed emotional passage to adulthood. By suspending the male characters in a state of childhood, the author achieves somewhat contradictory effects. The men continue to view all women as mothers, which can be sexist and reifying, but after all, young boys need their mothers, and so women retain some power. Moreover, by keeping the characters in a kind of childhood, Taraqqi suspends what is supposed to be their ultimate ascendance to mature heterosexuality. Because their sexuality is not yet decided or fully achieved, a certain potentiality remains immanent, and that potential—that threat—demands rather forcefully the separation of homosociality and homosexuality. And, indeed, Afsaneh Najmabadi notes that the "disavowal of homosexuality out of homosociality" represents "a cultural work that has continued into the present" (38).[5] Nevertheless, despite a growing interest in homosexuality in Iran, there have been few attempts to delineate the precise nature of this disavowal or the mechanisms that permit it in contemporary Iran.

SEXUAL NEGATION AND THE SYSTEMS OF DISAVOWAL

Najmabadi's observation, coupled with Taraqqi's narrative, prepares the way conceptually for a discussion of homosexual anxiety in 'Alizadeh's short story "Such." The story represents a complex system of missed opportunity and lost love. The disjointed text, which resists a fluid linear narrative flow and persists only as a series of segmented scenes, is organized around four middle-aged main characters. They, along with the minor characters, form a series of overlapping and intricate love triangles. The story opens with Ahmad Izadpanah, an unmarried antique dealer. The reader quickly learns that he remains a bachelor because he has never overcome a childhood crush on Leyli Nabavi. She ultimately marries Dr. Khosrow Shaqayeqi, who confesses his love for her cousin, Parichehr, during the course of the story. In the meantime, Farideh Mirboluki, one of three spinster sisters, approaches Izadpanah, hoping to sell him several antiques. Although Izadpanah's friend Navvab, a high school teacher, has requested Farideh's hand in marriage, she is in love with Dr. Shaqayeqi, whom she encountered only once, briefly, at a bookstore when they were both students. He left behind a white Pentel pen, which she took and continues to cherish.

In the middle of the narrative, the local university's president dies. Until this point, he has played no role in the story; however, his death shakes these middle-aged characters, reminding them of their mortality. Farideh and Izadpanah run into each other on the outskirts of the cemetery during the funeral. Suddenly confronted with the prospect of dying alone and struck by a mutual interest in literature, the two begin a courtship. They eventually marry and the story ends in the bedroom on the night of the wedding. Izadpanah, whose eyes are heavy with sleep, dreams of Leyli: "When he opened his eyes, Farideh was next to the window. [. . .] She said a prayer under her breath and threw the white Pentel pen toward the overturned jasmine" (246).

Critics have analyzed this story by attempting to reconcile the meanings of its title. "Such" is a nonsensical word in Persian, but it functions in the context of the story as an interjection. At the wedding reception, Farideh's father, recognizing that his daughter's future looks bleak, cries out with a shaky voice, "Such!" Hasan Asghari reads the word "Such" as an expression of the characters' realization of their discontent and suggests that the story signifies a kind of futility; that the "negation of one kind of life is the birth of another kind (561). Therefore, "Such," which is a powerful cry, serves as "a sign of the love and excitement that does not exist in the lives of the people of the story" (561). The present study does not attempt to overhaul Asghari's reading of the story but rather to add a nuanced dimension to it by locating homosexual anxiety as a contributing factor to the male characters' despondency.

Sedgwick positions homosociality as a prerequisite for homosexual panic. And indeed 'Alizadeh depicts a homosocial system that is similar in some ways to Taraqqi's *Khab-e zemestani*. In "Such," Ahmad Izadpanah has a group of old friends who, every day at noon, "would come looking for him during their lunch hour. They'd eat chicken sandwiches and drink Coca-Cola, discuss politics, stand by the window red with excitement, and smoke cigarettes. All of them had a wife and children" (212).

While Taraqqi's men embrace a lifelong immobility, 'Alizadeh's men represent a different kind of stagnation, woven directly into the story's despondent fabric.

Once vibrant, enthusiastic, and full of potential, the men of this group have stumbled into mid-life tedium. One character, for example, Amir-Hushang Mostowfi, "composed poetry . . . in his university days. Once SAVAK [the Pahlavi regime's secret police and intelligence agency that was known for detaining, torturing, and executing members of oppositional groups] arrested him for breaking windows. After that incident, he wrote political poems." And yet throughout the story, Mostowfi, who is preparing for the construction of his new house, talks "constantly about the quality and price of stones; marble, travertine, and porphyry." Similarly, Bahman Tafazzoli once travelled Europe and subsequently worked at the provincial theatre office, bringing important pieces of world-literature to the stage. However, "gradually his interest waned and for the past several years he has been content with a position in the office of the under-secretary of culture." The narrator goes so far as to describe him as "dull and taciturn. You'd think in the course of his life, he had done everything and realized that there was nothing new left under the sky" (212). Certainly, Tafazzoli's name, which means "charismatic," is indicative of the subtle humour that marks 'Alizadeh's writing. The author, therefore, carefully constructs her descriptions of these two characters, juxtaposing their previous ambition with their current acquiescence. "Such" features the same kind of paralyzing homosocial apparatus that the reader finds in *Khab-e zemestani*. It functions slightly differently in this context but produces the same crippling effects.

By noting that Izadpanah's friends each have a wife and children, 'Alizadeh makes an important distinction, separating Izadpanah, a bachelor, from the rest of the players on this homosocial field. "He had remained unmarried," she writes. "People said that he didn't have an interest in women. Gossipers spread this rumour to the point of discomfort" (212). Society prods his hetero-normative status by suggesting that he is uninterested in women. This threat generates an environment conducive to homosexual anxiety, as Izadpanah is an active participant in homosociality but not necessarily in heterosexuality. However, he is not the only character who fails to fulfill both terms of this interconnected dichotomy. The narrator suggests that in his youth, Khosrow Shaqayeqi "didn't pay any attention to girls" (218). These two statements form the foundation for a reading of this text with homosexual panic at its core. The narrator questions the characters' sexuality early in the story and devotes much of the subsequent text to the relief of an anxiety engendered by such public query.

In order to settle this score, Shaqayeqi and Izadpanah marry Leyli and Farideh, respectively. Such acts certainly put the rumours to rest, but the story's ending, which I examine in depth below, questions their sincerity. The women, consequently, become chips in a game, reduced to paltry anecdotage or anti-dotage pills. And, indeed, the male protagonists see the two women in these terms. Before employing them in defensive battle, Shaqayeqi and Izadpanah relegate Leyli and Farideh to the status of mere objects: prizes won in victory or fine paintings for show. This concretization of women, their presentation as items to be gazed upon, is an important feature of the text.

Just as the women of *Khab-e zemestani* are strangers or outsiders, the women in "Such"—at least in the eyes of the men—are static objects, occupants of an alien and external proximity. At times, 'Alizadeh's writing style appropriately reflects this distance. One example is the narrator's nostalgic description of Izadpanah's childhood crush on Leyli:

> The first time Izadpanah spotted Leyli, she was in the Spring Blossom Ice Cream Shop. A group of girls were sitting around a sticky table. Leyli put a spoonful of ice cream between her lips and sucked softly. Green spring flies circled all around the table. The afternoon sun was shining on her honey-coloured eyes and lit up the peach fuzz behind her ears. (213)

This scene strongly resembles a painting. Specifically, 'Alizadeh's use of light captures a kind of transcendent radiance. The afternoon sun and green flies set a lethargic tone, and even the most unspectacular details, like the flies and the sticky table, are cast in a nostalgic glow. More importantly, however, the scene traps Leyli: she endures as a figure in a romantic picture. Significantly, the description's first word, *didar* (view/sight), is directly related to seeing. Therefore, although the story is told from a third-person perspective, this particular image is mediated through the gaze of Izadpanah. It is important to note that this visually intense and highly descriptive writing is typical of 'Alizadeh's style; however, in the context of "Such," she employs it with regard to the women and in the presence of men.

The narrator offers this scene in response to Izadpanah's apparent disinterest in women, explaining that he had a "simple reason for abstaining from marriage: a broken heart in adolescence. Before finishing high school, he fell in love with Leyli Nabavi, the daughter of Colonel Nabavi of the Gendarmerie" (212). From adolescence to mid-life, then, he has taken cover under the pretext of a broken heart, thereby deflecting and refiguring questions about his sexual apathy. And yet the persistence of this rumour points to its ineffectiveness as a cover.

Izadpanah must approach this topic afresh and remitigate his anxiety by marrying Farideh, who is described as having an "outward appearance" that "consisted of thick gray socks, manly flat shoes, and furled up eyebrows" (216). In this way, 'Alizadeh denies Farideh her femininity. It is with some irony that 'Alizadeh assigns her a deep interest in the early twentieth-century poet Parviṇ E'tesami. Scholar Farzaneh Milani notes that throughout the twentieth century, many people were convinced that the author of E'tesami's *Divan* was a "man posing as a woman" (*Veils and Words* 106). E'tesami even battled this rumour poetically, claiming, "Some literary persons believe Parvin to be a man / She is not a man, this riddle better be solved" (qtd. in Milani, *Veils and Words* 106). Therefore, Izadpanah ultimately marries a woman who could be described as "manly." Jeffrey Eugenides's novel *Middlesex* (2002) helps to elucidate this description. In the book, an Asian-American woman says, "Haven't you ever heard that? Asian chicks are the last stop. If a guy's in the closet, he goes for an Asian because their bodies are more like boys" (184). By extension, we might suggest that Izadpanah's selection of a "manly" woman is telling in the same way.

Before the courtship even begins, however, Izadpanah objectifies Farideh in a fluid motion. During their first encounter, "Ahmad's eyes lit up. Everyone said that Mr. Mirboluki had nice, old goods in his house, and with a smile they'd add his daughter to this statement!" (219). Farideh thus joins the rank of object-for-sale. Once again, 'Alizadeh tellingly draws attention to the eyes. Although this classification of Farideh is ascribed to the general public ("everyone"), Izadpanah's ocular reaction marks his subscription to and excitement by the idea. Seeing her in the same terms as the antiques he sells allows him to clear the way for bartering, bargaining, and the regular exchange of goods. The use of lists marks an important feature of 'Alizadeh's text. The objects of each textual space are introduced not with full sentences but within lists. Izadpanah's antique store, Farideh's house, and Shaqayeqi's clinic are all described in this manner. As a result, the women of the text get lost at times among the objects that populate these lists.

Farideh's commodity value rises in Izadpanah's mind because of her relationship with Navvab. In *Between Men*, Sedgwick examines the power dynamics of this kind of male-female-male relation and builds on René Girard's study of erotic triangles. She suggests that in a society which at once encourages and depends on intense male bonds, but at the same time violently renounces homosexuality, men must navigate their intimacy through the currents of a female bystander (1–27). Sedgwick therefore refines Girard's triangular schema to accommodate the female mediation of a desire the two men have for one another.

In light of this argument, the introductory scene between Farideh and Izadpanah assumes new meaning because it comes to an end with Navvab's arrival. The two are chatting casually when "Ahmad looked to the street. Mohsen Navvab's Peykan [an Iranian-made car] was turning into the parking lot" (220). Although Farideh and Izadpanah are engaging in a rather personal conversation, upon seeing Navvab's car, Izadpanah abruptly steers its trajectory back to business, quickly bringing their pleasantries to a close. Then Farideh "opened the door and came face to face with Navvab. She bit her lip and quickly went out" (221). At this point in the text, both Izadpanah and the reader remain unaware of Navvab's pursuit of Farideh. This moment meaningfully marks 'Alizadeh's initial construction of the male-female-male triangle. The blocking in this scene is particularly important. Caught in the threshold of the door, Farideh is literally stuck between the two men.

The triangular formation posited in this scene comes to a head several chapters later, when Izadpanah learns of Navvab's intentions. Izadpanah asks, "Who's the bride?" and Navvab, winking at his friends, replies, "A really respectable person! Farideh Mirboluki" (228). This news clearly agitates Izadpanah:

> Facing the oval mirror, Ahmad saw his own tired face. He looked at the ground and thought it all over. [. . .] With the tip of a pen, he drew a line on the wooden table. [. . .] [H]e got up from the table and walked the length of the room. He grabbed the button on Navvab's coat and pulled, "If only you knew the antiques they have! Tomorrow or the day after I am going with a loan with interest and buying them all." (228–29)

Threatened by Navvab's positional coordinate point, Izadpanah angrily asserts his ownership of the antiques—and to that list he has previously added Farideh. Navvab's wink and Izadpanah's physical attack perhaps signify the kind of exchange of intimacy that Sedgwick charts in her discussion, and the conversation about Farideh (as object) negotiates this transference.

The asymmetrical gendered features of the erotic triangle provide it with complexity and depth, and this system does not simply generate a unilateral or linear product. In this case, although rivalry functions as the means through which the men express their desire, it is no less real for the men. Izadpanah and Navvab both contend for Farideh, and the former emerges as the victor. Ironically, the wedding reception is held at Navvab's house. Since Farideh rejected Navvab earlier in the story, the reception's location strikes the reader as strange, especially after the awkwardness of the encounter between Farideh and Navvab at Izadpanah's store. However, by situating the celebration in Navvab's house, 'Alizadeh actively reinforces the triangular formation—and her ironic writing style—to the end.

Male rivalry extends beyond Izadpanah and his group of friends. Indeed, 'Alizadeh broadens her observation to a theoretical level by also attributing this feature to Shaqayeqi. Two short chapters after the reader learns that, as a student, he did not pay attention to girls, he admits:

> Leyli does nothing for me. [. . .] Perhaps in the beginning I wanted her. I don't know. Do you remember? Half of the city's young men were her victims. I threw myself forward out of obstinacy, like a person who wants to be the winner of every competition, and snatched her from everyone else's clutches. [. . .] We are not each other's mate. (223)

In this revealing statement, Shaqayeqi himself suggests that a competitive drive roused his interest in Leyli. Just as telling are his moments of doubt. His wife has no sexual effect on him and he cannot recall if she ever has. In the course of this conversation, he sets side by side his sexual doubts and his professions of love for Leyli's cousin, Parichehr. Therefore, in a single gesture, he alludes to and attempts to resolve his anxiety. When Parichehr questions what he is looking for, Shaqayeqi replies, "As we men say, feminine allure. (He fixed his eyes on the sunset sky)" (223). This particular phrasing reveals a performance in his act. Rather than speaking to any specific attribute, he offers a generic answer that emphasizes his involvement in the masculine system. Yet once again, 'Alizadeh draws meaningful attention to the eyes. By looking away from the other participant in the conversation, Shaqayeqi undermines—and expresses discomfort with—his preceding statement. Therefore, just as he follows in suit as the young men of the city chase after Leyli, he blindly pursues "feminine allure" simply because it is what "we men" do. These actions together form a sort of social-sexual artificiality.

Although they are contemporaries, Shaqayeqi represents Izadpanah's future. Shaqayeqi's marriage has all but failed. The reader knows that despite Leyli's continuing beauty, he stays—or perhaps always has been—uninterested. Moreover, in the face of a long marriage, the couple remains without child, perhaps a symptom of Shaqayeqi's sexual apathy. And when he professes love for Leyli's cousin, Parichehr, she senses the insincerity of his confession, claiming, "I know men like the back of my hand. Tell the truth! How many women have you said this to?" (224).

Meanwhile, 'Alizadeh shows the reader Izadpanah's failing marriage before it has even begun. The book's final scene is particularly powerful, fraught with expectation, anticipation, and ultimately disenchantment:

> The nanny appeared in the doorway and offered a mysterious smile. She proudly looked at the room's bed and decorations. Farideh went toward her and kissed her on the forehead. She looked to the picture of her mother and after whispering something, they wept endlessly. The neighbour pounded his shovel against the wall. The man suddenly remembered the week before. While passing through Thirty-Meter Street, he had seen, among the masses of brick and cement, colourful pieces of tile. The shape of the peacock on the wall of Colonel Nabavi's house had taunted him for years. His eyelids felt heavy and he dreamed that he was lowering a bucket with holes into a well. When he opened his eyes, Farideh was next to the window. Her white wedding clothes were blowing in the wind on the back of a chair. The bride was wearing thick jeans with a long-sleeved cotton shirt. She said a prayer under her breath and threw the white Pentel pen toward the overturned jasmine. (246)

In the tradition of classical Persian literature, the nanny is present in the wedding chamber, mediating the couple's first encounter.[6] Her location is important because it signifies the ensuing consummation, yet the subsequent text clearly reveals that the couple fails to follow through with that act. The book ends and the marriage is, quite significantly, never consummated. Instead, Izadpanah falls asleep dreaming of Leyli. He is unwilling—or perhaps unable—to relinquish that fantasy and accept a future with Farideh. She, however, throws away her pen, abandoning her infatuation with Dr. Shaqayeqi in an act of practicality. "Such" thereby destabilizes Hasan 'Abedini's notion that 'Alizadeh's women are dreamers (50). In the moment of realization that Asghari posits (561), the men of "Such" are caught up in the delicate threads of their dream-web, but the women push forward and accept their lot.

The preceding discussion creates a space for sexual ambiguity in this text. Yet Sedgwick asserts that "so-called 'homosexual panic' is the most private, psychologized form in which many twentieth-century . . . men experience their vulnerability to the social pressure of homophobic blackmail" (*Between Men* 89). And so society (unlike the text) does not permit variant degrees. The global rise of a homosexual identity—whereby sexual practice constitutes lifestyle rather than physical act—demands that heterosexual men define themselves against this identity. Thus, heterosexuality becomes nonhomosexuality. It seems appropriate in that case to return to Asghari's classification of "Such" as a dual-negative, a site in which one disaffirmation leads to another (561). Might we, then, suggest that for Shaqayeqi and Izadpanah, the denial of homosexuality—through a submission to compulsory marriage—actually gives rise to the effective negation of their heterosexuality?

CONCLUSION: MALE HOMOSOCIAL BONDS AND FEMALE AUTHORSHIP

In her reading of Henry James's "The Beast in the Jungle," Sedgwick privileges the character May Bartram—as a woman—with the power of observation: "May Bartram sees and Marcher does not" (*Epistemology* 208). She contends that "it is always open to women to know something that is much more dangerous for any nonhomosexual-identified man to know" (210). Applying Sedgwick's idea of female observation to acts of authorship productively complicates our understanding of homosociality in Iranian literature. Suddenly, the female author (as woman) is charged with a certain kind of information about male desire to which even men are not privy. The implication for this chapter is that this observation on observation explains the sole presence of two female authors in a study of men, a value judgment grounded in and based on Sedgwick's notion that women have access to information too dangerous for a nonhomosexual-identified man.

No book more powerfully depicts these Iranian homosocial bonds than *Khab-e zemestani*. Goli Taraqqi draws particular attention to her exclusive commentary on men by narrowly depicting their world and thus limiting the role of women in the narrative. Her text, therefore, all but resists feminine reading and primarily concerns itself with the kind of critical information with which Sedgwick might privilege it. With the failed journey as a central motif, *Khab-e zemestani* constructs the homosocial system as a cage. The men of the book, caught up in each other—in their bonds and mutual desires—go nowhere and do nothing. They hide behind a shaky communal identity, too afraid and too comfortable to defy the group mentality. The two women of the story, typical of Taraqqi's use of archetypes, conflate into a single motherly figure, thereby demonstrating the men's inability to see women outside of the context of their mothers. Desire and intimacy, therefore, bounce among the men and within the group. These men, who function in a patriarchal domain, are not empowered by but rather imprisoned in their masculinity.

In light of Sedgwick's theory of female observation, this book signifies new meaning. Taraqqi, much like her female characters, is outside of the homosocial structure she builds, yet this external position provides her with a unique perspective. She is able, therefore, to write critically about men—about their extensive relationships with each other and their limited interaction with women. It is Taraqqi's status as a woman that affords her this opportunity. Undoubtedly, had a man written this novel, its evaluation of homosociality would have been markedly different. Taraqqi can recognize and subsequently comment on the intensity of male bonds precisely because she is outside of that system and cannot fall victim to homophobic panic. Ironically, then, her position as *female* author affords her this candid analysis. Therefore, the book as a whole represents a moment of subversion as Taraqqi finds freedom in her female authorship and concurrently locates masculinity as a limiting force.

While Taraqqi's text confines masculine space, imposing and supposing limit and restraint, Ghazaleh 'Alizadeh's story opens it up, creating a place in that homosocial arena for sexual ambiguity and thereby broadening masculine space to include new possibilities. While the women of *Khab-e zemestani* remain outside of the homosocial system, the two main female characters in "Such" function as mediators in this scheme, reconciling the men's desire for another and redirecting questions of male sexuality. They therefore occupy an intermediary and internal position. The men, whom 'Alizadeh describes as "uninterested" in women, subsequently reduce women to objects, which then function as currency in a desirous exchange. Meaningfully, by objectifying women, the men deny them their sexuality, and 'Alizadeh thus narrows their purpose. Sedgwick's erotic-triangle paradigm allows us to examine the nature of mutual masculine desire in this story. However, the text only points to possibility and, ultimately, functions as an endless chain of negation.

NOTES

1 Unless otherwise noted, all translations are my own.

2 For a compelling account of this system in classical poetry, see Julie Scott Meisami's "The Body as Garden," in which Meisami argues that the garden functions in the context of *amradparasti* as a signifier of the loss of and/or hope for bliss (271).

3 In his article "Modernist Re-orientations: Imagining Homoerotic Desire in the 'Nearly' Middle East," Joseph Boone complicates this dynamic between Europe and the Middle East by arguing that just as practices of Middle Eastern homoeroticism were being repressed (because of a scornful European gaze), the Middle East came to represent a new space for sexual possibility in the Orientalist imagination. He writes that "the sheer possibility of erotic contact with or between men of the 'Arabic Orient' has underwritten much of the appeal and practice of the phenomenon we call Orientalism" (566).

4 See, for example, her earlier work *Man ham Chegvara hastam: Majmu'eh Dastan* (*A Che Guevara in My Own Right: A Collection of Stories*) and later works like *Khatereh-haye parakandeh* (*Scattered Memories*).

5 In *Sexual Politics in Modern Iran* (2009), Janet Afary considers the modern manifestation of premodern homoerotic practices. However, her work focuses on open acts of sexual identification and in particular on *MAHA: The First Iranian GLBT e-Magazine*. She also describes the legal system built to control sexual transgression. She thereby establishes the political tension and exchanges of power among the individual, his sexuality, and the legal system in Iran. My reading of 'Alizadeh's short story suggests that literature has created a space for different and differing sexual identifications that do not necessarily aggravate cultural, legal, and political norms.

6 For more on this figure, see Milani, "Voyeurs, Nannies, Winds," and Mostasharnia.

WORKS CITED

'Abedini, Hasan. "Ro'ya-ii keh kabus mishavad: moruri bar asar-e Ghazaleh 'Alizadeh" ["A Dream That Becomes a Nightmare: A Look at the Works of Ghazaleh 'Alizadeh"]. *Zanan* 97 (Winter 2003): 50–53.

Abrahamian, Ervand. *A Modern History of Iran*. Cambridge: Cambridge UP, 2008.

Afary, Janet. *Sexual Politics in Modern Iran*. Cambridge: Cambridge UP, 2009.

'Alizadeh, Ghazaleh. *Chahar-rah* [*Intersection*]. Tehran: Entesharat-e Zemestan, 1373 (1995).

———. "Dar har roman shahr-e tazeh-i khalq mishavad: Goftegu ba Ghazaleh 'Alizadeh" ["In Every Novel a New City Is Created: A Conversation with Ghazaleh 'Alizadeh"]. *Gardun* 21/22 (1993): 50–53.

Asghari, Hasan. "Mokashefeh-ye delmordeh-gi" ["Revelation of Dejection"]. *Ba Ghazaleh ta na-koja* [*With Ghazaleh to Nowhere*]. Tehran: Entesharat-e Tus, 1378 (1999). 557–61.

Boone, Joseph A. "Modernist Re-orientations: Imagining Homoerotic Desire in the 'Nearly' Middle East." *Modernism/Modernity* 17.3 (2010): 561–605.

Eugenides, Jeffery. *Middlesex*. New York: Farrar, Straus and Giroux, 2002.

Floor, Willem. *A Social History of Sexual Relations in Iran*. Washington, DC: Mage, 2008.

Ghanoonparvar, M. R. "Postrevolutionary Trends in Persian Film and Fiction." *Radical History Review* 105 (Fall 2009): 156–62.

Halperin, David. *How to Do the History of Homosexuality*. Chicago: U of Chicago P, 2002.

Mahak, Francine. "Preface." *Winter Sleep*. Costa Mesa, CA: Mazda, 1994. vii–viii.

Meisami, Julie Scott. “The Body as Garden: Nature and Sexuality in Persian Poetry.” *Adabyat* [*Heaven*] 6 (1995): 245–74.

Milani, Farzaneh. *Veils and Words: The Emerging Voices of Iranian Women Writers*. Syracuse, NY: Syracuse UP, 1992.

———. “Voyeurs, Nannies, Winds, and Gypsies in Persian Literature.” *Critique: Critical Middle Eastern Studies* 8.14 (1999): 107–23.

Mostasharnia, ‘Effat. “Dayeh dar adabyat-e Farsi” [“The Nanny in Persian Literature”]. Diss. University of Tehran, 1978.

Najmabadi, Afsaneh. *Women with Mustaches and Men Without Beards: Gender and Sexual Anxieties of Iranian Modernity*. Berkeley: U of California P, 2005.

Sedgwick, Eve Kofofsky. *Between Men: English Literature and Male Homosocial Desire*. New York: Columbia UP, 1985.

———. *Epistemology of the Closet*. Berkeley, CA: U of California P, 1990.

Taraqqi, Goli. *Khab-e zemestani* [*Winter Sleep*]. Tehran: Entesharat-e Farzan, 1377 (1998).

———*Man ham Chegvara hastam: Majmu’eh dastan* [*A Che Guevara in My Own Right: A Collection of Stories*]. Tehran: Entesharat-e Nilufar, 1348 (1969).

Verkaik, Robert. “Iran Is Safe for ‘Discreet’ Gays, Says Jacqui Smith.” *The Independent* 23 June 2008.

CHAPTER SEVEN

Reading the Exile's Body

Deafness and Diaspora in Kader Abdolah's *My Father's Notebook*

Babak Elahi

In *My Father's Notebook*, Iranian-Dutch novelist Kader Abdolah explores the exile's sense of linguistic displacement. The novel is a metafictional account of a son's attempt to translate his father's notebooks from an unknown language into Dutch, the author and narrator's second or third language. The narrator's father, Akbar, was deaf and wrote his notebook in his own invented language using a cuneiform script he had learned from a cave inscription. The narrative begins in third person and shifts to first person as Ishmael, Akbar's son, tells the story of attempting to write a novel based on that notebook. I would like to suggest that Ishmael's experience is emblematic of the diasporic condition. He is so distantly displaced from his cultural identity that any return to that past is impossible. The language he writes in (Dutch) is at several removes from the father's invented language. However, what allows the protagonist to mitigate this sense of loss and linguistic displacement is, in part, memories of using sign language to communicate with his father. Sign language, far from the closed off and indecipherable written text of his father's notebook, is a relatively universal form of communication allowing for the physical embodiment of identity. Neither spoken nor written language can quite achieve this kind of linguistic embodiment of the self.

In a 2010 lecture titled "Literature as Resistance," Abdolah describes how Persian began to feel like a useless, even oppressive, language for him as an exile:

> I started writing my Persian books to continue my resistance against the Iranian regime. I had always fought against the dictator with my pen. My Persian words were bullets. But suddenly I couldn't fight anymore with my Persian words. The Persian words that I put on paper were sick. They had no power anymore. The Persian language became for me as a gun without bullets. I wrote. I wrote. But I felt sick. I felt like a dying writer.

Having written against both the Pahlavi regime and the new Islamic Republic's oppression of the Kurds, Abdolah found himself exiled from the language of cultural identity and political action. As his several novels and short story collections attest, Abdolah eventually turned to Dutch as a new language in which he could continue, with his words, to fight against the regime of the ayatollahs. Abdolah's discussion of having to write in Dutch rather than Persian bears out the idea that migration involves a transformation of self: Abdolah had been transformed, partly through the language that he inhabited and that embodied him, into a Dutch writer, but one clearly defined by his experience of diaspora. He had to write through the very experience of exile.

Abdolah's *My Father's Notebook* explores this dilemma of the exiled writer. However, complicating the writer's place between the language of home and host cultures is the third possibility of sign language shared between a deaf father and his son. In what follows, I argue that sign language offers an embodied sense of cultural identity that is not available either in written or in spoken language. Severed from spoken and written forms of Iranian cultural-linguistic identity, the protagonist of Abdolah's novel reinvents his familial and cultural identity through sign language as an embodied linguistic sense of self.

SIGN LANGUAGE AND THE DIASPORIC EXPERIENCE

Abdolah—whose given name is Hossein Sadjadi Ghaemmaghami Farahani—includes several linguistic and discursive themes in his novel *My Father's Notebook* (originally titled *Spijkerschrift* [*Cuneiform*] in Dutch). First, cuneiform script, with its ancient national origins, appears as the dead and empty language of the father. Second, spoken and written Persian are closely tied to national and cultural identity. As Ishmael—the narrator-novelist protagonist—tells his story in Dutch, he must come to terms with the national language (spoken and written) that he has left behind. Third, Dutch becomes the language of migration. As Ishmael puts it, Dutch is the new ground upon which he must dwell. Finally, and most importantly, the improvised sign language used between the deaf father and his children becomes the language of familial space and of an alternative sense of identity. The languages multiply, but we can group them into written, spoken, and gestural forms of communication. Each becomes a potent way to create and reinvent the self, but gestural language offers a way out of the speech/writing dichotomy and allows for a true embodiment of self. Improvised sign language, as the language of the narrator's father, links the narrator back to paternity and the nation, but without the ideological implications of either writing or speech. As an idiosyncratic familial invention in the protagonist's home, improvised sign language challenges the primacy of Persian or even the foundational ancient language of Old Persian inscribed in cuneiform. Furthermore, as an attempt to translate his father's notebook into Dutch, the novel itself links the adopted language of the diasporic writer back to the language of the father. Neither written nor spoken, neither Persian nor Dutch, gesture is a *third* language (a liminal linguistic space) that allows the narrator-author to triangulate these languages and translate the father's text.

The spoken word and the written word have certain implications for national identity. The spoken word manifests traditional culture, which, in the case of this novel, includes the recitation of medieval Persian poetry and Shi'a para-Quranic stories (like the tale of Mahdi, the messianic imam said to dwell in a cave on Saffron Mountain). The written word *constitutes* the nation—constitutions must, after all, be written. It can also link the nation's present to its past through monuments literally carved in stone and through literary or legal archives. The written word also modernizes the nation, as oral traditions become transformed into modern prose and poetry. However, by situating its own privileged language neither in speech nor in writing, but in gesture, *My Father's Notebook* offers a possible way out of the dichotomies of orality and literacy.

Deaf studies scholars Sarah Batterbury and Paddy Ladd, along with cultural geographer Mike Gulliver, recently argued that there are "significant parallels" between the experiences of Sign Language Peoples (SLPs, or Deaf communities) and "those of First Nation peoples" (2899). I would argue that these concepts of linguistic embodiment through sign language can also inform concepts of linguistic loss in diaspora. Batterby, Ladd, and Gulliver's observations about how SLPs use language and how the use of sign language results in the embodiment of identity can guide our reading of Abdolah's *My Father's Notebook*, in which the diasporic protagonist is also a member of a Deaf community. In an article on geography, sign language, and identity, they argue:

> Although the grammars of different spoken languages show tremendous variation in the ways that they map deep pragmatic and semantic concepts into the actual syntax of a speech act, those of different sign languages are remarkably similar, to the extent of being, by comparison, almost identical. This is not surprising when we consider that visuo-*gestural* languages *literally embody* almost biologically determined requirements, constraints, and expansionary principles. (2900; my emphasis)

Furthermore, Batterby, Ladd, and Gulliver argue that "evidence is mounting that the cognitive effects of embracing sign language and visual learning support SLPs' repeated statements that they embody a visually oriented 'intelligence' and geography, thereby providing support for their claims to an inalienable and valuable *physical embodiment* of cultural difference" (2904; my emphasis). Finally, Paddy Ladd has identified seven key tenets of Deaf discourse. He derives these tenets from speeches delivered by French Deaf leaders who held annual banquets in the 1840s as part of their efforts to promote Deaf culture and establish Deaf schools. At these banquets, Deaf people practiced and celebrated their different, rather than deficient, form of discourse. Drawing on a hearing journalist's account of one of these banquets, Ladd identifies certain key elements of Deaf discourse, aspects of discourse that make communication more effective rather than making it deficient. This journalist went so far as to write that witnessing the grace and eloquence of the gestures of the Deaf speakers was enough "to make us wish we could unlearn speech" (Ladd 111). Attending to the tenets of Deaf discourse that result in such enviable eloquence for a hearing observer might help us rethink diaspora outside of traditionally postcolonial emphases on textuality. These tenets shift the focus from textuality to the dichotomy and dialectic between orality and gesture. Batterby, Ladd, and Gulliver summarize them as follows:

1. Sign languages have a unique nature and power and can express things that spoken languages cannot.

2. There is greater ease of international communication between sign languages than between spoken languages.
3. Consequently, SLPs offer the world a model of global citizenship.
4. SLPs' existence on Earth is intentional, whether enacted by "God" or "nature," for the purpose of modeling these principles.
5. Non-Deaf people can be regarded as "sign-impaired," rather than SLPs being seen as "hearing-impaired."
6. Sign languages are offered as a gift which can benefit non-Deaf peoples.
7. There should be a commitment to the betterment of all SLPs, as opposed to an educated elite. (2906)

This manifesto offers some insight into how a CODA (child of a Deaf adult) living in exile might experience language. Furthermore, the first three of Ladd's principles, in particular, can help us think about how exile is experienced. If it is true that gestural, or signed, language is both more biologically grounded and more universally understood than written or spoken languages, then the language of gesture can be the bridge between home and host languages and cultures.

As linguist Sarah Taub, who studies ASL (American Sign Language), argues, sign language is iconic, containing an "abundance of visual imagery," and using iconic signs metaphorically to create abstract meanings (2). In fact, Taub challenges one of the foundational concepts of structuralist and poststructuralist critical theory, the Saussurian notion of the arbitrariness of the sign. In this tradition (familiar by now in the disciplines of philosophy, anthropology, literary criticism, rhetoric and composition, and other humanities and social science fields), the concept of the arbitrary nature of the sign claims, in short, that "the highest property of language" is a "*lack* of connection between a word's form and its meaning" (2). However, Taub counters that the "relative scarceness of iconicity in spoken language is not a virtue; it is merely a consequence of the fact that most phenomena do not have a characteristic noise to be used in motivating linguistic form" (3). She goes on to argue that while three-dimensionality is "crucial to language in many ways," speech is a "one-dimensional sequential medium" (3). She reports that

> researchers are now finding that iconicity is common enough to be of serious interest in the spoken languages of the world; if sound were not so limited in what it can iconically represent, they [spoken languages] would no doubt have even more iconicity. Signed languages, created in physical space with the signer's body and perceived visually, have incredible potential for iconic

expression of a broad range of basic conceptual structures (e.g., shapes, movements, locations, human actions), and this potential is fully realized. (3)

For an exile who is also a member of a Deaf community, the sense of linguistic unmooring so often a part of diasporic experience is mitigated by the deaf exile's sense of embodiment in a language both deeply felt within the signer's body and broadly shared beyond the national boundaries of spoken and written languages. Gestural or signed languages travel well. An exile who has experiential access to such a language can, potentially, resolve some of the dilemmas of diaspora: nostalgia and hope, loss and liberty, identity and community, and translation of identity. A close reading of *My Father's Notebook* can help us see these relationships among spoken, written, and signed language in the diasporic experience. In this novel, Ishmael's identity is deeply bound up with his shared use of gestural language with his deaf father. Thus, he is as much a member of a Deaf community or SLP as he is an Iranian or Kurd. By locating the most present and most clearly *embodied* language of the novel within sign language (that is, to locate the narrator-author's most direct link with his father not through spoken or written language but through gesture or ostensive meaning), Abdolah points us to a third option outside of the speech/writing dichotomy.

The experience of diaspora can be understood as a transformation of self. Discussing the effects of English-language instruction among South Asian immigrants to Canada, Vijay Agnew argues, "Learning and adopting a new language changes the individual because all languages permit slightly varying forms of thought, imagination, and play" (44). I claim that *My Father's Notebook* explores the possible ways in which the self can be re-embodied through language to re-create the self in exile. The unique place of an improvised sign language in this novel is especially important in helping to convey this sense of re-embodiment of self.

The novel explores the significance of language in diaspora by exploring multiple languages in a variety of forms. First, we have the ancient cuneiform script, as representing both an ancient language and the father's invented language. The antediluvian origins of the nation and the irretrievable memories of the father are thus superimposed onto one another—written in a forgotten script and conveying idiosyncratic meanings. The father's written language is doubly displaced: it uses a dead script and conveys a solipsistic meaning that the father alone understands. Second, we have Persian itself, which the narrator-author continues to understand, but which he relinquishes in favour of Dutch as the language of his novel. Third, there is Dutch, which is the author-narrator's adopted language, but one that he admits to struggling to master. Fourth, we encounter some untranslated sura from the Quran, formulaic verses that the narrator-author remembers without believing. One important sura—the story of the companions of the cave—figures prominently in the conclusion of the novel, which opens with the Quranic parable of the cave and explores the ways in which externalized, internalized, and embodied forms of language function both at home and in exile.

THE LITERATE SELF: WRITING AND NATIONAL IDENTITY

Books and writing play an important role in Abdolah's novel. For instance, ancient writing becomes national treasure, and legal documents construct civil identity. Even the novel inside the novel is a metafictional translation of the father's writing into the son's. Several important written texts—the Old Persian cuneiform inscription, the legal documents constructing Akbar's patrimony, the notebook (also in cuneiform) that documents Akbar's thoughts, and Ishmael's attempted translation of that notebook—punctuate the narrative of this novel as the exiled hearing son tries to find a sense of place in diaspora. It is only by trying to translate the writings of his deaf father that he is able to come to terms with his literate self.

Aga Akbar, a carpet mender, is taught in his youth by his uncle to write down his experiences and emotions in his own made-up language using a cuneiform script presumably based on the Old Persian or Pahlavi language that European Orientalists have uncovered in a cave on Saffron Mountain, a fictionalized setting that Abdolah situates within Senejan. The cuneiform inscription is the manifestation of Iran's "spiritual legacy" (39). However, written language in particular is also a means of control, especially in the colonial or semi-colonial context. A nation's dead or long-forgotten languages, some of which exist only in written form, convey not only the proclamations of ancient kings but also the means by which a colonized culture can be known and controlled. As Elleke Boehmer puts it, "The text, a vehicle of imperial authority, symbolized and in some cases indeed performed the act of taking possession" (13). But if control was textual, so, too, were challenges to it: "resistance to imperial domination—especially on the part of those who lacked guns or money—frequently assumed textual form" (15). In this Orientalist context, Akbar's notebook, written in a cuneiform script under the scrutiny of European Orientalists, constitutes both colonial constructions and postcolonial deconstructions of self.

We can think of the notebook as the kind of "hidden transcript" discussed by Jonathan and Daniel Boyarin in relation to "diasporic consciousness." The undecipherable text resists power structures that themselves rely on textuality: the "only modes of resistance, in diaspora, that are logical, that make sense, are those that will enable the continuation of . . . cultural and spiritual activity" (66). Hence, according to the Boyarin brothers, "in order for seditious discourse to be formed, there have to be 'autonomous social sites' either hidden from the eyes of the dominating population or hidden from their ears because of 'linguistic codes impenetrable to outsiders'" (66). When Akbar is introduced to a three-thousand-year-old cuneiform script by his uncle, Kazem, deep "inside the cave," it is clearly demarcated as a language of power, in that the "first king of Persia ordered that a cuneiform inscription be chiseled into the rock, beyond the reach of sun, wind, rain, and time" (Abdolah, *My Father's Notebook* 20). However, the inscription "has never been deciphered" (20). Initially, indecipherability excludes Akbar from power (in that knowledge, especially of a language, means power). He is excluded both from spoken language and from the ancient ancestral language of the early Persian kings that European Orientalists claim for themselves. However, Akbar is able to turn this power relationship around when he creates his own indecipherable languages, both written and signed. Indeed, the written language recuperates the language that the European scholars decipher from the cuneiform carvings. Then, once Akbar has used this script to create his own "written" word, the indecipherability of Akbar's notebook puts the narrator, Ishmael, simultaneously in the position of the "outsider" and in the role of the expert laying claim to the nation's cultural legacy. As the father's notebook falls into the son's hands, it takes on some of the qualities that the Boyarins associate with the indecipherable texts of diasporic consciousness.

The documents surrounding Akbar's name and patrimony present a different but similar set of problems in how the literate self, as I'm calling it, is constructed in this novel. Being both deaf and illiterate, Akbar has no access to the very documents that construct him socially. He is the illegitimate son of Aga Hadi Mahmud Ghaznavi Khorasani, a nobleman who arranged a temporary marriage with Akbar's mother, Hajar. Hajar had six other children, but Akbar is the only one born to Khorasani. Hajar goes to Khorasani and demands that Akbar bear his name: "I'm not asking you to make him an heir. Just to have Akbar's name recorded in an official document." Khorasani relents: "The imam wrote a few lines in a book, then drew up a document and had the nobleman sign it" (Abadolah, *My Father's*

Notebook 13). However, after the nobleman's death, Akbar loses even his name and title: "The document turned out to be worthless. After the nobleman died his heirs bribed the local imam and had Aga Akbar's name removed from the will." But for Hajar, "it hardly mattered. [. . .] Aga Akbar's parentage was known" (14). Here, the direct patrimony from the father takes on the questionable form of legal documents that can be reneged on, corrupted, and erased. Moreover, as a form of knowledge produced by clerics who serve the wealthy landowner, the legal document establishes power relations between social classes and castes.

However, Akbar eventually has access to a form of writing that falls outside both the nationalist/colonialist writing of ancient Persian kings and the corruptible documents written by religious legal scholars: the cuneiform symbols in his own notebook. When Akbar's uncle, Kazem, shows him the nobleman's library, Akbar discovers a new way of both expressing and understanding himself. "Oh, Allah, Allah, what a lot of books!" Kazem exclaims. They turn to one book in particular and Kazem says, "Hey, Akbar, come here. You see this book? It's been written by hand" (18). And it is at this point in Abdolah's novel that Kazem teaches Akbar to write his own book. The chiselled and inked documents of kings and *akhunds* (Muslim clerics) are replaced by the handwritten journal of the "literate" self. The Persian king *ordered* others to chisel cuneiform letters into the cave wall, and the nobleman *directs* an *akhund* to draw up a legal document. These are words and documents intended not to embody the self but to control others, to command. Kazem, in contrast, leads Akbar to write his own book. Akbar's book is both completely his own and that of the nation because it is written semantically in his own personal language but with a script associated with the nation's antediluvian origins. Kazem takes Akbar to the cave with the ancient inscription and tells him, "Now get out your pen and notebook. [. . .] I want you to write down the text. Look carefully at all the symbols, at all those cuneiform words, and write them down on the paper, one by one. [. . .] Just write" (21). But, of course, Akbar cannot and does not write. He resists, subtly, even the commands of his poet uncle. Rather, he draws: "Aga Akbar may or may not have understood what his uncle had in mind, but in any case he started copying the text. He stared at the cuneiform script and did his best to *draw each character*, one by one, in his notebook" (22; my emphasis). The semantic function of language is replaced by the tactile, visual, and aesthetic act of drawing the shapes of the letters. Rather than being commanded by the language of ancient kings or being defined legally by the documents of lawyers and clerics, Akbar makes the language radically his own.

Interestingly, as Orientalist scholars begin to decipher the cuneiform script, they give Akbar the key to open his own invented language. As Kazem tells Ishmael, "In those days he had quite a bit of contact with the foreigners who went to the cave, the ones who were trying to decipher the text. I think he'd learned something from those experts—something about other reliefs, or maybe even a likely translation" (23). Akbar finds himself caught between three forces whose power derives from textuality: the ancient Persian origins of the nation, the modern legalistic discourse of clerics, and the Orientalist appropriation of Persianness (both cultural and linguistic). And it is out of these that he manifests a self through textuality, a script that avoids either "the command of language or the language of command," to quote Bernand Cohn's phrase.[1] Finally, Akbar reads to Kazem what he has written: "I, I, I am the son of the horseman, the horseman from the palace, the palace on the mountain, the mountain across from the cave. In that cave is a letter, a letter from a king, a letter carved in the rock, from the time when there were no pens, only hammers and chisels" (24). The repetition of the incantatory first person traces Akbar's now auto-literate self back through ancestry, geography, and history. Later, in his work as a carpet mender, he comes across the script again. Saffron Mountain, in *My Father's Notebook*, is known for its carpets, and, in addition to images of birds, a "motif that made its way into their carpets was the cuneiform script" (26). Cuneiform is chiselled, written, and woven into Akbar's world. Akbar thus remakes the ancient Persian script and modern Iranian legal discourse into an indecipherable text over which he alone has power as author and translator, until the notebook falls into the hands of his son, who must decipher it in exile.

Ishmael's interest in books is often at odds with his father's illiteracy, but his literacy breaks down in diaspora in at least two ways: first, he must learn to speak and write in Dutch, and second, he finds himself unable to read his father's notebook. The father's radically idiosyncratic (even solipsistic) language reverses the roles of illiterate father and literate son. A bibliophile since his childhood, Ishmael finds that in exile, his words have been stripped of meaning, and his literate self bereft of identity.

One of Akbar's names for Ishmael is "The Boy Who Crawls Under the Covers and Reads" (156). The illiterate father fosters the son's love of books, bringing books home for Ishmael; unable to read their titles or know their content, however, Akbar's acquisition of texts falls short of Ishmael's desires: "They weren't books you'd read for fun. One old book he'd found at work, for example, was about cotton and thread. Another was filled with numbers and tables" (143).

Soon, neighbourhood kids begin to take these books from Akbar and taunt him. Embarrassed by his father, even Ishmael begins to taunt his father. Instead of reading the books his father brings him, Ishmael turns to Dr. Pur Bahlul, a dentist who treats Akbar's rotting teeth on credit and opens his library to Ishmael. Bahlul, it turns out, is a leading figure in the Iranian Left and is arrested a year after Ishmael meets him; his association with Ishmael also introduces the latter to political literacy, the brand of leftist politics emerging in Iran in the 1960s. The only book that Ishmael and his father seem to share an interest in is Sa'di's *The Rose Garden*, which I will return to below when I discuss gestural language. For now, it is important to note that with the exception of one of Iran's key national poets, the written word divides father from son. Indeed, father and son cannot even come to terms with the Holy Quran, which Ishmael tells his father "doesn't come from heaven. It's a book—a good book—but it has nothing to do with heaven" (168).

After Ishmael has joined Iran's leftist movement, the written word—specifically, print—takes on a material reality that leaves its imprint on his body. The leftists, though suppressed by Mohammad Reza Shah, survive the Islamic Revolution, but with their leadership almost completely eliminated. Ishmael's job in the new fight against Khomeini is to print revolutionary newssheets and slogans with a heavy industrial stencilling machine. Abdolah devotes several pages to describing how Ishmael acquires, transports, and stores this heavy printing press. The weight of the machine injures Ishmael's back so that he both literally and symbolically bears the burden of writing:

> I eased the machine off my back and set it down on the bed. I tried to straighten up again, but couldn't. [. . .] I spent the next quarter of an hour bent over, on my knees, until the pain subsided.
>
> To this day I'm still plagued by backaches. Sometimes when I've been sitting at my computer for too long, I feel a jab of pain when I try to stand up. I have to hunch my shoulders, then slowly straighten my back. (287–88)

Writing in an age of mechanical reproduction and in an age of revolution leaves its mark not only on paper and on the minds of readers but on the very body of the writer. Moreover, the burden continues to weigh on him as he sits at his computer, *writing* in exile.

What Ishmael is writing in exile interests us as well because Ishmael's diasporic writing is a return to Akbar's notebook. This relationship between the father's national script and the son's exilic writing is further complicated by the novel's metafictional structure, combining Ishmael's first-person narration with the limited-omniscient "voice-over" of a third-person narrator. The third-person narrator tells us at the outset that he will take us through Akbar's life and Ishmael's birth and coming of age but that then, Ishmael himself will take over because the book we are reading is, in fact, Ishmael's attempt to write a novel based on the translation of his father's cuneiform notebook. The literate self, then, is part of the very structure of the novel, not just a theme or subject within it. We move from the Iranian national context into the diasporic context of Holland through a narrative shift from an omniscient third person to a first-person narrator who has lost his linguistic power: having to learn Dutch and his father's cuneiform language at the same time. He must translate from an almost indecipherable language into one that he barely understands. It is out of this radically indeterminate linguistic space that the novel itself emerges. What I call the "literate self" is born in the space between "author" and "narrator," and between an illiterate father and a son writing in a second language.

Abdolah's novel is modelled, at least in part, after Dutch author Multatuli's (Edward Douwes Dekker) *Max Havelaar*, in which the narrator distinguishes himself from the writers of verse and theatre, whose genres amount to forms of lying (either to serve the dictates of rhyming or to cover real-world vice with imagined virtue), and states: "Well, reader, this book owes its existence to my inviolable love for truth, and my zeal for business. I will tell you how all this has happened" (Multatuli 9). Ishmael (and Abdolah through Ishmael) quotes the opening passage of *Max Havelaar* directly and makes a similar claim to truth to the point that author and narrator seem to merge. When he receives his father's notebook from an aunt, he tells the reader, "I've never written a book before, but I'd like to try and write one now, because if it's at all possible, I'd like to put my father's writings into a readable form" (99). Ishmael/Abdolah acknowledges the distance between his own story and that of his father: a linguistic gap between Dutch and Farsi, between speech and gesture, between computer font and cuneiform script. "I'm sitting at my desk in the attic," Ishmael writes, "staring out the window. Everything in the Flevopolder is new: the soil still smells of fish, the trees are young, and the birds build their nests with fresh twigs. There are *no ancient words*, no ancient love stories, no ancient feuds" (100). By contrast, "Everything in my father's notebook is old: the mountains, the well, the cave, the cuneiform relief, even the railroad. That's why I don't put pen to paper. I can't imagine writing a novel in this new ground" (100).

And yet he does write. Later in the novel, in fact, he tells his Dutch friend Louis, "I've got a story for you, Louis. [. . .] I'm writing a book. A novel. In Dutch." He goes on to explain that the book is about his father, who kept a diary all his life but "wrote it in an unknown language—a kind of cuneiform that he invented himself." So Ishmael has to decipher it: "I look at a passage, then try to read it and transcribe it. No, 'transcribe' isn't the right word. I try to translate it into Dutch" (195). He is attempting to carry over a story from an unknown language written in a dead script into a known language and a living script. He compares himself to the small part of the great sea now "diked in by the Dutch. Much as I, a little patch of ancient Persian culture, have been surrounded by a Dutch dike" (100). Retrieving the past whole, like trying to re-create the sea, is impossible. However, he concludes, "Just as Holland invented this ground, this landscape, I can use my father's cuneiform writings to invent something new" (100). The novel we are reading is the author-narrator's attempt to make a living story from a dead language, to reanimate the fleshless word of diaspora. Ishmael's father, Akbar, comes across a handwritten book in his own biological father's library and is inspired (and encouraged by his uncle) to write his own. Ishmael comes across his father's handwritten notebook and is inspired to translate it into Dutch. However, in each case, the writer attempts to inscribe the self, to make the self legible. Although this challenges certain discursive forms of power and resists the marginalization of exile, it does not quite *embody* the self. The oral/aural self—and the gestural self, in particular—begin to do so more fully.

THE ORAL/AURAL SELF: SPEECH AND CULTURAL IDENTITY

The third-person narrator of the first third of the novel tells us: "The following story cannot be found in the Holy Book, or in any other book, and yet the villagers on Saffron Mountain believe it and tell it to their children" (57). The story in question is the key tenet in the Twelver form of Shi'a Islam, which states that Mahdi, the twelfth imam in the line of succession from the Prophet Mohammad, went into occultation as a child and will return on the day of judgment. The inhabitants of Saffron Mountain believe that the Mahdi climbed up the mountain, where he took refuge in a cave, and is still hiding in their well:

> If you take an oil lamp and go into the cave, all the way to the very back, you will still see, even today, the ashes from his fire.

Mahdi wanted to stay in the cave even longer, but the Arabs following him had managed to track him down.

So he climbed even higher, until he reached that miraculous rock face. There he realized that he was going to be Muhammad's last successor and that he had to hide in the well and wait until he was called.

Many centuries have gone by since then. He's still waiting in the well. In the well of Mahdi ibn Hassan Askari. (57)

The story depicts "Arabs" as the villains who "tried to kill Mahdi." Like the mountain assimilating the modern railroad, this story suggests that Iranians assimilated Islam into their own sense of national identity. The oral narrative of the well as a sacred place within Iran turns the religious and political message of Arab invaders into a naturalized representation of a distinctly Iranian version of Islam.

In addition to this oral myth from Twelver Shi'ism that affords Akbar a communal sense of identity through orality, his relationship with his uncle, Kazem, gives him a more individual and personal sense of identity through the spoken word. For example, Akbar's marriage is fostered by Kazem's poetic voice. Searching for a place to rest for a few nights on one of his many journeys away from the village, Kazem approaches the house of a fellow opium smoker but is confronted by the man's hard-headed daughter, Tina. When she rejects his plea to let him into her father's house, Kazem says, "I'm not your average opium smoker. [. . .] I read books and I know hundreds of poems by heart. I also write them. If you open the door, I'll write a poem especially for you" (85). Although he refers to written poetry, he presents these things in the form of sweet talk—the persuasive and seductive voice of the poet. Tina is eventually persuaded to meet and ultimately marry Akbar, and a spoken recitation from the Quran marks the marriage ceremony, during which the "imam recited a short melodious sura: *'Ar-rahman, alam al-Qur'an, Khalaqa al-insan, 'allamahu al-bayan. Ash-shams wa al-qamaru be-husbanin, wa as-sama'a rafa 'ha wa waza'a al-mizan*'" (90).[2] These lines—untranslated in both the Dutch original and the English translation—are the first five lines of the fifty-fifth sura of the Quran ("The Beneficit"), one of many sura that point to signs of proof of Allah's existence and his beneficence. As untranslated transliteration, the brief passage underscores the importance of *recited* rather than written or silently read verse. Moreover, it points to language itself as one of those merciful and beneficent creations of God: "*Khalaqa al-insan, 'allamahu al-bayan*" can be translated as "He created man, and taught him speech."

In contrast to this orthodox Quranic verse that sanctifies Akbar's marriage, it is the mystical words of Hafez, spoken by Kazem, that bless Akbar's birth. When Ishmael is born to Tina and Akbar, the play between written and recited poetry and between silence and sound establishes Ishmael's infantile and subconscious identity as an outgrowth of that play. When Tina gives birth, there is "an ominous silence": "According to family tradition, no one was allowed to break the silence yet" (91). Once Ishmael is brought in to the men, no one is to speak until the appropriate words are spoken into Ishmael's ears:

> A while later the oldest woman in the house took Ishmael in her arms and brought him into the guest room. No one spoke, because the first word, the first sentence to reach the baby's unspoiled mind had to be a poem—an ancient melodic verse. Not a word uttered by a midwife or an aunt's joyful cry, not an everyday word from the mouth of a neighbor, but a poem by Hafez, the medieval master of Persian poetry. (91)

Kazem then takes a volume of Hafez from the shelf:

> Kazem Khan brought his opium-scented mouth to Ishmael's ear and whispered:
> [. . .]
> A nightingale once sat with a bright petal in its beak,
> But this memento of its loved one merely made it weep.
> "Why bewail this token of your heart's desire," I cried.
> "It makes me long for her all the more," the songbird sighed. (91–92)

However, this mellifluous poetic whisper is contrasted by the misguided scream of an anxious deaf father. In one of the few "quotations" from the father's notebook, the narrator explains why Ishmael has always had trouble with his left ear:

> I didn't know if the baby had been born yet. Suddenly I saw Kazem Khan's gold tooth gleam. I knew then that the baby had been born. My aunt came in with the baby in her arms. I was afraid the baby would be a deaf-mute like me, and I wanted to see if he was deaf. I know it was wrong, but suddenly I stood up, ran over to my aunt, took the baby from her, put my mouth to his ear and spoke into it. The baby screamed and turned blue. Kazem Khan snatched him from me and shoved me out of the house. I went and stood at the window. Everyone frowned at me. I had shouted into the baby's ear. Everyone said it would be damaged for good. It was stupid of me, stupid. Akbar is stupid. (92–93)

The narrator's commentary on Akbar's description, however, redeems Akbar by suggesting that the deaf father's *voice* marks the son, embodies his identity physically in the ringing in his ear: "Damaged? No, not really, but whenever Ishmael was sick, or under stress, or feeling discouraged, whenever he fell down and had to stand up again, a voice shouted in his ear. His father's voice. Aga Akbar was always inside him" (93). Clearly, the father's embodied voice and its bodily presence in Ishmael's ear gives Ishmael an oral/aural sense of self, despite the father's deafness. Like the heavy stencil machine that Ishmael uses in his work with revolutionary leftists and that leaves its mark not only on paper but on Ishmael's body in the form of physical pain, so too does the spoken word make a permanent change to Ishmael's body. But in both cases, the physical mark is not "damage" so much as a reminder of how Ishmael is the embodiment of discourses and languages (written, spoken, or, as we shall see, signed) that speak through him.

THE GESTURAL SELF: SIGN LANGUAGE AND INDIVIDUAL EMBODIMENT

By contrast to the national identities established by spoken and written languages, the novel presents a distinctly familial and personal identity established through signed language. Abdolah's narrator tells us,

> The family, especially his mother, communicated with him [Aga Akbar] in a simple sign language. A language that consisted of about one hundred signs. A language that *worked best at home*, with the family, though the neighbours also understood it to some extent. But *the power of that language manifested itself most in the communication between Mother and Aga, and later between Aga and Ishmael.* (7; my emphasis)

Here, we have a third form of language, one situated neither in oral/aural forms of cultural identity nor in the written forms of national monuments. The gestural language of sign is associated with the familial space. Mother tongue becomes the entire maternal and paternal body, not just through Aga Akbar but also through Aga Akbar's mother and, later, through Ishmael and his sister, Golden Bell.

For Ishmael, embodying his father through gestural language is often a burden. He describes how the sons of blind and deaf men "became their fathers' eyes" and ears, and the bodily connection between them was a key to the survival of the father and the identity of the son (101). He goes on to elaborate: "The moment the baby started to crawl, the blind father placed the palm of his left hand on the baby's shoulder and showed him how to be his guide. The child soon realized that he was an extension of his father" (101–02). Clearly, the son's inheritance is embodied in the touch of the hand to the shoulder, the movement of the body guiding another, even in infancy. "The sons of the deaf-mutes had an even more difficult task," Ishmael writes in a passage that he, apparently, has excised from the final version of the book. These sons "had to serve as the mouths, minds, and memories of their fathers" (102). Again, the sons become the embodiment of the fathers, but in this case, the embodiment of their language: mouths, minds, memories. They are no less embodied, though, than the filial guides of blind fathers. They are the word made flesh, quite literally. They must express the "minds, mouths, and memories" of the father through the movement of hands and bodies. The word of the father exists as the very body of the son.

The work of Taub, along with that of Batterbury, Ladd, and Gulliver, cited above, clearly suggests that gestural language is an important way in which the self is linguistically embodied and that this embodiment has ideological implications for what Batterbury, Ladd, and Gulliver call "Oralism." These claims are also supported by cognitive evidence in the work of Jordan Zlatev. Zlatev argues that the "gap between language and embodiment" can be minimized through "bodily mimesis," defined as the "volitional use of the body for constructing and communicating representations." Bodily mimesis, furthermore, leads to the broader concept of "mimetic schemas," or "body-based, pre-linguistic, consciously accessible representations that serve as the child's first concepts" (Zlatev 301). Admittedly, Zlatev's concept *excludes* sign language because, as he claims, sign language is organized through a set of symbolic conventions and manual letter shapes; thus, the movement of the body is completely abstracted into ideographical representation and a hand alphabet. In other words, it has the same arbitrariness that structuralist linguistics and poststructuralist theory associate with written and spoken language. However, as Taub has argued, even within a formally conventionalized symbolic system like American Sign Language, the relationship between bodily and manual movement relies on certain mimetic relationships. In the context of my own argument, bodily mimesis and bodily schemas make sense in that the "sign language" at work in *My Father's Notebook* is not a formally established and recognized language like ASL but rather a homemade form of communication using the body to represent objects, images, and ideas that the interlocutor can understand by reference to the visual world and to his or her own body.[3]

The way that Akbar names Ishmael, for example, is significant both in Akbar's use of sign language to form a proper name and in Ishmael's remembered sense of self through his father's gestures rather than his spoken or written words. The first name Akbar gives Ishmael is "Mine": "He had different names for all of us, and he changed them whenever there was a major change in our lives. For example, in the beginning I was called Mine" (156). What's interesting here is that the designation of proper names coincides with "major changes." Every crisis or triumph calls for a new name. But even more interesting is that these names are given through gesture: "When he put his right hand to the left side of his chest, everyone knew he was referring to Ishmael" (156). Thus, it is the movement of the father's body, not the sound of a father's voice, that signifies Ishmael. The hand-to-heart gesture metaphorically points to ownership, which, by analogy, points to paternity. Furthermore, it is also the son's movements and physical presence that win him other proper names such as "The Boy Who Crawls Under the Covers and Reads" to designate Ishmael as a boy, "The Man Who Wears Glasses" to refer to him as a young adult, "The Man Who Is Never Here" for Ishmael as a student, and "The Man Who Went Away" after Ishmael leaves Iran. The very naming of self relies on these uses of language as the body both of the namer and the named (Abdolah, *My Father's Notebook* 156).

In discussing the importance of writing and its failure to embody fully Ishmael's self and to reproduce completely his relation to his father, I noted above that books created a wall between Ishmael and his father rather than bringing them closer, with one exception: the book that bonds the son to the father is Sa'di's *The Rose Garden* as Ishmael attempts to "translate" Sa'di's work through bodily mimesis. The *hekayah*, or "stories," rendered in verse range from the morally didactic to the broadly satirical. Most importantly, Abdolah narrates the exchange between Ishmael and Akbar about Sa'di through gesture and signs. The *hekayat* that Ishmael attempts to interpret into bodily mimesis is the story of the centipede. Ishmael attempts to show this through gestures (which are conveyed to us only through a retranslation of those gestures into dialogue): "A centipede, you know, the insect, the little insect with lots of legs that crawls so fast . . . hold on, I'll bring the oil lamp a bit closer." The narrative switches from dialogue to the description of bodily movements: "I drew a centipede in the dust with a stick and made a rapid movement with my finger" (146). The story tells of a man without arms or legs who swats a centipede and kills it. But Akbar, for whom legs and arms are so crucial, latches onto the logical conundrum: "'How can he swat an insect if he doesn't have any arms or legs?' my father signed" (147). In fact, Ishmael's interpretation of the story as having to do with the inevitability of death fails to persuade. Nevertheless, the physical embodiment of the narrative and the father and son's gestural conversation lead Akbar to reflect: "That was clever of the writer. Can you read another story?" The bond that Ishmael and Akbar fail to cement through books is established more fully through gestures and signs, through the body.

Similarly, when Ishmael attempts to describe astrophysics to his father, we once again turn to the intensely embodied language of gesture and the body. This embodiment of outer space is an outgrowth of their conversation about the existence of God. Attempting to prove to his father that the universe was not created by a God but emerged from the big bang, Ishmael first turns to a book (again, attempting to rely on literacy, which proves inadequate) but must revert to the intimate and direct language of sign. Ishmael recalls, "I got up and hunted around for a book on outer space, one with lots of pictures of stars." When these pictures fail to convince Akbar that such vast empty spaces and orbital relationships exist, Ishmael uses his hands and body: "I did my best. I tried to tell him, in our simple sign language, all that I had learned. But he stared at me in perplexed silence" (169). Ishmael recounts what he tried next:

> I gestured toward the stars, collected all those stars in my left hand, added the river that ran through our town, threw in the mountains for good measure, placed my father on top, squeezed them all together into a ball, and then transferred that ball of matter to my right hand. I held it up in front of his eyes and suddenly let it explode: "B-o-o-m! Stars, stars, more stars, then the sun, then the earth, then the moon then my father and then me . . . do you understand what I'm saying?" (169–70)

However, Ishmael's increasingly outward view of the world—as an exile but also in this focus on "outer space" as a way to explain his atheism—takes him away from a connection with his father. He remembers that, no, "he didn't understand. I didn't either" (170). He reflects, "I'd wandered far away, so far away that I could no longer connect these theories with my 'not praying'" (170). Ishmael also recalls his father as a man who "went away," who wandered and went up into the mountains to stay for an extended period. "My father went away again for a long time," he says (170). And then Ishmael himself goes away. I would like to suggest that this movement away is not just into exile from the nation, but a movement away from embodiment, a movement away from the body. Borrowing terms from cognitive linguistics, and the work of Zlatev in particular, we can see the experiences of Ishmael, Akbar, and Golden Bell as some combination of interoceptive (perceptual focus on internal sensations of, for example, the organs), exteroceptive (experience of the self's relationship to the world around it), and proprioceptive (sensory focus on the body itself, and its movements). Ishmael and Akbar attempt to communicate in proprioceptive space, but each in his own way is steeped in exteroception—moving away. It is through the intercession of Golden Bell, who moves inward and helps Akbar articulate his embodied self, that some of this dilemma of gestural communication is resolved.

CAVE ALLEGORIES

The third and final "book" of Abdolah's novel, like the first, is titled "The Cave," while the second one is "New Ground." In addition to moving back from first- to third-person narration, Book 3 intertwines the narrative of Ishmael's departure from Iran with that of Golden Bell's imprisonment within Iran: "Golden Bell had been arrested six weeks after Ishmael's escape" (289). Ishmael, before going to Holland, spent some years in the Soviet Union and stayed there after 1989. The contrast between Soviet and post-Soviet society, even for expatriates like Ishmael, is categorical and almost traumatic: "The entire social system had been turned upside down. [. . .] It took him months to realize where he was and what had happened" (287). Like the Kahafians who dwell in the cave for three hundred years to emerge into a society they do not understand, Ishmael lives in exile in a society that goes through a radical revolution (the end of the Soviet system), and its changes are tantamount to centuries of transformation, leaving the system upside down and the exile lost. This is like Jemiliga, one of the companions of the cave, in the allegory as Abdolah quotes it in the opening and closing pages of the novel: "Jemiliga then left the cave with the silver coin in the palm of his hand. When he reached the city, he saw that everything had changed and that he did not understand the language" (319). By contrast, Golden Bell is sent into an internal exile just as Ishmael leaves for an external one. Much of *My Father's Notebook*, in fact, concerns Ishmael's attempts to overcome his bewilderment. His exile leads him to be disconnected from Iran's reality and the reality of the Kurdish nationalist movement within the nation. He is left to decipher languages that have lost their reference points for him.

Not only are their forms of exile (one internal, the other external) diametrically opposed, but Ishmael and Golden Bell's relationships with Akbar are also markedly different. Both Ishmael and Golden Bell try to teach Akbar what they have learned in books about physics. In the days during which Akbar and his wife, Tina, seek to learn what has happened to Golden Bell, who fails to appear during a prison visit, Akbar "thought about the fact that Golden Bell was more patient than Ishmael. She explained things to him with endless patience" (301). More specifically, "Ishmael always talked to him about big things—the sky, the stars, the earth, the moon—but Golden Bell always talked to him about little things" (301). As Ishmael attempted to move Akbar's thinking outside his world, Golden Bell attempted to lead him further into it:

> One time she picked up a stone. "There are tiny things moving around inside," she said.
>
> "Inside the stone?" Akbar couldn't believe it.
>
> "Yes. Little tiny things that revolve around each other," Golden Bell explained, "the way the earth revolves around the sun."
>
> He still couldn't believe it. "That's impossible," he signed. "A stone is just a stone. If you smash it with a hammer, you wouldn't see a thing. No earth, no sun."
>
> Golden Bell handed him a hammer. He smashed the stone. "You see, no sun."
>
> "Make it even smaller," she said.
>
> He did it. Smaller and smaller and smaller. He banged away at the stone until it was just a heap of sand, and it couldn't get any smaller.
>
> "The sun is inside the tiniest grain of sand," Golden Bell said.
>
> Akbar laughed out loud. (301–02)

Mirroring the contrast between Ishmael's exile and Golden Bell's imprisonment, their embodied uses of language situate Ishmael in the external world (the "New Ground" of the Netherlands, space, the universe) and place Golden Bell squarely within (inside the stone, inside the cave, inside Evin Prison). Like the Mahdi, and like the companions of the cave, Golden Bell's imprisonment is a movement into an internal exile. Golden Bell takes this further as she tries to take Akbar inside himself, both physiologically and, one might argue, spiritually:

> She's smart, he thought as he neared the prison. She gets all of that from books. He remembered another of Golden Bell's explanations. One time she laid her head on his chest and said, "Boom, boom, boom."
>
> "What do you mean, 'boom, boom, boom'?" he signed.
>
> "Here, just under your ribs, you've got a motor," she replied.
>
> "A motor?"
>
> He laughed, but she opened a book and showed him a picture of the motor under his ribs that went boom, boom, boom. (302)

Unlike Ishmael's extraverted or exogamous linguistic self-construction, Golden Bell's self-construction is endogamous. An exogamous way of knowing the self reaches out for an identification of self in relation to others. Ishmael reaches out through exile, through his knowledge of astrophysics, and through his interest in Dutch culture and literature. This is parallel to what Shaun Gallagher calls exteroceptive perception of the world—an outward visceral orientation between self and other (279–80). Figuratively, this can be thought of as the Orientalist's desire to gain command of a foreign language. By contrast, endogamous ways of knowing the self turn inward. Figuratively, again, this might be the orientation of the nationalist whose know-nothing view of the external world can become chauvinistic. However, in a more positive sense, endogamous ways of knowing are analogous to what Ghallager calls interoceptive perception (279–80). In the novel, Golden Bell pursues this interoceptive or endogamous sense of identity. She turns inward, embracing a cultural identity under attack, and she corrects Ishmael's astrophysicist view of the universe with a cellular-level sense of the physical world.

CONCLUSION

This contrast between Golden Bell's inner world and Ishmael's outer space is, however, only part of the answer, and a deeper reading shows that Abdolah's novel does not restrict itself to such tidy dichotomies. In fact, Ishmael eventually *has* to turn inward, and Golden Bell's political activism constitutes a radically *outward* approach to the world. Furthermore, unlike the Orientalist's relationship to cuneiform script, Ishmael's command of the ancient writing technology brings him closer to the domestic language of his father rather than the foreign language of empire. Thus, each character's sense of self is, and must be, closer to an embodied sense of self balanced between endogamy and exogamy, between interoceptive and exteroceptive forms of perception. This embodied identity is not just a middle ground, but something akin to what Maurice Merleau-Ponty calls the "minimal bodily equilibrium" of perception (122). It is an enactment of the self at the site of the body. An invented familial sign language is a key way in which the self is enacted at the level of the body. Akbar's language of gesture is the novel's central image of this kind of embodiment of the self. The significance of all other languages in the novel, whether spoken or written, European or Asian, and all other senses of the self derive their form from, and must be understood in relation to, Akbar's embodied language of gesture.

NOTES

1 This is the title of the second chapter of Cohn's *Colonialism and Its Forms of Knowledge*, in which he claims a functional importance for the Persian language as a pragmatic means of legal control. See esp. pp. 16–19.

2 This remains untranslated in the novel. From M. H. Shakir's translation of the Quran, we have this: "The Beneficent God taught the Quran. He created man, taught him the mode of expression. The sun and the moon follow a reckoning" (359).

3 Iranians had access to schools for the Deaf beginning in the 1920s, but in the remote, fictionalized Senejan of this novel, such access is limited. A man of Akbar's generation would probably not have attended one of the schools opened by Jabbar Baghchehban, the trailblazing Iranian teacher who established the first schools for Deaf children in 1928. See Jabbar Baghchehban's autobiography, *Roshangar-e Tariki* (*The Illuminator of Darkness*).

WORKS CITED

Abdolah, Kader. "Literature as Resistance: A Lecture by Dutch-Iranian Author Kader Abdolah." Berkeley, CA. YouTube, 15 Apr. 2010. 19 Apr. 2010. http://www.youtube.com.

———. *My Father's Notebook*. Trans. Susan Massotty. New York: Harper Collins, 2000.

Agnew, Vijay. "Language Matters." *Diaspora, Memory, and Identity: A Search for Home*. Ed. Vijay Agnew. Toronto: U of Toronto P, 2004. 23–47.

Baghchehban, Jabbar. Roshangaran-e Tariki: Khodnevesht-hayeh Jabbar Baghchehban, edited by Safih Mir-Babai. Tehran: Institute for the History of Children's Literature, 1389 (2010).

Batterbury, Sarah C. E., Paddy Ladd, and Mike Gulliver. "Sign Language Peoples as Indigenous Minorities: Implications for Research and Policy." *Environment and Planning A* 39.12 (2007): 2899–2915.

Boehmer, Elleke. *Colonial and Postcolonial Literature*. Oxford: Oxford UP, 1995.

Boyarin, Jonathan, and Daniel Boyarin. *Powers of Diaspora: Two Essays on the Relevance of Jewish Culture*. Minneapolis: Minnesota UP, 2002.

Çohn, Bernard. *Colonialism and Its Forms of Knowledge: The British in India*. Princeton: Princeton UP, 1996.

Gallagher, Shaun. "Phenomenological and Experimental Contributions to Understanding Embodied Experience." Ziemke, Zlatev, and Frank 241–63.

Ladd, Paddy. *Understanding Deaf Culture: In Search of Deafhood*. Clevedon, UK: Multilingual Matters, 2003.

Merleau-Ponty, Maurice. *The Primacy of Perception, and Other Essays on Phenomenological Psychology, the Philosophy of Art, History, and Politics*. Evanston, IL: Northwestern University Press, 1964.

Multatuli (Eduard Douwes Dekker). *Max Havelaar: Or the Coffee Auctions of the Dutch Trading Company*. Trans. Baron Alphonse Nahuys. Edinburgh: Edmondston and Douglas, 1860.

Qur'an. Trans. M. H. Shakir. New York: Tahrike Tarsile Qur'an, 1999.

Taub, Sarah F. *Language from the Body: Iconicity and Metaphor in American Sign Language*. Cambridge: Cambridge UP, 2001.

Ziemke, Tom, Jordan Zlatev, and Roslyn M. Frank, eds. *Embodiment*. Berlin: Mouton de Gruyter, 2007. Vol. 1 of *Body, Language, and Mind*. Cognitive Linguistics Research 35.1.

Zlatev, Jordan. "Embodiment, Language, and Mimesis." Ziemke, Zlatev, and Frank 297–338.

CHAPTER EIGHT

Persian Literature of Exile in France

Goli Taraqqi's Short Stories

Laetitia Nanquette

The literature of exile and the figure of the exiled artist have been given a romantic interpretation in the past century. However, as Edward Said rightly remarks:

> Exile is strangely compelling to think about but terrible to experience. It is the unhealable rift forced between a human being and a native place, between the self and its true home: its essential sadness can never be surmounted. And while it is true that literature and history contain heroic, romantic, glorious, even triumphant episodes in the exile's life, these are no more than efforts meant to overcome the crippling sorrow of estrangement. (173)

The concept of exile has been transformed into an enriching motif in modern culture, but in Said's view, exile cannot be made to serve notions of humanism in a world where it is the consequence of warfare and totalitarian rule (174). In the case of Iran, life in exile has indeed sparked creativity, and yet Said's warning does apply: the experience of exile has been traumatic for many of the Iranians who fled the Islamic regime after 1979.

The consequences of leaving Iran are reflected in the texts written abroad, and it is this shared reflection, which emerged as a massive trend after the 1979 Revolution, that I speak of as the "literature of exile." I argue that such literature is defined by three characteristic uses of the experience of exile—thematic, stylistic, and generic. My argument begins from the premise that this literature is a new phenomenon. Although, prior to the revolution, Persian literature had sometimes been produced by writers living abroad, never had exile functioned as more than a thematic device. Nor, until the post-revolutionary period, had exile ever been narrated in such proportions, or by so many different writers.

A distinction is commonly drawn between immigration, which is assumed to be a matter of personal choice, and exile, which is forced upon the emigrant (typically for political reasons) and therefore connotes suffering. Whereas critics such as Maliheh Tiregol thus argue that exile constitutes a unified category of experience that is qualitatively distinct from the experience of immigration, I prefer the broad definition of exile proposed by Peyman Vahabzadeh, for whom this dichotomy does not apply in the case of Persian literature. "Many of the exiled and banished of yesterday," he writes, "who longed for a vindicating return to their homeland transformed into today's emigrants who have come to terms with their permanent conditions of alterity and foreignness" (496). Regardless of the reasons—personal or political—that prompted them to leave their homeland, both exilic and immigrant writers are caught between two nations: sentiments of alienation from both the new country and the homeland are shared in the same sense of loss and the desire for a return. Although, in terms of the psychological impact of leaving the country, differences do exist among exile, refugee, expatriate, and eimgrant, I contend that these differences are reflected in literature only to a limited degree. Therefore, I do not make a distinction between the literature of exile (*adabyat-e tab'id*) and the literature of emigration (*adabyat-e mohajerat*).

In what follows, I will focus on the use of exile as literary device in the short stories of Goli Taraqqi. Taraqqi is an apt subject not only because the notion of exile imbues all aspects of her writing, from language to structure and theme, but also because she offers a discourse on the subject, in the "metatext." Moreover, her stories exhibit so many of the characteristic features of the Persian literature of exile, and in such dense concentration, that they can be viewed as representative of the whole trend.

GOLI TARAQQI AND EXILE

Taraqqi, one of Iran's most prominent writers, left the country during the Iran-Iraq war and now lives most of the year in France; she publishes all her texts in Iran and travels back to Tehran at least once a year (personal interview, 6 May 2009). Interestingly, although she belongs to a privileged category of exiles (she is not banned from Iran and is relatively comfortable in financial terms), her texts are some of the most convincing in terms of a reflection on exile, precisely because of her "in-between" status, the product of her perpetual shuttling between the two countries. As she puts it:

> I have double nationality: I am an Iranian with a capital I, but a French citizen with the smallest possible "F," almost invisible. This phantom-like citizen is the size of an ant, in comparison with my gigantic Iranian being. Nevertheless, this small ant exists and claims its individuality and civil rights. . . . She's a modern ant, and in spite of her small size she has the force and the audacity to occasionally kick out the other part, meaning the Iranian self. This double life has marked my literary imagination; it has become the central theme of almost all my writings. (qtd. in Nafisi)

The "double life" affecting her literary imagination is predominantly found in her attempts to find a home through literature: one example is her *Do donya* (*Two Worlds*), a collection of short stories in which the opening story depicts a committal to a psychiatric clinic in a suburb of Paris, while the last story ends with an exit from this same clinic. In between, the process of writing has taken place, starting with remembrance and the writing of childhood memories. The homodiegetic narrator herself states in the last short story that she was saved by literature. A new beginning emerges, in a new country, where she can finally visualize the possibility of a future while also creating and re-creating her past through her childhood remembrances. This very process is present in the title, which insists on the existence of a here and a there.

Jennifer Langer uses an interesting metaphor for writers like Goli Taraqqi, for whom literature is a question of life and death: she compares them to Shahrzad (Scheherazade) of *The Thousand and One Nights*, who started telling stories in order to stay alive (267), an experience that is precisely the subject of *Do donya*. Indeed, most authors of the Persian literature of exile are Shahrzad fighting for their lives through language, even if the role of the sultan Shahriyar is undetermined and varying.

"Anar banu va pesar-hayash" ("The Pomegranate Lady and Her Sons"), "Madam Gorgeh" ("The Wolf Lady"), and "Adat-haye gharib-e Aqa-ye 'Alef' dar ghorbat" ("The Bizarre Comportment of Mr. Alpha in Exile") are three short stories emblematic of Taraqqi's exilic writing.[1] I will compare them in order to achieve a synthesis on exile as a theme, as a style, and as a genre. I hope to show that exile is inscribed in the writing at all these levels. All three of these stories have been translated into English.

"Anar banu" is an autobiographical short story in which the narrator leaves Iran to return to France, where she lives most of the year. At the airport in Tehran, she meets an eighty-three-year-old woman who has left her village in the province of Yazd for the first time in order to visit her sons, who have lived in Sweden for twelve years. The old lady is illiterate, which adds to her difficulties in travelling; she complains about having to leave her dear homeland and her village, where she was born under a pomegranate tree. The narrator helps the pomegranate lady on the journey and tries to point her in the right direction at the Paris airport, where she has to change flights, but realizes three days after their parting that by mistake, she has kept the lady's plane ticket from Paris to Sweden. No matter how hard she tries, she cannot find any information about what has become of the old lady. The end of the story becomes surreal, as the narrator imagines her happy in Sweden, surrounded by her sons, preparing traditional Iranian food for them. This surreal end becomes the dream of the narrator to find her roots again.

"Madam Gorgeh" relates the story of an Iranian woman living with her two young children in a Parisian building, and their conflict with the downstairs neighbour. It is told by a first-person narrator, who can again be easily compared to the author. More precisely, it is a fable, where the narrator's neighbour is portrayed as a she-wolf whose constant complaining about the noises coming from the upstairs flat eventually leads the Iranian mother and children to avoid laughing, playing, or inviting friends to their home. The situation changes one day when the narrator, absolutely certain that there is no noise in her flat even though the neighbour is still complaining at the door, realizes that she can shout back, thus ending the tyrannical game: the neighbour reverts to being her silent, lonely old self, and the narrator resumes her normal life.

In "Adat-haye gharib-e Aqa-ye 'Alef' dar ghorbat," told through a heterodiegetic narrator and forming part of a novel not yet completed, the main protagonist, Mr. Alpha, is a middle-aged Iranian history teacher whose pupils attack him in his classroom during the Islamic Revolution, after which he emigrates to Paris. In an interview published in the magazine *Bokhara*, Taraqqi explained how she met the person—a lonely Iranian man giving bread to pigeons in a Parisian park—who inspired the character of Alpha (Fani and Dehbashi 43). In Paris, Alpha lives alone, is jobless, and wanders aimlessly through the city streets and inside his own memories; he remembers his past in a middle-class Tehrani background and his platonic love for Mrs. Nabovat, the physical education teacher of his school. Because he has always lived in a confined environment, Alpha is unable to adapt to France. Moreover, he has exiled himself out of fear, without thinking, because of his inability to make choices and his tendency to follow the crowd.

THE THEME OF EXILE

In "Anar banu"

The sense of being a wanderer permeates "Anar banu," from both the viewpoint of the old lady, who travels from Yazd to Sweden so as to die in the arms of her sons, and that of the narrator, a figure of the writer: "O my sons, what am I going to do with you? I wish I could stop loving you, so that I would not become the wanderer that I am today" (53).[2] Wandering and exile are indeed recurrent and important features in the narrator's emotional life. The first lines of the short story are emblematic of this importance:

> Mehrabad Airport, Tehran. Air France, Flight 726
> Two o'clock in the morning: sleepless night. Confusion, tiredness, hurry
> are mixed with nostalgia, anxiety and crazy ideas like the one of leaving and
> never coming back or, on the contrary, the one of staying here in my beloved
> Tehran, with all its good and bad and not to move away from there anymore:
> one of these even more crazy ideas! Well, a bloody life of wandering, of eternal
> comings and goings (eternal compared to my lifetime), of middle-of-the-night
> flights, opening my suitcase, going through customs (this bridge of paradise)
> and the humiliating inspection of the body, the shoes, the pockets, the bag, the
> ears, the nose. (45)

The space of the airport is symbolic of the space of exile and its unreality. It is significant that the short story is entirely set within the framework of these middle spaces, Mehrabad and Charles de Gaulle airports, and that the places about which the two characters talk (Iran and Sweden) become unreal places for reinventing the past and dreaming the future. Even though the characters stop in Paris, the city is not mentioned as a place where people live: it is just one stop before Sweden, where the lady's family reunion is supposed to happen, and just another Western place, as unknown to the old lady as Sweden is.

Exile has plagued the lady's family, and its sorrow has been the cause of her husband's death. Both husband and wife lamented their boys' exile, both sons having lost their Iranianness, according to their parents, through occidentalization and marriage to foreign women. The husband, especially, thought when he saw their pictures that they had become effeminate, and he died from shame and anger.

However, the painting of exile is nuanced, carrying overtones of exile itself as a way to reunify Iran symbolically. The unification of the homeland happens in the story through the relationship between the two antagonistic Iranian women. The pomegranate lady functions as a synecdoche for Iran. It is a recurrent and valid argument of postcolonial studies that women are linked to the land, their bodies compared to the nation's soil (McClintock, Mufti, and Shohat), and the pomegranate lady embodies this tie. The narrator is a modern occidentalized woman, hurried and intolerant of the old lady's failures to understand her surroundings, while the old lady represents the traditional Iran lost by the narrator, an image of the lost nation. Yet through their exile, the two female characters realize that they both represent Iran and are longing for it. Though the narrator finds some of the old lady's reactions exasperating, she describes her in a sympathetic way:

> She has a gentle voice and her eyes laugh. She is round, plump, and short. Her feet do not reach the cabin floor. Her face resembles a red pomegranate, ready to be squeezed, with red cheeks and full lips. She is a delightful and lively old woman. (55)

This short story is similar in its design and themes to "Khaneh-i dar asman" ("A Mansion in the Sky"), another text by the same author, in which an old Iranian woman wanders between European cities to be with her children, who live in different countries and eventually come to consider her a nuisance. However, in "Anar banu," the narration evolves in a positive way: antagonisms between the two kinds of Iranians—one modern, occidentalized, and living in both lands; the other traditional, staid, and never stirring from the home country—disappear. The narration shows the reunification of Iran through the encounter of two characters, as opposed to "Khaneh-i dar asman," which is precisely the narration of the rupture between these categories. In "Anar banu," exile becomes the only status and identity along which the two characters can define themselves, and it eventually comes to be understood as a positive state. On the last page of the story, the narrator indeed explains to the old lady that exile and looking for a new place are themselves ways of life and that as such, they probably make her sons happy.

In "Madam Gorgeh"

"Madam Gorgeh" is another embodiment of exile, as well as a satire of Parisian life, where neighbours are an omnipresent nuisance. While "Anar banu" is set in the abstract space and time of exile and of air travel, "Madam Gorgeh" unfolds in the daily-life space of exile, when an exiled person is not at home even in her own flat and relives the constant threat of displacement. Even home is not the last secure bastion against a hostile world: exile is represented as a constant battle. Life in exile has become a miniature of earlier life, shrinking human beings and making them claustrophobic. In "Madam Gorgeh," this is exemplified by the comparison between the tiny scraps of nature found in Paris in the two square metres of the family's balcony and the big parks of Darband in Tehran (143). The term "garden parties" applied to the former becomes an ironic reflection on this diminishing of the self and on the claustrophobic tendencies of exiles. The children suffer even more acutely, as they cannot understand the reasons for leaving their loving family for a cold foreign place: "They have been exiled to a cold, sad, unkind place from the bosom of their grand-mother, their aunts, from an abundance of love and affection, charming airs and caresses" (143; trans. Vatanabadi and Khorrami 132). The story's happy ending, however, depicts exile as a temporary and conceivably constructive period.

In "Aqa-ye 'Alef'"

"Adat-haye gharib-e Aqa-ye 'Alef' dar ghorbat," an early short story by Taraqqi, introduces the theme of exile through a nostalgic narration, the most recurrent form within Persian literature written in exile. The character of Alpha is an abstract embodiment of exile: in fact, Alpha—who symbolizes various concepts by his very name—is more the personification of an idea than a short story character. He has no proper name other than Mr. Alpha, a letter, and the first of a series yet to come. Even as a child, he was called "Little 'A'" (213): just a practical appellation carrying no reference to his identity and given solely to avoid confusing him with other children. This sense of anonymity is reinforced by the name being enclosed in quotation marks.

In the story, Mr. Alpha does not belong with the majority of Iranian immigrants in France, whose comfortable financial circumstances and good educational background make them familiar with French mores and culture; he is thus faced with redefining his own social status. In this sense, Taraqqi's text on the difficulty of exile and the miseries of an undocumented resident in the big city of Paris is universal. Alpha is an archetype, with whom the reader cannot identify. He is designed as such to let the narrator draw on her main subject: exile as the transforming experience of the loss of one's own being.

In the story, Mr. Alpha is feeling all his "-ness" disappearing: his Iranian-ness, his Alpha-ness, the very essence of his own self:

> He felt as if he had been transformed into someone else, someone he did not particularly like. [. . .] He sustained a deep anxiety that his foreign sojourn, like an acid, would corrode his "Mr. Alpha-ness." [. . .] Life beyond the windowpanes seemed to have no relation to him. (190; trans. Farrokh, 123–24)

He summarizes his feelings in a letter to his colleague, Mr. Fazeli:

> I am lost and bewildered here. [. . .] I do not understand things. My past is all lost to me, and my vision does not extend beyond the end of the week. [. . .] Sometimes I even doubt my mental health and fear that in this foreign atmosphere I may lose the meager balance of my sanity. (175: trans. Farrokh, 119)

The narrator depicts exile as an unreal experience and draws on Alpha's feeling of being lost in time and space. The relation between the characters and the representation of space is revealing in this story: the experience of exile is a deep and physical one. The first pages of the text deal with Alpha's waking up to a new environment (97). All his senses experience new and strange feelings: hearing (with the sound of the bell), smell, touch, sight; only the sense of taste is safe from this trauma. Time is also physically experienced as foreign: Alpha does not know how to adapt to the new temporality; unable to adapt to the present, he is perpetually confused about the time of day. Since exile is an experience of remembering, it is significant that Alpha's most used adjective is "known" and its various opposites, because Alpha finds security in the known and cannot adapt to new situations. He defines things according to two categories: known and unknown.

The discourse of this text is complicated by the fact that Alpha is an anti-hero without personality. We see him becoming another man through the experience of the Revolution, as he becomes another man through the experience of exile: he has no specific traits; he is ductile; there is no such thing as his Alpha-ness. However, if exile is depicted in a negative light, this is somewhat mitigated by the fact that Alpha is an anti-hero and cannot therefore be considered a model.[3]

It is hardly surprising that a writer with a life experience such as Taraqqi's would write on exile. In the next section, I address the way the theme has led her writing through a stylistic evolution. This change is illustrated through comparing the use of metaphors and structure in "Aqa-ye 'Alef,'" "Anar banu," and "Madam Gorgeh."

WRITING EXILE: METAPHORS AND STRUCTURE

The pomegranate lady is both a plausible and an extreme figure of the Iranian exile. She has no clue about her new environment and thus looks at things in a fresh and innocent manner. The narrator sees the reflection of her own suffering in the sense of loss and feelings of sadness expressed by this old woman. The home country, embodied in this rural woman, thus becomes a dream-like country, idealized in its traditions as represented by basic activities such as cooking and sharing food.

The pomegranate fruit is important to this embodiment of the nation in the lady, who bears such an otherwise improbable name. The pomegranate is indeed a symbol of Iran through its long association with an array of meanings deeply embedded in Persian literature.[4] The fruit almost becomes a fetish, a talisman protecting the character of the old lady against the West. The pomegranate represents not only the native products of Iran but also the country's cuisine, which the old lady invokes as a reason for pride—even a reason for returning to the home country (58). Exile is thus inscribed within the text through the metaphors of the lost homeland, as represented by its cuisine. This fetishization of Iranian objects, especially culinary ones, is another component of the Persian literature of exile. The pomegranate plays an important role, therefore, as a national fetish.

In "Madam Gorgeh," the metaphor around which the text is structured centres on the linguistic element. The story is a description of the power of language and of the battle to overcome and appropriate such power—an important problem in the life of the exile, for whom language is both a question of belonging and of survival in the new country. The narrator is harassed by her neighbour because of her inability to speak French. When she finds in herself the words to fight the neighbour's verbal attacks and overcome the French language, she becomes the winner: "I chirp like a nightingale and swim in the ocean of words. My thoughts are the same as my language" (153, trans. Vatanabadi and Khorrami 140). "Madam Gorgeh" is both a metaphor for language and a statement on its empowering force. In this sense, the story is a tale: it is structured as the initiation process of the heroine, who is held up as an example for potential readers.

As for "Aqa-ye 'Alef,'" the text is more realistic than metaphoric, its most striking feature in terms of style being linked to the structuring of the narration through the alternation (almost equal in quantitative terms) between narrative sequences set in Paris and memories of the past. The psychological loss experienced by the character resonates in the narrative structure so as to make the reader participate in the sense of uncertainty and confusion as to space and time. In fact, Parisian scenes are pretexts for the analepses of Alpha's life in Iran. In exile, the present has no real consistency; what is meaningful is the space of dreams. There is no space of any solidity: one is in the unstable dimension of exile, between old dreams and reality. Exile is thus the feeling of not being able to distinguish between dream and reality, and of looking for the in-between that allows for avoiding decisions and taking refuge in memories. Thus the very structuring of the story around this dialogue between past and present evolves from the theme of exile.

The three short stories have a style directly linked to exile—for "Anar banu" and "Madam Gorgeh," through metaphor, and for "Aqa-ye 'Alef,'" through structure. In the next section, I will demonstrate how exile is also part of the writing process within a specific genre.

THE GENRE: BETWEEN REALISM AND TALE

An evolution can be noted in Taraqqi's writing from the realistic genre of "Aqa-ye 'Alef'" to the use of tale conventions in the other later short stories. I contend that this evolution reflects the maturing of Taraqqi as a writer, who detaches herself from her first-hand experience of exile to create stories out of it and get some distance from the trauma of the arrival in France. Iranian writers within Iran often insist, in interviews, that one of the ways to avoid censorship is through the use of the conventions of tales and fables. I would argue that this is also a characteristic of Persian literature abroad, where most innovations on the tale are reproduced even when censorship is no longer a direct threat. The determining factor is a stylistic trait characterizing the whole of Persian literature. Indeed, the tale realizes the potential of a contemporary literature using all the richness of its tradition. Balaÿ argues that this use is linked to fragment-writing, dominant as much in the novel as in the short story. In the case of the tale, this argument is fitting and demonstrates that Persian literature abroad can use the form of the tale even when censorship has ceased to be a direct threat.

"Aqa-ye 'Alef'" appears less innovative in terms of genre, precisely because it does not use the efficient device of the tale and restricts itself to a classical realistic short story. I argue that for Taraqqi, who wrote this story at the very beginning of her life in Paris, exile was still deeply bound with her emotional state and that the motif had not had sufficient time yet to transform her writing. In fact, "Aqa-ye 'Alef'" is peculiar in Taraqqi's writing economy because of its unfinished aspect. In an essay titled "Ashna-ii ba Aqa-ye 'Alef'" ("Encounter with Mr. Alpha"), Taraqqi describes the difficulties she encountered when the story, initially conceived as the first part of a novel, was submitted to censorship. She tells of having to alter the ending, bringing Alpha back to Iran, because the censor objected that such a good man might be perverted by life in Paris (569–70). Taraqqi thus had to cut the narration of his exile, which meant that she did not finish the story and that the novel was left unachieved. I contend that this loose structure and the consequent failure to complete the novel are the reasons for the lessened effectiveness of the short story.[5] In the *Bokhara* interview, Taraqqi states that she vowed to finish the novel about Alpha (thus confirming that she does conceive the text as a novel), if that were the only thing that she was to finish in her life. She speaks about the novel as a genre, and how much energy it requires, insisting that she is not the kind of writer to write novels and that she can be content with short stories (Fani and Dehbashi, 43). She seems to me very lucid when she states that the text of "Aqa-ye 'Alef'" resists her. A comparison with the two other short stories shows that a more innovative generic use is beneficial to the treatment of exile. This is especially true of the use of the tale conventions, sometimes verging on the moral tale and sometimes on the fable, using animals or imaginary figures.

In "Anar banu," the elements of tale come mostly from the character of the pomegranate lady. She actually bears an unlikely name that refers directly to myths; her birth under a pomegranate tree and her being bred by trees are also mythical, harking back to the myth of the Iranian nation, in which the pomegranate is an essential intertextual element. In the same mythic vein, the pomegranate lady's narration transforms her own journey into an arduous adventure in which she crosses mountains and oceans to achieve her goal, with the courage and prowess worthy of a fairy-tale hero. The story's imaginary happy ending also confirms that Taraqqi had the tale form in mind when writing this text. The ending is indeed very close to the traditional fairy-tale ending—"And they lived happily ever after .

. ."—although in this case "they" are not a prince and princess but rather a mother and her two sons.

"Madam Gorgeh" is a story about tyranny and the necessity of revolting against unjust rules, as well as a tale on exile and adaptation to the new country, especially through language. The narration follows the structure of a fable, with the heroine-narrator getting rid of the monster-neighbour when she succeeds in ridding herself of her own fears (about the language). The devices employed in the story also appear in the choice of images used, especially in the animal form taken by the characters: the neighbour-she-wolf and, by extension, the lamb as the wolf's prey. At the beginning of the story, the narrator is the lamb, but the situation is ultimately reversed, with the neighbour subdued by the narrator, who transforms herself into all sorts of monsters: "I [. . .] have grown taller, and my teeth have grown like those of Dracula's. I've grown horns and a beard; I look like a dragon and I love it" (153; trans. Vatanabadi and Khorrami 141). This fantastic style helps to transform exile into a universal fable, where the issue of empowering is as important as the particular experience of exile. The need to master the host country's language is underlined in humorous passages. The use of the tale, as analysed above, plays a different function in stories of exile than in stories written in Iran, where it is mainly used in order to escape censorship. In exile, the tale is used as a tool to reinforce discourse on the Other, as it is also a device for narrations on faraway lands and strange indigenous people. The tale in stories written in exile demonstrates that the Other is like the Self, if not identical.

In the following section, I argue that France is one of the elements forging a representation of the Iranian Self and that a complete analysis of exile needs to look at the place from which the story is written and against which the narrators define their exilic status. I further argue that the Persian literature of exile is as much acted upon by the representation of the Self as by the representation of the Other, as exile is precisely defined by this state where redefinitions of identity happen, when the confrontation with the Other has become mandatory. It is through the redefinition of France and the French that the narrators' selves are delineated in Taraqqi's texts.

THE REPRESENTATION OF FRANCE IN THE THREE STORIES

"Anar banu" is not concerned with France in a precise way, though the country is always in the background—part of a West unknown to the old lady, for whom both

France and Sweden are distant and incomprehensible locations. Paris is an indeterminate Western space where people are in a hurry: a pretext for generalizations on Western society. For instance, the discipline of the French passengers on the plane is remarkable, whereas the Iranian passengers continuously leave their seats until the French flight attendant finally gives up on them. Also, Westerners are shown to be indifferent to the plight of others: at the airport in Paris, without thinking of stopping or giving help, they pass the old lady as she sits on the floor helplessly repeating "Sweden." When the narrator realizes that the suffering pomegranate lady needs to be carried, she helps her onto a trolley and tries to comfort her and shield her against embarrassment: "I say: 'Dear Mama, nobody knows you here. Nothing is inappropriate in the West'" (65). The strict opposition between the West and Iran is, however, blurred by the fact that the narrator is herself representative of Westerners: she insists on having a thousand things to do and is abrupt when addressing the old lady. Only from time to time does she remember the tradition of generosity of her country and resolve to continue giving help.

"Madam Gorgeh" also posits an opposition between the French and Iranians, the former portrayed as serious, self-contained people who prefer meeting friends in a café rather than opening their homes to them. There is a funny depiction of French people taking an inordinately long time to open their doors with their many locks and making sure that the person who knocks is reliable, while the Iranian narrator says her door is always open, a welcoming cup of tea ready for anybody who might like to come in (62–63).

There is definitely a criticism embedded in this story, employing as it does the extended metaphor of the wolf-lamb dyad to present Western society as a place of constant struggle where the weak are necessarily dominated by the strong. At the end of the fable, the weakened neighbour disappears without anybody noticing: this implies that Western society is a place where a person can become lost and disappear. But, as in "Anar banu," the criticism is also applied to the narrator herself, who knows how occidentalized she has become: at the end of the story, busy preparing dinner for the friends she is expecting, she herself forgets about the loneliness of a tramp in the street and the despair of her downstairs neighbour alone in the cold. Mixed with negative Western characteristics, the Iranian Self can no longer be purely Iranian; as such, the criticism of French society is also a self-criticism.

The narrators of "Aqa-ye 'Alef'" and "Anar banu" often use the term *Farang* to refer either to France or to the West. This is a significant word choice, considering that they could use the modern term *Faranseh*. The choice of *Farang* refers both to a poetic symbol, the ancient term being evocative of travelogues and poetic images, and to a political stance, because *Farang* and *Farangestan* are also generic terms to designate the whole Western world and can have negative connotations. In an interview, Taraqqi remarked on the element of irony in her association of the term with the Qadjar era, stating that she had used it because of its humorous connotations (personal interview, 9 Jan. 2009). In the case of "Aqa-ye 'Alef,'" this choice of vocabulary is confirmed by the fact that for Alpha, France is a Western country of exile like any other. Alpha has no particular attachment to French values. The only ones he approves of are Western and general: for example, he praises the civility of the people. In his depiction of the West, the narrator deals with the topos of a busy, self-absorbed place (203). For Alpha, Notre Dame Cathedral incarnates Paris, with its frightful solidity and all its weight of stone, symbolizing the chill of the country—its beautiful, ancient, but inaccessible nature. Paris is generally depicted as a cold city with unfriendly people, cold weather, and an impenetrable beauty, definitely too sumptuous and far too distant for Alpha's expectations. It is also described as an anonymous city where one does not want to hear or befriend one's neighbours, solitude being the corollary of coldness, as in "Madam Gorgeh." Sometimes, the positive topos of Paris as the most beautiful city in the world tempers this depiction: Mrs. Nabovat, Alpha's platonic love relation, is particularly representative of this opinion in the letters she writes to him (118). Taraqqi does not hesitate to use topos and clichés of the country, or to mix positive and negative ones. This balance between negative and positive representations, and between self-criticism and criticism of France, is another way for Taraqqi to present a nuanced way of looking at the Other.[6]

In this essay, I have compared three short stories by Goli Taraqqi to illustrate how Persian literature of exile uses thematic, stylistic, and generic devices. Many Iranian writers living in France can be compared to Taraqqi and be included in Persian literature of exile in France, including Reza Qassemi, Chahla Chafiq, Javad Javaheri, M. F. Farzaneh, and Mahasti Shahrokhi. These writers range from authors who have integrated themselves into French society and participate in it as full citizens—such as Chahla Chafiq, a published sociologist and activist—to authors like Goli Taraqqi, who tend to mix mostly with other Iranians and rarely speak French. Nuances have to be applied when including them in the broad trend of Persian literature of exile, but the common characteristics of exilic writing along thematic, stylistic, and generic lines necessitate a comparative approach.

NOTES

1 The first of these stories is from Taraqqi's collection *Ja-ii digar* and the second and third are in the collection *Khatereh-haye parakandeh.*

2 In translating Taraqqi, I have consulted published translations in English and French, and, on occasion, I quote from one of the available English translations (as indicated). All other translations from the Persian are my own.

3 I do not read Alpha as an embodiment of Taraqqi, although she did compare her story with his in an interview (Fani and Dehbashi).

4 The pomegranate is also present in other literary imaginaries, such as the Turkish or Armenian.

5 The genealogy of "Aqa-ye 'Alef'" is an example of the fluidity of Persian literature within Iran and abroad. Although living mostly in Paris, Taraqqi is determined to publish her books in Tehran: censorship thus remains a weighty issue affecting her life and work.

6 It is also important to remember that Taraqqi received an English education and that she experienced France through the prism of an Anglo-Saxon outlook (personal interview, 6 May 2009).

WORKS CITED

Balaÿ, Christophe. "Stylistique du récit court dans l'oeuvre de Zoya Pirzad." 17 Sept. 2008. 2 Dec. 2009. http://www.zulma.fr/datas/files/stylistique_pirzad.pdf.

Fani, Kamran, and Ali Dehbashi. "Goftegu ba Goli Taraqqi" ["Conversation with Goli Taraqqi"]. *Bokhara* 19 (2001): 31–54.

Farrokh, Faridoun, and Mohammad Ghanoonparvar. "Portraits in Exile in the Fiction of Esma'il Fassih and Goli Taraghi." *Iranian Refugees and Exiles Since Khomeini*. Ed. Asghar Fathi. Costa Mesa, CA: Mazda, 1991. 280–93.

Langer, Jennifer. *Silver Throat of the Moon: Writing in Exile*. Nottingham, UK: Five Leaves, 2005.

McClintock, Anne, Aamir Mufti, and Ella Shohat, eds. *Dangerous Liaisons: Gender, Nation, and Postcolonial Perspectives*. Minneapolis: U of Minnesota P, 1997.

Nafisi, Azar. "Reading of Between Two Worlds, by Goli Taraghi." *Lifelines: The Literature of Women's Human Rights*. Washington, DC: Lib. of Cong., 7 Mar. 2001. 17 Nov. 2010. http://www.loc.gov/locvideo/womensday/.

Said, Edward. *Reflections on Exile and Other Literary and Cultural Essays*. London: Granta, 2001.

Taraqqi, Goli. "Adat-haye gharib-e Aqa-ye 'Alef' dar ghorbat" ["The Bizarre Comportment of Mr. Alpha in Exile"]. Taraqqi, *Khatereh-haye parakandeh* 181–231.

———. "Anar banu va pesar-hayash" ["The Pomegranate Lady and Her Sons"]. Taraqqi, *Ja-ii digar* 43–72.

———. "Ashna-ii ba Aqa-ye 'Alef'" ["Encounter with Mr. Alpha"]. *Naqd va barresi-ye asar* [*Textual Criticism*]. Ed. Ali Dehbashi and Mehdi Karimi. Tehran: Nashr-e Qatreh, 2003. 567–73.
———. *Do donya* [*Two Worlds*]. Tehran: Nilufar, 2002.
———. *Ja-ii digar* [*Another Place*]. Tehran: Nilufar, 2000.
———. "Khaneh-i dar asman" ["A Mansion in the Sky"]. Taraqqi, *Khatereh-haye parakandeh* 157–79.
———. *Khatereh-haye parakandeh* [*Scattered Memories*]. 1992. Tehran: Nilufar, 2004.
———. "Madam Gorgeh" ["The Wolf Lady"]. Taraqqi, *Khatereh-haye parakandeh* 139–56.
———. "The Bizarre Comportment of Mr. Alpha in Exile." *A Mansion in the Sky*. Trans. Faridoun Farrokh. Austin: U of Texas P, 2003. 117–54.
———. Personal interviews. 9 Jan. 2009 (Paris); 6 May 2009 (Tehran).
Tiregol, Maliheh. "Si sal adabyat-e Farsi dar tab'id" ["Thirty Years of Persian Literature in Exile"]. N.d. 6 Feb. 2008. http://www.asar.name/2004/06/blog-post.html.
Vahabzadeh, Peyman. "Where Will I Dwell? A Sociology of Literary Identity Within the Iranian Diaspora." *Comparative Studies of South Asia, Africa, and the Middle East* 28.3 (2008): 495–512.
Vatanabadi, Shouleh, and Mohammad Mehdi Khorrami, eds. and trans. "The Wolf Lady." *Another Sea, Another Shore: Persian Stories of Migration*. Northampton, MA: Interlink, 2004. 130–42.

CHAPTER NINE

Farang Represented

The Construction of Self-Space in Goli Taraqqi's Fiction

Goulia Ghardashkhani

Focused on personal thoughts, memories, and relationships, Goli Taraqqi's fictional works are set against a background that reflects the contemporary history and social milieu of Iran during the last three decades of the Pahlavi dynasty as well as the author's later life in diaspora, following the Islamic Revolution in 1979. Taraqqi's pre-revolutionary publications include the novel *Khab-e zemestani* (*Winter Sleep*, 1972) and a collection of short stories titled *Man ham Chegvara hastam* (*A Che Guevara in My Own Right*, 1969), both of which deal with the routines and obsessions of disoriented characters. The first three collections of short stories that appeared following her emigration to France—*Khatereh-haye parakandeh* (*Scattered Memories*, 1992), *Ja-ii digar* (*Another Place*, 2000), and *Do donya* (*Two Worlds*, 2002)—are mostly autobiographical and deal thematically with the traumatic sense of displacement and the nostalgic reconstruction of homeland.

One of the key concepts in Taraqqi's later publications is the notion of "Farang" and its signification. Etymologically, the term *Farang* is the Persianized version of the word France. The adjective *Farangi* is thus generally used to indicate an association with Farang, that is, with France and, by extension, with Europeans and Christians (see Dehkhoda, vol. 11, "Farang"). According to Mohammad Ghanoonparvar, the terms *Farang* and *Farangi* were once used to refer to "the people and lands of Christendom," but since the late eighteenth and early nineteenth centuries, they have come to refer to "the West and Westerners in general, more specifically to the lands and peoples of Europe and North America" (2–3). Almost all the stories in Taraqqi's later collections deal, in one way or another, with the notion of "Farang."[1] Although Taraqqi does not necessarily locate Farang as the central theme of these stories, the word itself, its connotations, and the ironic references to the notion permeate her narratives.

FARANG IN TARAQQI'S SHORT STORIES

Generally speaking, the concept of "Farang" in Taraqqi's work comes up in two types of stories. The first consists of stories that open in a diasporic setting but that continue with the reconstruction of a temporally and spatially remote homeland, mainly depicted in the author's autobiographical flashbacks. Examples are "Otubus-e Shemiran" ("The Shemiran Bus"), "Dust-e kuchak" ("My Little Friend"), and "Gol-haye Shiraz" ("The Flowers of Shiraz").[2] The second type is made up of stories that are specifically set in diaspora and narrate the very experience of displacement, examples being "Madam Gorgeh" ("The Wolf Lady") and "Adat-haye gharib-e Aqa-ye 'Alef' dar ghorbat" ("The Bizarre Comportment of Mr. Alpha in Exile"). While in the stories belonging to the former group the concept of "Farang," alongside its attributes, is represented positively, those of the latter group reflect a counter-Farangi discourse.[3]

Taraqqi's upper-middle-class characters, when located in Iran, are depicted as individuals infatuated by Farang and the sociocultural connotations it communicates. Their passion for Farang is generally represented in the ways they try to imitate the Farangi ideal, their emulative attitude being reified in their everyday manners, cultural activities, values, and ambitions. In this respect, if Farang (in the first place, a spatial term) is socioculturally perceived as an ideal, then it can be logically inferred that the individual's transition from the location she or he already inhabits (home/Iran) to the desirable and spatially remote space of Farang (France) would result in that person's general satisfaction. However, Taraqqi's account of her characters in France discredits that hypothesis. These characters are depicted as disillusioned, dissatisfied, and disoriented. In this respect, the following question is raised: What function does Farang fulfill in the sociocultural space of home/

Iran that it fails to perform in France, which is allegedly the very embodiment of the notion? In order to answer this question, it is important to clarify some ambiguities regarding the concept of "Farang."

FARANG SIGNIFIED

Farang, like any other concept, depends for its meaning on discursive practice. That is, both the denotative and the connotative significations of the term are constructed and communicated within an intricate network of cultural and contextual interactions and power relations, which make it impossible for the term to retain a stable and fixed meaning. In this respect, one major question to be explored, here, is the meaning of Farang.

In "The Work of Representation," Stuart Hall explores the theoretical development and the dynamics of the relationship between the subject and meaning in a cultural context. Drawing upon Saussure, he points out that language is a representational phenomenon that functions through signs and difference. That is, any particular signifier (word, item, colour) represents the signified (meaning, message, concept) through its difference from other signifiers. The relationship between the signifier and the signified is arbitrary and generally agreed upon in any culture (30–31). In this sense, meaning is *constructed* in a particular sociocultural context and is dependent on "conventions" rather than "nature." Accordingly, Hall argues that "if meaning is the result of . . . our social, cultural, and linguistic conventions, then meaning can never be *finally* fixed" (23). Here, "discourse" (in its Foucauldian sense) takes over language as a "system of representation." Discourse is understood as "a group of statements which provide the language for talking about—a way of representing the knowledge about—a particular topic at a particular historical moment" (44). But the construction of meaning is not exclusively based on what can be linguistically communicated. Meaning is also conveyed through social practices such as ceremonies, rituals, behaviours, dress codes, and relations. Since "all social practices entail *meaning*, and meanings shape and influence what we do . . . all practices have a discursive aspect" (44). Therefore, if meaning, practice, and the sociocultural context are so closely connected, then meaning is prone to change based on the conduct of the *subject* as well as his or her historical and geographical standpoint. In other words, it becomes unavoidable for the subject to be defined by—and in—the discourse in which she or he is located. The discourse forces the subject into a specific "subject position" and thereby defines him or her (56).

The same rules apply to the signification of the term *Farang*. The meaning of the word *Farang* is not fixed: it changes on the basis of the discourse in which the concept is articulated—first, on the basis of how, where, and when the term is used and its meaning thus constructed and expressed and, second, on the basis of the social practices it stimulates. In Taraqqi's stories, the most important factor influencing the meaning of *Farang* is the subject's transition from one sociocultural space to another (here, from Iran to France)—a movement that shatters the word's previous connotations and makes it ambiguous. In this sense, the intricacies and ambiguities concerning the signification of the term *Farang* in Taraqqi's stories are closely related to the concept of space. This is not simply because Farang primarily denotes Europe as a geographical locale but rather because its denotative and connotative meanings shift in accordance with the location of the perceiving subject (character). Regarding the perceiving subject, I emphasize that owing to Taraqqi's autobiographical style and her somewhat class-conscious approach to the events that she incorporates into her narratives, the reader typically perceives the narratives from the vantage point of the Iranian upper middle class. In this respect, in exploring the multi-layered signification of the term *Farang* in Taraqqi's stories, I limit my discussion to the perspectives of those characters who, at a certain point in time and place, are infatuated with Farang and its attractions rather than the ones who are intimidated by it. Accordingly, by the location of the perceiving subject, I mean the spatial relation between the geographical standpoint of the subject both to Europe (which is primarily what Farang refers to) and to what Farang denotes in a more sociocultural sense.[4]

In this sense, there are at least three layers of meaning within the concept of "Farang" in Taraqqi's stories. The first is related to what Farang signifies for the subject living in Iran for whom it is perceived as a geographical point of orientation and a desirable object of emulation. The second layer is related to the moment of confrontation: the moment when the geographical distance between the subject and destination is overcome and, as a result, the subject is confronted with disillusionment and new interpretations of the concept. The third layer is related to how the signification of Farang is altered when the old and the new definitions of the term are reconsidered. In this case, the admiring and emulative attitudes of the subject in Iran are reviewed by the subject who has already been exposed to a newer signification of the term after emigration. The perceiving subject, accordingly, experiences a slippage in the signification of the concept of "Farang." For him or her, Farang is no longer an admirable object of imitation nor is it only associated with the biting experience of disillusionment. The meaning of *Farang* becomes vacillating and the truth of the term is disturbed. Although the first and the second attitudes toward the concept of "Farang" function as Taraqqi's raw materials for her narratives, her retrospective authorial stance leads to an ironical style that undermines both. In other words, she tells us the stories from an in-between position—from "other narrative spaces" (Bhabha, *Location* 177–78).

IRONY AND THE THIRD SPACE

Here, I would like to draw some links between irony, as a linguistic and literary trope, and Homi Bhabha's notion of cultural translation. Taraqqi's later stories are generally narrated in an ironic and somewhat objective tone. At the same time, they are narrated from the specific subject position of a marginalized migrant—the position that Bhabha refers to as "the third space" (Bhabha, "Interview" 211). The point here is that Taraqqi's ironical style is not merely a matter of choice but is also a result of the discursive position she occupies as a migrant author writing about her own experiences—an in-between hybrid subject position from which two or more cultures (and hence two or more discourses) go through the process of cultural translation. It is only through this "third position of removal and distance" that the subject is able to "objectify and judge the different strata of culture" (Byrne 32). Through distance and objectification, the representational aspect of culture is revealed. This means that what is generally signified as the stable *truth* in a cultural discourse can be approached as merely a conventional *representation* of a message through cultural translation in the third space. In this way, the authority of truth is destabilized and the effect becomes ironic.

As an Iranian writer living in France and writing about nostalgia, homeland, and diaspora, Taraqqi occupies a third-subject position—a position that enables her to go back and forth between two cultural discourses. In this sense, she is constantly engaged in an act of translation in order to produce meaning. During the process of cultural translation, the authority of truth is destabilized and the representational function of cultural practices is revealed. In the story "Gol-haye Shiraz," for instance, Taraqqi provides the reader with the stereotypical images and sociocultural practices that both convey and construct the Farangi discourse. What makes the story amusing and ironic is the fact that through her authorial stance (positioned in between Iran and France) and certain narratological strategies, Taraqqi illustrates the ways in which Farang is represented in the discourse of the upper and upper middle classes in the Iran of the 1950s. I will come back to this issue with more detailed discussions in the analysis of the story "Gol-haye Shiraz."

REPRESENTATION, IDENTIFICATION, AND THE SELF-SPACE

Before dealing with the textual analysis of the stories "Gol-haye Shiraz" and "Madam Gorgeh," I return to a question posed earlier in order to formulate the central premise of this paper: What function does Farang (as a discursive construct) fulfill for Taraqqi's characters in the sociocultural space of home/Iran that it fails to perform in France? The answer to this question can be comprehended in terms of the relation between identification and the possibility to construct self-space in a specific discursive domain.

If the subject is defined by discourse, then identification (i.e., the construction and the communication of the meaning of self) becomes a discursive phenomenon, too. That is, identification becomes dependent on—and only possible in—a specific discourse. In other words, the identification strategies developed by an individual in a particular discourse fail to function in another discourse. The subject, therefore, has to develop other strategies (through language and practice) to be able to *represent* the self in the new discursive space that she or he occupies. In this sense, what lies beneath the discontentment of Taraqqi's characters in Farang has to do with their inability to preserve the same identification strategies for the representation of the self, and thereby, the construction of self-space.

Since any discourse is developed in a specific social and cultural territory, identification becomes space-dependent. This, however, is not the only factor that relates identification to the notion of space. The relation between identification and the concept of space stems also from the fact that the construction of identity functions through symbolic or "signifying practices." If identity is constructed and communicated through difference (as is the case with any other signifier in a sign system), then there should exist a virtual (or even actual) borderline delineating the difference (Hall, "Introduction" 3)—there should exist *boundaries* that outline the territories of the self.

In this respect, the present essay will be engaged with the textual analysis of two of Taraqqi's stories: "Gol-haye Shiraz," from the collection *Do donya* (2002), set in the Tehran of the 1950s, and "Madam Gorgeh," from the collection *Khatereh-haye parakandeh* (1992), set in Paris during the 1980s. The analysis of the former story will be concerned with the relation between identity formation and the notion of space vis-à-vis Farangi values, and that of the latter, with displaced identities and the relation between sign systems and space (re)construction in the very space of Farang.

"GOL-HAYE SHIRAZ": SIGNIFYING THE FARANGI AND THE CONSTRUCTION OF SELF-SPACE

"Gol-haye Shiraz" delineates a city on the verge of change. The story is set in the summer of 1953 and sketches the streets of Tehran from downtown Laleh-zar to the northern district of Shemiran. Amid the confusion during the overthrow of Mosaddeq's government, the fourteen-year-old narrator gives us the account of the background setting of the narrative in a rather lighthearted but ironical tone. Wandering down the streets of Tehran, she is enticed by the sparkling shop-windows, cinemas, bistros, bookstores, colourful ads and posters, fashionable dandies, and bantering vagabonds.

Concerning the sociohistorical setting of the story, it is relevant that European cultural practices—such as dress codes, foods and beverages, arts and entertainment, and moral conventions—helped to create a new value system during the reign of the Pahlavis. These "Farangi" cultural practices came to exercise hegemony over the already familiar for at least three reasons: first, because they were promoted by the state authorities; second, because they were new, unfamiliar, and exotic; and third, because of the economic superiority of the social class that consumed them. The construction of this value system elicited, in consequence, certain reactions from the individuals exposed to it. This reaction or attitude fluctuated between the extremes of "Europhilia" and "Europhobia" (Tavakoli-Targhi 19). In another sense, this value system functioned as a point of orientation based on which subject positions or identities were constructed.

The change that the city in "Gol-haye Shiraz" is about to undergo is of a spatial nature. Not only is the change rooted in remote places and geographies (such as Europe or America), but it also constructs new boundaries within the larger space it enters. The introductory paragraph of the story is full of nouns and modifiers designating different social and cultural spaces within the setting of the narrative. For example, the Armenian Madam Yelena, who teaches dance to children, has formed a group, Gol-haye Shiraz, whose young members give public performances (attended mostly by parents and family friends) in spaces rented for the occasion, such as Talar-e Farhang and Cinema Metropole (Taraqqi, "Gol-haye Shiraz" 95). Not only do these cultural spaces function as performance venues for the newly imported cultural products (such as international dance, films, and plays), but they also vividly signify newly constructed exotic spaces through their very names. In addition to Cinema Metropole, for instance, two other cinemas mentioned in the story have Euro-American names: Cinema Mike (103) and Cinema Rex (109). Even Cinema Bahar (101) is immediately described as the cinema screening American films.

Apart from this, Talar-e Farhang, because of the phonetic similarity of the word *Farhang* to the term *Farang*, signifies a discursive tension between the geographically indefinite notion of "farhang" (culture) and the spatially specific word *Farang* (Europe). This tension arises from the connotations of the term *farhang* in Persian: the word is in no sense a value-neutral term. Although it is an objective reference to the notion of culture in general, it is also widely used in everyday conversation—in combination with prefixes and other words—to engender complimentary or derogatory terms and phrases such as *bi-farhang* (uncultured), *ba-farhang* (cultured), and *farhang-e paiin* (low culture). Of course, an equivalent usage can also be seen in European languages: for example, uncultured, *unkultiviert*. The difference, however, lies in the fact that the tension communicated by the term *uncultured* in a European context can be explained in terms of class dialectics. In the Iranian context, however, this is not exclusively the case, since the matter of class in the contemporary society of Iran, in addition to its economic and educational dimensions, is rather defined by the extent of the acquisition of the standards of Western culture by the subject in question. That is, the signification of *farhang* is constructed through the discourse of "civilized West versus uncivilized East." In this sense, the concept of "farhang" (culture) cannot be exclusively interpreted, and hence communicated, without its spatial connotations.

When it comes to the relationship between identity and cultural practices, it is interesting to note that the introduction of certain cultural practices into a society also means that they are introduced into the social sign system of that particular region. That is, they are practiced to be perceived, and when perceived, interpreted. Stuart Hall refers to this phenomenon as cultural "representation" ("Work of Representation" 15 and 21). In cultural representation, a certain behaviour goes through a two-stage procedure before the process of signification is completed. First, a meaning is *encoded* in that certain behaviour, and then it is *decoded* and interpreted by the perceiver. The encoded and decoded messages play a significant role in the construction of an identity and its communication; in other words, "codes make it possible . . . to establish the translatability between our concepts and our languages which enables meaning to pass . . . and be effectively communicated within a culture" (22).

In order to explore the representational aspect of Farangi social practices in "Gol-haye Shiraz," it is useful to see what Farang and Farangi are associated with in the text of the story. The word *Farang* and its derivatives appear only four times in the text of "Gol-haye Shiraz." However, what gives the reader the impression that the story is permeated with the concept and images of Farang is the kind of discourse constituted around the very term. Regarding this issue, the descriptions about Gol-Maryam's father provide the reader with appropriate examples.

Gol-Maryam is the narrator's newly found friend. She is also the focal point of the narrative. Although the narrative does not begin with Gol-Maryam's story, somewhere in the middle, she attracts the narrator's attention, after which the story continues and finishes with a focus on her and her father. Gol-Maryam's father used to be a doctor but has stopped practicing medicine as a result of some undisclosed bitter experience. He is described as a person who "lived abroad for many years, in France, in Switzerland, and Belgium. He knows several languages and has read thousands and thousands of books" (Taraqqi, "Gol-haye Shiraz" 104). A few pages later, another descriptive passage about the father appears. The passage more or less reiterates the same points but ends emphatically with a brief conclusion: "My father is a doctor. He has spent most of his life abroad, in France. He has always thought rationally and scientifically. *Like Farangiha*" (106; my emphasis).

In the sociocultural context of Iran, the fact of having travelled to or lived in Europe communicates a Farangi identity. Science, rationality, and the command of knowledge, implicitly juxtaposed to superstition, emotionality, and ignorance, are also associated with the West. Thus, embedded in Gol-Maryam's description is the colonial relation between West and East, with the emphasis falling on the resemblance of her father to the former. Since Gol-Maryam's father is not originally European, however, but rather *like* Farangiha, he is presumably engaged in a process of emulation in order to communicate the resemblance. The practice of emulating what is attributed to Europeans results in the formation of cultural signs: that is, titles (such as "Doctor"), claims to knowledge (through books, for instance), and a rational and scientific point of view all become signals for the perceiver's interpretation. In other words, these cultural signs represent and communicate a discursive message, namely, that the person displaying them has an identity based on the imitation of that which is *attributed* to Farang—thus, a Farangi identity.

Regarding Taraqqi's ironical style, it is through irony and during the process of cultural translation that the authority of truth is destabilized and the representational function of cultural practices is revealed. At this point, therefore, it is relevant to explore the ironic elements used in describing the character of Gol-Maryam's father, for instance, in order to better comprehend how Faranginess shifts from being a stable truth to merely a representation of a particular concept.

Gol-Maryam's father is regarded as a Farangi person, since he is allegedly rational and has a scientific point of view. This description is, however, followed by the paradoxical information that he regularly holds meetings to summon ghosts and claims to have contact with the ghosts of the dead (105, 106). Here, superstition and rationality are put side by side quite matter of factly, as if they were not in conflict. The narrator's objective tone adds to the ironic effect. In the message transmitted to the reader, the father's rationality (which is a Farangi attribute) is destabilized. In other words, rationality is no longer a truth about the father but only an attribute that makes his character *signify* as a Farangi person. The term *rationality*, in this respect, becomes only an arbitrary signifier of a Farangi identity to the perceiver who shares and has knowledge about the sociocultural conventions of the same discourse.

The Farangi identity, in this sense, is represented through certain stereotypical images and characteristics. The word *image*, here, is a key term, since the function of an image in communicating messages is the closest to the function of a signifier in a sign system. Another descriptive passage about Gol-Maryam's father allows me to elaborate on this issue. The narrator is spending an evening with Gol-Maryam and her father at their place:

> That evening's program after dinner is looking at the photo album: the photos of Mr. Doctor in different cities all over the world: with an umbrella, a hat, and a raincoat in front of a church; in swimming gear on the beach; in a black frock coat, a white official shirt, and a bow tie; arm in arm with a blond woman; on a bike; on a horse; in the park; at the zoo; at the museum; lying down; standing up; sitting down; and so on. (109)

Taraqqi captures the character of Gol-Maryam's father in caricature-like snapshots. The fact that the photos are arranged in an album and watched in the company of a stranger emphasizes that they have been primarily taken with the intention to be *shown*—with the intention of transferring a message to the perceiver. Farang and the message "I am very much like Farangiha" emanate from the photos. The garments and the accessories mentioned are particularly interesting: for instance, the umbrella, hat, raincoat, swimming gear, frock coat, and bow tie all belong to the category of Western clothing. The places referred to are also quite telling: the beach, the park, the zoo, and the museum. Although the equivalents of these spaces have also been constructed in Iranian urban space, these spaces and the very cultural practices performed within their structures originated in the West. So the photos reflecting Gol-Maryam's father, dressed and performing "like Farangiha" in the very space of Farang, indicate and communicate his Faranginess. What undermine the very concept of Faranginess, however, are the humorous tone and the ironic implications of the narrator as she describes the father. The narrator is reporting on the events of the evening that she spends at her friend's home. Although the photos are supposed to be entertaining, they bore the narrator. She is "yawning" all the time and is "exhausted with all the photos and memories" (110). The tempo of the text also has an ironic effect. The narrator starts describing the photos—first, in long descriptive clauses but then switching to briefer prepositional clauses read with a faster tempo: "on the bike; on the horse; in the park; at the zoo; at the museum" (109). Finally, the description is closed with references to the father's body postures: "lying down; standing up; sitting down" (109). The visual image of the snapshots, one moving after the other with an increasing tempo, calls to mind the movements produced by a flip book or motion-picture animation. The whole description of the father becomes, therefore, caricaturized. In this sense, the seriousness of Faranginess is destabilized, and thereby, the symbolic (representational) function of Farangi practices is revealed.

If we accept that Gol-Maryam and her father resemble a Farangi identity to a certain degree in a certain discourse, then it is interesting to see where and how the borderlines of their difference are delineated. Gol-Maryam and her father live in a lonely castle-like house in Shemiran, surrounded by "tall pine trees" (107). They have isolated themselves from the rest of the world and rarely have contact with other people. From her very first encounter with Gol-Maryam, the narrator points to the invisible borderlines between Gol-Maryam and the rest of the dancers. She drives back home in a car that has dark gray glass. The narrator wonders "why the inside of the car cannot be seen from outside" (106). She describes Gol-Maryam as someone exceptional, someone who is different from others (*tafteh-ye joda bafteh*) and "belongs to another tribe" (99). The descriptions about her difference continue with the narrator's comments on her beauty, which is explicitly attributed to her similarity to Europeans:

> [She is] thin and pale with dark, big, black eyes. She is beautiful and her beauty is of a special kind as if she were half European, half French, half Russian. Her name suits her. Her skin is as white as tuberoses and, contrary to other Shiraz Flowers, she smells good. Madam Yelena is in love with her. (99)

The position of the aesthetic criteria in this excerpt is an unstable one. Gol-Maryam, with her "dark, big, black eyes" and light complexion, does not necessarily resemble the most typical European visage. Therefore, the narrator's comparison of her beauty to Europeans does not stem from an actual resemblance; rather, Gol-Maryam is generally recognized as a Farangi type in a specific sociocultural context (because of her manners, conduct, lifestyle, and, of course, being the daughter of a Farangi father). As a result, her beauty is interpreted as "a special kind," not because she looks like Europeans but because she resembles the Farangi.

In "Gol-haye Shiraz," a Farangi identity is also communicated through having a Farangi mentality. Since thoughts and ideas cannot be concretely displayed in public, the subject in question has to adopt certain behaviours and use certain objects in order to render the intangible mindset communicable. The narrator in the story, seemingly naïve but endowed with an ironic voice, foregrounds such behaviours and items not only to represent (signify) a specific disposition but also to caricaturize it. What exactly constitutes a Farangi disposition is not directly discussed in the story, but according to the text of the narrative, a person who thinks like Europeans is relatively open-minded in regard to the social relation of the sexes. The parents of Parviz (a friend of the narrator), for instance, allow him to throw mixed parties and "dance with girls his age or even older" (113). A person with a Farangi outlook should also be politically involved and have great affinity with books and all sorts of other print publications. In this respect, smoking, political engagement, journals, and even books come to be linked with the characters' Farangi mentality in the text of the story.[5]

Smoking while in deep thought is a hackneyed and stereotypical pose signifying intellectualism. The pose can be observed in photographs of prominent Iranian poets, artists, actors, and political activists of the 1950s up until 1980s, who are, in many cases, even dressed in Western garments. In "Gol-haye Shiraz," Taraqqi reproduces the stereotype in descriptive passages about some of the characters through a certain narratological strategy. The following two passages provide examples of these techniques. The first passage depicts Gol-Maryam's father, and the second describes Parviz, the dandy teenager of the neighbourhood, and his parents:

> Mr. Doctor [. . .] is wearing his pajamas—silken pants and shirt, in dark blue with a yellow collar. His room smells of cologne and cigars. His whiskey glass is half full. He himself is also half asleep, half drunk. Everywhere is full of books and magazines, from the floor up to the ceiling, bookshelves, bookshelves, bookshelves, covering the four walls. On the bedside table, there is a big framed photo of Dr. Mosaddeq. (108)

> [Parviz] gives political lectures. His father and mother think like Farangiha. [. . .] Every Friday afternoon, we gather at his place and hold a literary and political session. Parviz lends us the books he has read and talks bigger than our juvenile minds. He has pinned the picture of Lenin to his wall and intends to change the world. His parents are members of the Tudeh Party and smoke cigarettes. (113)

On the narratological level, the functional objective of both of these passages is characterization. By representing the characters in question alongside certain items and actions, the author not only introduces the characters but also presents them as stereotypical. The cliché, as mentioned above, is the image of the smoking Farangi intellectual. The linkage among intellectualism, smoking, and Faranginess in each passage is established by the employment of descriptive sentences, the subject matter of which is similar in the two excerpts. In other words, the existence of similar characteristics in certain entities produces types. In both excerpts, for instance, the characters are portrayed as Farangi—in the former through the way the father is dressed, the glass of whisky, and the odour of cologne and, in the latter, through the explicit description of the parent's mental outlook. It is worth noting here that the exact phrase "like Farangiha" (106) has been used earlier in the story with reference to the father's way of thinking. Moreover, books and political issues are mentioned with a certain degree of ironic exaggeration and the photos of political leaders are displayed in both excerpts. Smoking is another subject common to both descriptions—in the former, the action is terminated but the effect is perceptible through the very smell of cigars, and in the latter, the act of smoking is referred to as the parents' habit.

In order to comprehend better the irony of these passages, it is useful to consider the type of narrator from whose vantage point the story is rendered. The seriousness of the quotations above is questionable because these are the words and comments of a teenage girl about the weird father of a friend and a fascinating sixteen-year-old boy, who, so to say, "gives political lectures." The teenage narrator observes and categorizes naïvely; nevertheless, her point of view is merged with that of the cynical author who remembers and despises. The ironic voice of the author is heard, for instance, later on when the narrator wonders "what this man [Gol-Maryam's father], who deals with ghosts and indulges in the events of the past, has to do with Mosaddeq" (121).

The teenage narrator observes, associates items and actions with certain meanings, and imitates in order to perform within a semantic system. For example, her association between Farang and smoking is illustrated in the comparison she makes between the taste of Farangi cherry ice-cream and the joy of smoking stealthily (119). Similarly, she uses books in order to communicate specific messages. The symbolic function of books, for instance, is highlighted when the narrator walks back and forth in front of Rahi Mo'ayyeri (an Iranian poet and lyric writer [1909–68]) carrying two thick books that she has specifically brought to the course with the intention of attracting Mo'ayyeri's attention (97). The irony is accentuated by the fact that Mo'ayyeri was never married during his lifetime (Sabur 13).

Categorization, or determining semantic borderlines, is performed by the subject in the dynamic process of constructing semantic systems. Such categorizations can be observed in the prevalent usage of the word *ahl* in combination with politics and printed materials in the text of "Gol-haye Shiraz": phrases such as "ahl-e she'r va ketab" (a person interested in poetry and books) (97), "ahl-e bahs" (a person interested in taking part in discussions) (98), "ahl-e ketab va ruznameh" (a person interested in books and newspapers) (99), "ahl-e siyasat" (a person interested in politics) (121). The idiomatic use of the word *ahl* as seen in the structures of these phrases indicates a person who is considerably *involved* with books, magazines, and politics. But apart from this, the literal meaning of the word *ahl* (inmate, inhabitant) once again denotes geographies and boundaries that connote inclusion and exclusion.

The boundaries of identity, and their struggle for hegemony, can also be observed in the setting of the story, in the breech between *shahr* (city) and Shemiran (102, 104, 113)—with the latter being located on top of the former, for instance—or even more emphatically, in the descriptions about Tajrish Square where "up on the bridge, Tajrish is divided into two parts" (118). Sa'd-abad Street, which resembles a glorious party furnished with fashionable men and women, is decidedly juxtaposed to the "the other side" of Tajrish—the bazaar entrance and the district of Darband—which, being "dim and less crowded," belongs to taxi and bus drivers, women wearing chadors, street fights, shouting machos, and drunken vagabonds.

The borderline between the two sides of the square is emphasized by the narrator's statement that she and her friends "are not allowed to cross to the other side" (119). They always meet in front of "Villa Ice-Cream Store," where they can have the brand new Farangi fruit ice-cream: "the ice-cream that smells of another world, a world on the other side of the borderlines" (119). The two parts of Tajrish construct a spatial binary. The spatial binary also represents Farang as the source of joy and as the ideal object (space) of desire. The names of the streets are also quite telling: Sa'd-abad (place of prosperity) and Darband (captive). But the spatial binary also implies that all this joy takes its significance from the fact that it is juxtaposed with the world of the common. In other words, the process of identification functions through inclusion *and* exclusion. Identification would be a loose term without the emphasis on difference and without the interpreting eye of the other.

In "Gol-haye Shiraz," Farang, in the way it is represented and interpreted, is perceived as an ideal object of imitation and a point of orientation. In the socio-cultural context of the story, elements that are representative of Farang (including characters) are symbolically associated with rather positive notions such as knowledge, rationality, intellectualism, freedom, flexibility, exotic appeal, joy, and beauty. Certain social and cultural practices, similarly, come to signify an individual's association with Farang and what it stands for. The emulative attitude toward Farang therefore leads to the formulation of social codes that can be deciphered by an observer who recognizes and understands the discursive conventions. It is through this act of decoding that the boundaries between social groups are delineated and social identity thus defined. The borderlines of social difference in "Gol-haye Shiraz" are traceable everywhere in the setting of the story—in cultural spaces such as cinemas and theatres, in the dichotomous charting of neighbourhoods, in the categorization of people into different groups, in the characters' specific lifestyles. In other words, in "Gol-haye Shiraz," Farang functions as a shared point of cultural reference that enables the construction of self and social spaces.

In "Madam Gorgeh," however, the term *Farang* loses its previous connotations and stops signifying joy, beauty, or knowledge; instead, it signifies being "cold, sad, and unaffectionate" (Taraqqi, "Madam Gorgeh" 141).The Farangiha, too, are not regarded as rational or flexible but rather are referred to as "greedy, superficial exploiters" (140). The previous signification of the term *Farang* is shattered in the new discursive space—the space that, paradoxically enough, has the same geographical dimensions as the Farang of homeland. In this new and ambiguous discursive space, the protagonist of the story is struggling to construct self-space.

"MADAM GORGEH": TROUBLES WITH SPACE CONSTRUCTION

"Madam Gorgeh" is apparently an autobiographical account of Taraqqi's life in a small flat in central Paris, where she lived for several years with her two children. The plot of the narrative focuses on the relationship between the autodiegetic narrator of the story and her nagging neighbour (Madam Gorgeh), who is always blaming them for making excessive noise. The story's climax is built upon the narrator's extremely harsh argument with the neighbour after discovering that all her claims about the irritating noises have been unsubstantiated.

One of the major problematics of the story is the construction of space in the setting of the narrative. The narrator is incessantly obsessed with the question of space and repeatedly complains about the lack of self-space in Paris. The concepts of space, borderlines, rooms, home, and the like are frequently mentioned in the story. The very opening lines, for instance, indicate that "life in diaspora, in Paris, is full of hidden anxieties and the guilty feeling that one is the outsider who has come from the other side of the borderlines and has usurped the space of the insiders" (Taraqqi, "Madam Gorgeh" 140). Throughout the story, the narrator refers to her apartment with phrases such as "small and limited," "a mouse nest" (142), "four walls" (147), "a hand-span space," and "a place in which one cannot stir" (143). Not only is the narrator's space small and limited, but the very act of possessing it is also denied her, for, after all, she is an outsider—an outsider who can, of course, be the usurper but definitely not the owner.

The actions of the narrator and her children are also restricted and repressed in the very space of the apartment. In order not to disturb Madam Gorgeh, they have to "be cautious," "stay silent," and "walk quietly" (147). They even receive a letter from the neighbour "emphasizing that they should stay at home less and rather try to spend their time outside" (147). Later in the story, the narrator draws a comparison between her present situation and her previous life in Tehran, where she was "not horrified by the neighbours and was able to scream, caper about, laugh, cry, and dance" in her private territory (150).

This latter example correlates the concept of space with an individual's capability of self expression. If we interpret the absence of self-expression as the nonexistence of the self, then it is possible to link the concepts of space, identity, and language (or any other shared sign system through which self-expression becomes possible). The interrelation among these three concepts is better clarified in the following excerpt, where the narrator, describing her efforts to placate Madam Gorgeh, ironically compares "silence" to "death":

> I'd promise her that all these inhuman voices would never be repeated again [. . .] and that I'd fly away, without my feet touching the floor, like a light mosquito, to the end of the corridor; and I'd spend three days and three nights under the mattress, or under the bed if necessary, in the silence of death. I would try my best to stick to the rules of this land and adhere to the principles of its people. (142)

Here, two actions—the muting of "inhuman voices" and the shrinkage of the self to the size of a "mosquito"—result in the erasure of the self. The same relations can also be detected in the narrator's death wish, the entombment imagery, and the association between death and silence. In other words, what results in the nonexistence of the self has both semantic and spatial significance. In this sense, identification can also be defined as the ability to construct self-space through mastery over a particular sign system: that is, mastery over the rules of encoding and decoding. Accordingly, the trauma of displacement is not merely caused by transference from one particular space to the other but rather by transference from one "semantic realm" (Syzska 11) to the other. This issue is verified in the last sentence of the above excerpt, where the narrator talks about adherence to the "rules" and "principles" of the "land" that she has recently entered.

The location of the narrator in the story of "Madam Gorgeh" is a liminal one. However, not only is she geographically displaced, but she also occupies a space that has shifted semantically from her original. This issue, by itself, foregrounds the significance of language in the formation of Bhabha's in-between position—as "a new area of negotiation of meaning and representation" ("Interview" 211). By significance of language, I do not exclusively refer to the fact that the subject in question (here, the narrator) has not yet acquired the foreign language with which she has to deal in the new locality but rather the semantic ambiguity caused by displacement—an ambiguity that gives way to the subject's interpreting attempts, an ambiguity that is the generative force behind "cultural translation" (209–10).

The displaced subject is exposed to a new sign system that has to be learned and internalized before identity formation is ever possible. In other words, integration precedes identification. Several times in the story, the narrator points to her inability to make sense of the ambiguous situation in which she is trapped. She refers to the neighbour, for instance, as "the ominous ghost who has a perpetual, invisible presence" in her "chaotic" life (Taraqqi, "Madam Gorgeh" 141). Some lines further, she indicates that having just arrived, they "don't know the whys and hows of living in Farang, [. . .] have been thrown up to the other side of the world and turn around each other like sleepwalkers" (141). Here, we can see that the concept of "Farang," which in the story of "Gol-haye Shiraz" is assumed as *already known*, becomes ambiguous. In order to render the new space intelligible, the narrator frequently articulates generalized descriptions about the manners and lifestyle of Parisians and thereby attempts to construct narratives about her surroundings:

> People, in this town, do not sit out on the balcony of their houses; they do not chatter and giggle over nonsense; they don't spend their invaluable time for happy-go-lucky blather. [. . .] The French do not easily open up the doors of their houses [. . .] greetings, here, are not regular. (143–44)

Along the same lines, it is also relevant to pay attention to the concept of rights. What determines an individual's right to a certain behaviour in a social context? In addition to the scripted version of rights, generally known as the law, there is an unwritten convention that ascertains the rights of an individual in any community. This conventional legal system is embedded in the behavioural sign system of that community. That is, in order for a person to know about his or her rights and act upon them, it is indispensable for that individual to have enough knowledge about the discourse in which she or he is communicating. In "Madam Gorgeh," the ambiguity of the narrator's situation is due to the fact that she is not yet able to recognize what her rights are. She is constantly obsessed with a vague sense of guilt. Contemplating her situation, she refers to herself as "the Iranian, accused of an unknown guilt," a person who does not "have the right to object" (143); later, commenting on her intimidated relationship with the neighbour, she muses, "[L] ittle by little we have forgotten that we, too, are human beings and everyone is free in his own house [. . .] we are not used to defending our own rights, since we do not know them in this very land" (147).

Significantly, the rising action of the plot is also initiated at the very instant when the narrator becomes assured of her *right* to act. It is midnight and the children are in bed when the neighbour knocks at the door complaining about the noise they make. With increasing excitement, the narrator relates:

> I stand still. I listen. There is sheer silence. [. . .] There is no need for the French language; there is no need for any knowledge about the cultures of East and West. It is the simple logic of all humankind. There is no sound inside, and the neighbour from the lower floor is wrong. This time, I won't be bullied, since I am right; and being right is a great privilege that gives me power and courage. (151–52)

Upon recognizing her right, the narrator explodes, abuses the neighbour, and harshly chases her away. The neighbour never comes back, and in this way, the first self-space is constructed in the setting of the narrative. The narrator describes the life of herself and her children in the absence of Madam Gorgeh: "life regains its natural form," "we talk cheerfully with no fear," "we sit on the balcony and laugh with no apprehension," "we go out when we want and staying out is not an obligation" (154).

The framework of a home, as one of the most symbolic terms referring to the concept of self-space, is finally delineated in the setting of the story. Although, from a narratological point of view, the conflict of the plot is somehow resolved, the text of the story bears witness to the continuing obsession with an original homeland: "Years pass and we still dream about going back" (155). The present tense of the verb "pass" indicates that probably there will be no end to the obsession with the idea of an ever-postulated return and the troubled sense of belonging. This issue is even better emphasized in the original Persian text, where the verb "pass" is in the present continuous tense—*sal-ha migozarad*—inducing a sense of perpetuity as if the oscillation of the self in between two spaces, once inaugurated, might never be completely resolved.

CONCLUSION

In Taraqqi's stories "Gol-haye Shiraz" and "Madam Gorgeh," the reader is exposed to two different significations of the term *Farang*. Its meaning and connotations, and what it generally signifies for the subject/character communicating in a specific discourse/setting, vary extensively from one story to the other. While the word *Farang*, in the former story, appears to represent a concept already known and signifying positive notions such as knowledge, beauty, and joy, in the latter (paradoxically set in the very geographical dimensions of Farang), the term loses those connotations and becomes ambiguous.

In the setting of "Gol-haye Shiraz," Farang functions as the ideal point of orientation for the identifying self. Through what Farang represents and how it is interpreted in the semantic system of the setting of the story, the differentiation of the self becomes possible, and thereby, the boundaries of identification can be constructed. However, in the case of "Madam Gorgeh," the displaced subject, having entered into the ambiguous semantic realm of Farang, faces difficulties with the construction of self-space. Self-expression, as the indispensible prerequisite for the existence of the self, becomes problematic in the new sign system and, thereby, the construction of identity. The ambiguity associated with Farang (the subject's new geographical standpoint) is therefore not merely directed to a specific locale but rather to a liminal *semantic* situation that disturbs the certainties exposing the subject to an array of possible interpretations. The encounter with the ambiguous, in consequence, leads to the subject's urge for narration.

NOTES

1 Included in the collection *Ja-ii digar* are three stories—"Derakht-e golabi" ("The Pear Tree"), "Bozorg banu-ye ruh-e man" ("The Great Lady of My Soul"), and "Ja-ii digar" ("Another Place")—that do not specifically address issues surrounding Farang and the diasporic situation, although, in keeping with the title of the collection, they do deal with the concept of space. In addition, Taraqqi's most recent collection, *Forsat-e dobareh* (Second Chance, 2014), contains several stories that do not concern matters of emigration and displacement.

2 Considered on its own, "Gol-haye Shiraz" might seem an exception, as the story is not explicitly framed within a diasporic setting. However, the collection *Do donya* is framed by two narratives, one at the beginning and the other at the end of the book, both of which are set in France. In these two stories, the autodiegetic narrator declares that the stories in the body of the book, of which "Gol-haye Shiraz" is one, are the result of her obsessive retrospections during her residence at a mental hospital in France.

3 Three of these stories—"The Shemiran Bus," "My Little Friend," and "The Bizarre Comportment of Mr. Alpha in Exile"—are included in *A Mansion in the Sky*, an anthology of Taraqqi's stories translated by Faridoun Farrokh. All translations in this essay are, however, my own.

4 No doubt the signification of the term *Farang* and the way it influences an individual's sociocultural practices is also a matter of class. But in this essay, I have chosen to limit myself to the matter of space.

5 Books and other published materials function as symbols in "Gol-haye Shiraz." Several times, the story implies or directly expresses an association between books and Farangi characters. In this sense, certain items, subjects, and images such as photos, books, magazines, and political issues are signs used to express a certain message, which not only imparts the character's desire to be perceived as learned but also conveys an association with Farang. Nevertheless, I emphasize that this in no sense implies a factual association between books and the West in Iranian history and culture. What is at issue here is that in this *specific* story, such an association is implied: books and other published materials are presented ironically and not literally, and the characters affiliated with books (as symbolic items) and political causes are the ones who are also described as Farangi.

WORKS CITED

Bhabha, Homi. "Interview with Homi Bhabha: The Third Space." *Identity, Community, Culture, Difference*. Interview by Jonathan Rutherford. Ed. Jonathon Rutherford. London: Lawrence and Wishart, 1990. 207–21.

———. *The Location of Culture*. London: Routledge, 1994.

Byrne, Eleanor. *Homi K. Bhabha*. London: Palgrave Macmillan, 2009.

Dehkhoda, Ali Akbar. *Loghat-nameh-ye Dehkhoda* [*Dehkhoda's Dictionary*]. 16 vols. Tehran: Mo'asseseh-ye Entesharat va Chap-e Daneshgah-e Tehran, 1998.

Ghanoonparvar, M. R. *In a Persian Mirror: Images of the West and Westerners in Iranian Fiction*. Austin: U of Texas P, 1993.

Hall, Stuart. "Introduction: Who Needs 'Identity'?" *Questions of Cultural Identity*. Ed. Stuart Hall and Paul Du Gay. London: Sage, 1996. 1–17.

———. "The Work of Representation." *Representation: Cultural Representations and Signifying Practices*. Ed. Stuart Hall. London: Sage, 1997. 13–74.

Sabur, Dariush. *Rahavard-e Rahi* [*The Souvenir of Rahi*]. Tehran: Entesharat-e Zavvar, 1375 (1996).

Szyska, Christian. "Introduction." *Erzählter Raum in Literaturen der islamischen Welt / Narrated Space in the Literature of the Islamic World*. Ed. Roxane Haag-Higuchi and Christian Szyska. Wiesbaden: Harrassowitz, 2001. 9–17.

Taraqqi, Goli. *Do donya* [*Two Worlds*]. 1381 (2002). Tehran: Entesharat-e Nilufar, 1387 (2008).

———. "Gol-haye Shiraz." Taraqqi, *Do donya* 93–126.

———. *Khatereh-haye parakandeh* [*Scattered Memories*]. 1371 (1992) Tehran: Entesharat-e Nilufar, 1387 (2008).

———. "Madam Gorgeh." Taraqqi, *Khatereh-haye parakandeh* 139–156.

———. *A Mansion in the Sky*. Trans. Faridoun Farrokh. Austin: U of Texas P, 2003.

Tavakoli-Targhi, Mohamad. "Women of the West Imagined: Persian Occidentalism, Euro-Eroticism, and Modernity." *Journal of Iranian Research and Analysis* 13.1 (1997): 19–22.

CHAPTER TEN

Film as Alternative History

The Aesthetics of Bahram Beizai

Khatereh Sheibani

Recovering forgotten history is one of the main themes in Bahram Beizai's cinema. Through the use of mythological motifs and historical references in his films, Beizai invites the viewer to revisit formal history, that is, the generally accepted version of history as narrated by historians. In this chapter, I focus on two films, *Perhaps Some Other Time* (*Shayad vaghti digar*, 1988) and *The Stranger and the Fog* (*Gharibeh va meh*, 1974), in order to examine Beizai's rehistoricizing of the past and the way it problematizes the status quo. I explore how Beizai deconstructs and reconstructs the conventions of Iranian visual and performing arts and reframes concepts such as "the past," "the present," and "identity" by dislocating formal history, focusing instead on private spaces and highlighting the culture of the past. As we will see, in *Perhaps Some Other Time*, the filmmaker relies on the alternative history found in family albums and personal memories to interrogate what is conventionally regarded as "documented history." Through its themes and formal structure, *The Stranger and the Fog* further questions the aesthetic conventions of mainstream Iranian cinema, which, for over half a century, has depicted and thus normalized a patriarchal and sometimes rather misogynistic world view.

Beizai's films, especially those made after 1974, are charged with mythological references and highly allegorical meanings, prompting some critics to describe them as difficult to comprehend (Eshqi 288; Akrami 295). Nonetheless, they are popular among Iranian filmgoers. For instance, *While We Are Sleeping* (*Vaghti hameh khabim*, 2009) won the People's Choice Award at the 27th International Fajr Film Festival, as did Beizai's previous film, *Dog Eat Dog* (*Sag-koshi*, 2001, a film also known by the English title *Killing Mad Dogs*). Although Beizai has been the target of censorship—the Ministry of Culture and Islamic Guidance (Ershad-e Eslami) suspended a number of his film projects—one of his plays, *The Tragedy of Professor Makan and His Wife, Rokhshid Farzin: A Passion Play* (*Majles-e shabih: Dar zekr-e masa'eb-e Ostad Makan va hamsarash Rokhshid Farzin*, 2005), which has similar implications for standard views of the past, became the most profitable play in the history of Iranian theatre. Identifying with the past has been a formative element in the shaping of modern national identity in Iran, which could explain Beizai's box office success.

The construction of the modern Iranian self is grounded in a conscious awareness of national identity in the sense that modern history and historiographical works have had a significant impact in shaping the understanding of individual self. Approaching film as history, Beizai raises questions about the modern sense of self-identity and reactivates Iranian collective memory, which makes his cinema yet more popular among Iranian spectators. Refashioning Iranian history in the modern era is not merely a twentieth-century phenomenon. It dates back to the eighteenth and nineteenth centuries, when Persian texts such as *Shahnameh*, the first national epic in the modern Persian language, were reread and reviewed in order to shape new national identities. As Tavakoli-Targhi states:

> In the emerging Iran-time, the mythical tempos of *Dasatir, Dabistan-i Mazahib, Sharistan*, and *Shahnamih* increasingly *displaced* the sacred time of Islam. Reading and (re)citing these Iran-glorifying texts in a period of societal dislocation, military defeats, and foreign infiltration during the nineteenth century allowed for the rearticulation of Iranian identity and the construction of alternative forms of historical narrations and periodizations. The authorization and popular (re)citation of these narratives resulted in a process of cultural *transference* that intensified the desire for a recovery of the "forgotten history" of ancient Iran. (97)

Through the revival of Zoroastrian and Persian texts that replaced the established Islamic texts, the national identity in Iran was altered in the modern era. The globo-Islamic identity, created through a crucial and decisive scheme in the Islamic empire that pronounced all its citizens as a unified nation (*ommat*), was to be changed by a more regional and national (*melli*) discourse around Iranian identity.

However, the common trait in both the Islamic and nationalist accounts of identity construction is their construing of a coherent, homogeneous, and unified history. In both the Islamic and Iranian historical accounts, history is treated as a rigid and unchanging sequence of events. For instance, whether historical and artistic texts have portrayed the biblical Adam or the Zoroastrian Kiumarth as the first human being, in both cases, a monological cultural explanation, based on fixed propositions of a single culture and ideology, is sustained. This self-glorifying approach to history still informs many current Iranian historiographical texts and art productions (in both government-funded and private sectors). Beizai's refashioning of history, however, diverges from the nationalist and Islamist interpretations in the sense that it problematizes the "established" and institutionalized elements of Iranian culture and history.

In Beizai's films, one hardly finds a coherent and homogeneous world based on a monological perspective.[1] For instance, the space in his films represents not only real places but imaginative and realist ambiances in the present or in historical times. On one hand, Tara in *The Ballad of Tara* (*Cherike-ye Tara*, 1979) and Ra'na in *The Stranger and the Fog* overcome challenges created by historical and supernatural creatures, respectively. On the other hand, Kyan, in *Perhaps Some Other Time*, deals with half-real, half-imaginative hallucinatory dreams that eventually help her to understand her childhood and find her lost family. In their search for identity, the figures portrayed in Beizai's films are deterritorialized as they challenge established cultural and societal beliefs.

It is worth bearing in mind that Beizai's reinterpretation of history—in opposition to both the Islamic-oriented accounts and the nationalist narratives—does not rely on formal texts. His films are based on mythology and history, yet they are not directly informed by canonical texts in Persian, like *Shahnameh*, or Islamic texts, such as the Quran. Similarly, his aesthetics owe more to popular artistic conventions such as those of Iranian theatrical traditions. Also, for Beizai, examining issues from subjective and personal perspectives takes precedence over probing social issues such as war or national history. The social issues stay as the background while the individual's journey of personal growth is highlighted. Beizai's conscious exploring and highlighting of private stories overpowers the importance of socio-historical themes.

Whether he tackles a national historical event, as in *The Death of Yazd-gerd* (*Marg-e Yazd-gerd*, 1983), or a very personal issue, as in *The Crow* (*Kalagh*, 1977), Beizai does not limit his cinematic gaze to representing "facts" from any particular viewpoint such as a national or a religious one. His films have a humanist approach in the sense that they are about people, but they also encompass universal themes: the challenges that his characters encounter could be applied to humanity in general. Beizai's films therefore provide alternative interpretations of history; they historicize cinematically, the forgotten self in conventional, accepted histories.

HISTORICIZING THE FORGOTTEN SUBJECT

The lead character in *Perhaps Some Other Time*, Kyan (Susan Taslimi), does not know who she is. Her real identity is lost in the past, and, in order to discover her self, she must recover a missing history. Historicizing the self thus plays a crucial role in Kyan's reconstruction of her identity. Through her search, the viewer faces questions of remembering, forgetting, and alienation. The leading characters in most of Beizai's films are women who, in their search for identity, must revisit their past. In the process of recovering memory and through the recurring themes of time and space, *Perhaps Some Other Time* invites the viewer to participate in remembering and *reconsidering* formal history. In its linking of personal identity with the process of reconstructing the past, the film also aptly illustrates Beizai's ongoing exploration of the historical roots of Iranian culture and the relationship of this history to the definition of the modern Iranian self.

Kyan, pregnant and struggling with scattered, bitter childhood memories and a psychological illness, discovers that she is not her parents' biological child. She begins searching orphanages and birth archives to locate her biological parents. When she does not find a satisfying answer, she ends up delving into her memories and family albums. Finally, she finds her answer but not in the documented files. Her true identity was ultimately found in Vida's (Kyan's sister) home and albums—domestic, private places that are far from the official documented history.

Kyan's husband, Modaber (Dariush Farhang), is involved in making documentary films for Iranian National Television Broadcasting. Early in Beizai's film, Modaber is shown in a studio, where he is working on dubbing a documentary about pollution. This montage sequence contains highly metaphorical images and abrupt juxtapositions of shots. The camera initially focuses on a familiar scene of the streets of Tehran. When it zooms out, we realize that what we have just seen was a silent film projected on a screen in a studio. The camera cuts to a low-key lighting composition of the film crew and finally zooms in with a medium shot of an unflattering composition of Modaber's face in a hard light. Then Modaber moves toward the screen to answer the phone. The projected documentary, at this point, provides a background for Modaber's conversation scene in a shallow focus. The old Tehran images, initially in the background, move to the foreground in sharp focus; they present an old Tehran quite different from the contemporary capital. The documentary portrays an elegant and tranquil city adorned with nineteenth-century buildings, wide streets, trees, and a few old cars. Interestingly, though, the images of the old city inserted in the documentary are just paintings, not "real" photographs. The fragmented montage is complemented with parallel shots of Kyan in a phone booth in the midst of busy downtown Tehran. On Kyan's side, we only hear the noise of the street. The montage continues to contrast the old elegant Tehran with the modern city depicted in present time (Kyan's parallel shots) and the filmic version (Modaber's documentary), with jammed traffic and unattractive condensed apartment complexes in medium to far shots. Traffic lights, exhaust pipes, a baby in a stroller, and the tire of the stroller are framed in close-up and extreme close-ups in the documentary. A few workers with masks are depicted in a very polluted setting. The images of the workers and the editing group in the studio are shown through the shot/reverse-angle shots. Modaber indicates that the smoke in the scene seems extremely "unreal" for a documentary. Paradoxically, his colleague confirms that this is the only real smoke they managed to shoot. The whole sequence problematizes what is portrayed as reality, whether in documentaries or other forms of documentation. Particularly, it depicts the manipulative practices exercised in the process of making "documentaries."

In a shot that is shown on the screen in the studio, Modaber locates a woman who looks remarkably like Kyan and who is riding with a strange man in a red car. Modaber loses his concentration and fails to dub in the film. Since he cannot continue the work, the crew decides to postpone the job for the next day. Modaber, however, does not leave the studio. He is determined to recover the truth regarding the strange man whom he saw, in the film, with his wife. Modaber and his colleagues now discontinue dubbing in the film or, in other words, "adding" to the filmed "reality." Instead, because of Modaber's concern, he wants to find the "unedited" film stock in order to see the whole sequence that was "elided" through editing. Thus, Beizai suggests the existence of another layer of reality, where the "facts" are not eliminated or added through editing and dubbing. In this way, the viewer is led to question the reliability both of a filmed event—documentary and fiction alike—and, in a broader sense, of the extant documented historical accounts.

The dubbing is suspended and most of the crew leaves for the day. Modaber returns to the room. He watches the same scene over and over to find the plate number of the red car, but to no avail. In a set of matching cuts, we see Kyan, who looks down the street through a window. The low-angle point-of-view shots illustrate a breezy, cloudy autumn day, with people on the street. The falling golden leaves and the dusky setting create a melancholic mood. Modaber is then shown calling his wife, but when Kyan answers the phone, he remains silent. The use of medium shots rather than a closeup shot to portray Modaber depicts the pictures of the old city in the background. Then the camera move to foreground—although still in a medium shot to highlight the picture of the picture of the old city. The sequence that started with images of old Tehran finishes with the same images. Thus, Beizai's editing of the closing sequence parallels and repeats the beginning scene, but with the positions reversed. By employing this technique, the sequence that began with pictures of the old city on the screen ends with pictures of the old city on the wall. In the opening scene of the sequence, the pictures of old Tehran focus the documentary on the present situation, while in the closing scene, the same pictures of the past are highlighted to emphasize the ties of the people of today to their past. Modaber lives and works in the present; nevertheless, recovering the past opens a new chapter in his life. In this manner, *Perhaps Some Other Time*, which begins with an ordinary present-time situation, turns its cinematic focus on objects from the past.

Modaber suspects Kyan, thereafter, of having an affair with another man. Kyan's distrustful behaviour—because of the new findings regarding her true identity, a psychological illness, and her pregnancy, which she hides from her husband—merely stirs Modaber's suspicion. From this moment on, Kyan and Modaber's relationship moves into a stage where everything looks dubious. In order to know about his wife's in/fidelity, Modaber has no other avenue but to search in the film stocks. It seems that these highly constructed documentaries are the closest he can get to reality.

Kyan's nightmarish dreams are portrayed through Beizai's masterful and accelerated blue-tinted montage. The excessive camera movements, the jump cuts, and the lighting, which varies from gloomy and dark to extreme high-key lit scenes, have a disorienting effect and emphasize a state of severe instability. As Kyan learns more about her past, the dreams occur more frequently and with more details. Through the montage techniques—such as editing fragmented images, rapid travelling shots, and fading—the spectacle enters an expressionistic space in which Kyan duels with her nightmarish memories and a dual identity.

In a blue-lit scene, Kyan is shown on her bed sleeping, but apparently, she is struggling with bad dreams. A fast travelling shot shows Modaber in the same room searching through Kyan's wardrobe to find the dress he saw in the documentary. The viewer realizes that the other side of the room, where Modaber stands, is not tinted blue but almost grey, barely lit with a lamp that Modaber holds. In this way, Beizai aesthetically makes a physical and spatial separation between Modaber and Kyan, who are virtually living in two separate worlds. Modaber ruthlessly throws one dress after another on the bed where Kyan is sleeping. The frenetic tracking shots move from right to left to show Modaber's hysterical behaviour and Kyan's suffering in her sleep. These rapid travelling shots are repeated several times, but in the last tracking shot from right to left, first we see Modaber. Then the camera moves rapidly and the viewer expects to see Kyan but, surprisingly, sees Modaber once again. It takes few seconds to realize that this is not his image but its reflection in the mirror. The camera travels another half circle to focus on him again. This seeming violation of the 180-degree rule would metaphorically suggest that Modaber is extremely absorbed in his thoughts. The sequence is shot with a wide-angle lens in medium to close-up shots, which results in the distortion of the image of Modaber, the shape of the room, and Kyan's bed. The sequence illustrates the way in which Beizai engages in the interplay of images and memories and raises questions about the reliability of image and memory in recovering the past and reality. This idea recurs, albeit in different forms, throughout the film.

The close-up shots in which Kyan's face fades away with a dazzling light suggest the change of time and space as she passes from the "real" present time to a surreal moment in the past. These scenes particularly focus on the inner life of a character and her personal pains, which is emphasized by the graphic account of her nightmares that Kyan relates to her therapist. The scenes with the therapist are clipped and the dialogues are elliptical and accompanied by an illustrated account of her surreal dreams. In illustrating the dreams, long takes are used frequently, showing Kyan running in an endless hallway. Kyan keeps on going through a long hallway but she arrives nowhere. In these scenes, Kyan is filmed in a far shot and the ceiling of the hallway is highlighted through high angles——to emphasize her enframed powerlessness. Long takes also recur in the rainy scenes, accompanied by the sound of thunderstorms, where Kyan passes an alley or steps down never-ending stairs while Modaber is shown spying on her from his car.

The past, in general, is signified by black and white shots, including the scenes that visualize Kyan's mother. Other instances are the old Tehran paintings and the pictures of the film crew, which show them in the process of filming the documentary. All of these black and white images—which are less clear than those in colour—are actually more explicit and even illuminating in terms of revealing Kyan's past than the many images of Kyan in the present. For instance, when Modaber interrogates Kyan, who is tired and distressed, the reverse-angle shots that show Modaber from Kyan's point of view are blurry and unclear. It is as if Kyan feels more at ease with her internal thoughts than with the external reality. External reality is merely an intrusion of her consciousness. The deliberately blemished editing of *Perhaps Some Other Time* matches Kyan's deeply problematic identity.

Perhaps Some Other Time, like many of Beizai's films, engages fast editing along with fast camera movements that involve occasional long takes. This incorporation of a montage-based filming, along with mobile camera movements, puts a brake on the realist effects of the narrative. In a similar way, the light contrasts in this film enhance a dramatic and emotional effect. The black and white scenes, while signifying the past, also connote a historical aura as these scenes resonate with the rhythm of *ta'zieh*, the Shi'ite Passion Play. In a *ta'zieh*, all of the players wear black and white or neutral-coloured outfits except for one character, Shemr, who is to murder Imam Hussein and who usually wears red. After the death of Imam, all characters are represented in black except for Imam's murderers, Shemr and Yazid. Employing black and white scenes and light contrasts in the film is reminiscent of a *ta'zieh* scene, which in turn brings a historical connotation. All these effects enhance the viewer's consciousness of the fact that a narrative, like a play, is a manipulated and constructed product.

Finally, Modaber locates Haqnegar, the man whom he suspects of having an affair with Kyan. He finds out that Haqnegar owns an antique shop and arranges to visit him personally. Surrounded by antique objects, Modaber enters a world that has little to do with the present time. By viewing these objects in a dark cellar that looks distant from the outside world, Modaber becomes somewhat conscious of (the significance of) the past. The antique shop is reminiscent of formal history and the objects and accounts that are—selectively—preserved from the past.

Paradoxically, in his quest to know his wife, he discovers a great deal about formal history and historically "significant" objects. For instance, he sees a watch given to Nasser al-din Shah by Queen Victoria, Shah Hassan's armour, and Changiz Khan's stamp. These objects, however, fail to attract Modaber's attention. On the contrary, it is a "historically insignificant" picture, as Haqnegar calls it, that captures Modaber's interest and increases his suspicion, since the woman in the picture noticeably resembles Kyan.

Both Kyan and Modaber find little evidence in the official, documented history in their separate but related quests. Neither the antiques that embody the official history, nor the birth archives, nor Modaber's documentaries reveal the past. On the contrary, Kyan's true identity is recovered through a reconstruction of Kyan's personal memory, as well as through her search in more intimate spaces like pictures, family albums, and homes. In Haqnegar's home, both Modaber and Kyan are surprised when they see Vida, who looks strikingly like Kyan. In fact, by portraying the resemblance between Kyan and Vida, many questions are answered for both the characters and the viewers. In succeeding shots taken with static cameras, we see the twin sisters, who both look troubled. Subsequently, the fragmented shots of Kyan represent her trauma. The subliminal flashbacks signify another expressionistic moment in *Perhaps Some Other Time*. They portray Kyan and her shadow on the wall, and yet the shadow/parallel shot does not match Kyan's position in the room. In fact, the shadow resembles Kyan's mother in her routine activities. This is a vital moment for both twins, Kyan and Vida, as it reveals the past.

Vida—who feels that her mother blames her for having had to give up her twin sister (since the mother could only take care of one of them)—tries to recreate the lost history. She presents a picture of herself and her lost twin sister, Kyan. The viewer is now fully informed that the time and space in the present are in fact anchored in the past and that history has intruded on the present through the old pictures of a family album. This recalls a passage in André Bazin's "The Ontology of the Photographic Image" in which Bazin describes the "charm of family albums":

> Those gray or sepia shadows, phantomlike and almost undecipherable, are no longer traditional family portraits but rather the disturbing presence of lives halted at a set moment in their duration, freed from their destiny; not, however, by the prestige of art but by the power of an impassive mechanical process: for photography does not create eternity, as art does, it embalms time, rescuing it simply from its proper corruption. (14)

In a similar fashion, family albums turn into a significant space in the film, even more significant than the hegemonic and institutionalized written history. It is in this family album, or "embalmed time," that Kyan finds her lost identity. She can finally see her childhood image "at a set moment," in Bazin's words, belonging to the past—a past she never saw in the family albums of her adopted parents. She is seemingly living in the present time, but as the pictures represent, her identity is fully attached to the past; it is "change mummified," as Bazin says (14–15). Nevertheless, Kyan's identity is not destined to be mummified in her past. Having been estranged from her self, she now moves to free the self from the photographs, as well as her past, in order to craft a new identity through reconciliation with the present moment. When Modaber says, "We should go and visit the lady and gentleman who raised you," she replies, "mother and father." The whole set of events in Vida's house—from the moment the film crew sets up the filming equipment, to Kyan and Vida's first sight of each other, and finally, to Modaber's response to their invitation ("perhaps some other time, we will visit you")—signifies a ritual through which Kyan transforms to embrace her adopted parents as her "real" parents. More importantly, in a ritualistic manner, Kyan, who has been so concerned about her past identity, transcends time and comes to terms with her own past.

As in many other films by Beizai with similar figures, Kyan metaphorically signifies the modern collective identity lost in the institutionalized history. She recovers her identity and refreshes and refashions her memory in less formal but cozier spaces forgotten in our collective memory. In these informal, domestic spaces, insignificant objects, such as pictures and paintings, become significant. The antiques and the picture of Kyan's mother in Haqnegar's store, Vida's expressionistic paintings, Modaber's film stocks and other film equipment, and Kyan's family albums all attract the viewer through shots with limited movements, pans, and tilts. In *Perhaps Some Other Time*, antiques denote the characters' ties with the past. This is reminiscent of Alain Renais's *Muriel ou le temps d'un retour* (1963), in which objects define the clichéd lives of the characters in the film. In *Muriel*, as Crissa-Jean Chappell observes: "These middle-class people live in a world of objects. In a way, their banal existence has allowed them to become objects as well. Their hopeless lives revolve around objects instead of communication with others. They can't free themselves from their rigid patterns of existence. The characters' wasted lives resemble dusty antiques." In contrast, the characters in *Perhaps Some Other Time* manage to leave history behind. In their journey of recovering and re-establishing their identities, they strive to know themselves and the past. Nevertheless, the objects and their signification of the past do not imprison these people in history. Their examination of the past merely paves the way for the characters' growth in the future. Therefore, while Renais employs antique objects to reveal the characters' imprisonment in past memories, Beizai uses the same objects to liberate the characters from past. In *Perhaps Some Other Time*, although the portrayal of these objects emphasizes the significance of the past in a modern understanding of the notions of self and identity, the objects do not constrain the characters in their move toward the future.

It is important to note, however, that although Kyan transcends time and comes to terms with her past, knowing her past is crucial in her definition of the self. In other words, the "present self" in *Perhaps Some Other Time* is not separated from the "historical self." What was missing in Kyan's search for her identity was her mother, who recurs in her dreams. In fact, for Kyan, getting to know her mother, and thus a part of her historical self, becomes vital because it is the reconstruction of her past that reconstitutes the interactions of her present. In the closing sequences of the film, Kyan finally succeeds, through her newly found sister, in reconstructing her past. She learns about her mother and finds a meaningful answer to the question of her identity. Thus, it is the existence of her mother that adds contextual meaning to Kyan's life. *Perhaps Some Other Time* interrogates the relevance of the modern social subject unaware of her past.

Beizai's film raises similar questions about imagistic authenticity in documentary, a genre engaged with realities of the world. As mentioned above, in the documentary about air pollution, the apparently natural smoke, we are told, is artificially made. In contrast, the heavy smoke that looks unnatural to Modaber is said to be natural. The woman in the documentary who is identified by Modaber as Kyan turns out to be Vida. The film's conflation of fact and illusion is also evident in Beizai's ironic choice of the surname Modaber, meaning "prudent" or "far-sighted," for Kyan's husband, who is unaware of Kyan's thoughts, fears, and real identity. Another question that arises is to what extent Haqnegar—literally, "the one who sees the truth"—is accurate about the history of the antiques he describes. Furthermore, in a broader perspective, viewers might wonder if Beizai, to convey his point, is manipulating them by confusing fact and fiction.

Beizai's reflexive cinematic techniques problematize our understanding of facts on a different level of reality—the off-stage reality. Susan Taslimi's performance as three different figures—Kyan, Vida, and the mother—provides a self-referential frame to the potential artificiality of so-called reality as the basis of history. Owing to the deliberately similar makeovers for Taslimi in her three roles, the audience easily recognizes her as the same person and is encouraged to remain critically distant from the fictional layer in which she plays three different roles. This keeps the viewer conscious of the dramatized nature of a constructed historical account. Another self-conscious decision—a counter-cinematic practice that blends fact and fiction—relates to Kyan's rediscovery of her sister being shot by Modaber's film crew. Kyan's new identity is to be "documented" in the same way in which the official history was recorded. In a text-oriented culture, people, accustomed to "documented" history, tend to accept it uncritically. The sequence with the presence of a film crew to document a historical moment, however, challenges our unconsciously uncritical acceptance of documents. This "performed" sequence of the film suggests the idea that history is "made" or "constructed."

The thematic structure of *Perhaps Some Other Time* relies on the power of the image, as this is a cinematic production that challenges history by reimagining its neglected aspects. Moreover, the film is anchored in the concept of "imagination" in its portrayals of Kyan's dreams, Modaber's false speculations, and Kyan and Vida's imagining and recovering of the past. For instance, Kyan observes, reproduces, and retains images in her memory. Remembering and recovering identity in Kyan's life does not take her to the past. Kyan, as a modern person, was a stranger to her self because she did not know about her past identity. The power of the imagination, by the end, separates her from the past as well as from reality as she faces the future. As the title of the film suggests, she may return to her roots to reconsider the past "some other time." In the present, though, she looks forward to embracing future possibilities.

The notion of constructing history is not only seen in *Perhaps Some Other Time*. In fact, much of Beizai's filmmaking is deeply engaged with the (re)construction and deconstruction of modern history. In particular, the filmmaker has explored extensively the issue of reconstructing the image of women. No other Iranian director has considered gender issues and the remythification of women's representation more thoroughly than Beizai.

CULTURAL AMNESIA AND THE REHISTORICIZING OF WOMEN LOST IN (FILMIC) HISTORY

The release of *The Stranger and the Fog* (1974), Beizai's fourth feature, unleashed new possibilities in the Iranian film industry. *The Stranger and the Fog* was a landmark film because of its mythic language and, more importantly, because it established a cinematic convention that was to historicize and remember women. In terms of form, as both Iranian filmgoers and film critics have noted, this film was an innovative and groundbreaking experience in Beizai's filmmaking (Naficy 277; Mehrabi 167). Before the making of *The Stranger and the Fog*, Beizai was mostly engaged in directing realist films with explicit social concerns, as in *Uncle Moustache* (*Amu Sibilu*, 1970), *Travel* (*Safar*, 1971), and *Thunder Shower* (*Ragbar*, 1971). In *The Stranger and the Fog*, however, Beizai employs an unprecedented mythological style in narrating the story of Ayat and Ra'na and their challenges with mysterious forces that they encounter both on land and in the sea. The people who are portrayed in this film do not seem to belong to any particular ethnic group; rather, they are mythical figures in an unknown time and location. The village in which the story is set is a mysterious coastal community, the narrative is allegorical, and the plot is unrealistic. The motivation behind the characters' actions and fights seems very simple but unknowable. In narrating the story of the villagers and the sea inhabitants, Beizai uses a metaphorical language. This film was praised mostly for its complex and novel *mise en scène* and film grammar. As Naficy notes, Beizai spent two years and more than $300,000 to accomplish this project (277).

In my view, the importance of this film lies in its unparalleled focus on women and their exercising of power. In fact, *The Stranger and the Fog* initiated a different kind of cinema that disturbs gender conventions to historicize the portrayal of women, who have generally been depicted in Iranian cinema through a culturally normative lens. This approach is seen not only in explicitly commercial films—what is known as the *filmfarsi* genre—and popular movies but also in Iranian new wave films.

The 1960s was a defining moment in the history of Iranian cinema with the birth of the new wave movement, which enriched the national cinema and brought international gravity to Iranian films. Although these films were highly engaged with social problems and were momentous productions in terms of their original cinematic stylistics, they dealt primarily with male issues, with few exceptions. *Bita*, made by Hajir Dariush in 1972, was one of those rare films with a central theme of femininity. The fact that the film script was written by Goli Taraqqi, a prominent female writer of the time, may explain this unprecedented focus. Googoosh, the most popular pop singer in the pre-revolutionary period, played the role of Bita. Although Dariush had, both intellectually and aesthetically, invested in the film by hiring Taraqqi and Googoosh, *Bita* was not recognized as an important movie in the 1970s. This film, along with its gendered focus, was soon forgotten and largely omitted from the history of Iranian cinema.

To explore how the new wave films dealt with gender issues, I re-viewed many of these films. Surprisingly, both locally and internationally acclaimed films like *The Cow* (1969), *Gheisar* (1969), *Reza motori* (*Reza, the Cyclist*, 1970), *Aqa-ye Halu* (*Mr. Simpleton*, 1970), *Sadeq, the Kurdish* (1971), *Still Life* (1974), *The Secret of the Treasure of the Jinn Valley* (1974), and *The Deer* (1974) either ignore women altogether or give them a secondary and conventional role.

During this period, even critically acclaimed films such as *Still Life* and *The Cow* that dealt with poetic representations of life from a philosophical standpoint did not offer a realistic depiction of women. Although the new wave films made at this time had a socialist political agenda, the themes are explored through the male gaze. Generally speaking, the dominant trend in those years was to focus on the representation of masculinity, which resulted in either ignoring women or in a shallow personification of female figures in subservient roles. Women in such films appear in one-dimensional roles like victims of sexual mistreatment (in *Gheisar*), sufferers of male harassment (in *The Postman*, 1972), and seductresses (*The Secret of the Treasure of the Jinn Valley*). In the absence of a real portrayal of women, films such as *Gheisar* and *Sadeq, the Kurdish*—impacted by the cultural currents of the time—typically emphasize the personification of male actors who embody the characteristics and representations of power or the frustrated masculine power that is suppressed. The main themes in these films relate to social class, social mobility, and injustice.

In the realm of popular cinema, the robust masculine physique of actors such as Mohammad Ali Fardin, Said Rad, and Behruz Vosuqi, complemented by the powerful, deep voices of actors like Nasser Malek-Moti'i (because the voices were not synced in most of these films, the directors had the option of choosing the most pleasing voices for dubbing), established a male-dominated aesthetic in the Iranian film industry. The persona of these actors was characterized by energy, charm, and sexual vigour. In this era of Iranian film history, male authority is a given: it never meets with female resistance. Thus, the representation of femininity suggests a voiceless and static role for women to "sustain" the social control and the "normal" parameters of gender behaviour. The starlets—including Googoosh, Foruzan, and Puri Banaii—were chosen from the most beautiful actresses and singers of the time to meet the standards for portraying the objects of desire of the handsome actors. These female figures were "important" to the narrative because of their supporting role to the male figures. Moreover, by employing these young starlets with their attractive physical attributes and expressive bodies, the directors and producers were responding to the market imperatives of the time. Minor actresses would usually perform in dance sequences to fulfill the masculine gaze by displaying the female body. Although new wave cinema was addressing social problems, it operated in this stylistic mode, to a certain extent, in films such as Hatami's *Touqi* (1970) and Kimiai's *Gheisar*. Most of these films were narrated in a realistic style; however, the gender representation was not based on the reality of Iranian society because the films erased the multi-layered and diverse identity of half of the Iranian population, being women.

Although Beizai chose a surreal *mise en scène* in *The Stranger and the Fog* and employed a highly allegorical language, the film's concerns are realist since it reimagines both men and women who are confronting problems that could occur in everyday life. As already mentioned, this film portrays the relationship between Ra'na, a widow living on the seacoast, and Ayat, a stranger who mysteriously appears on the shore. Sea creatures peristently haunt Ayat, even following him from the sea to the village; they symbolize the mystical or "unknown" forces of life as we do not know who or what they are. At one point, when Ayat acquires new scars while stabbing a sea creature, the viewer may wonder whether these creatures actually do exist or whether they symbolically represent different aspects of Ayat's personality. Similarly, Ra'na is troubled by her dead husband's ancestors. The village council decides that if Ayat wishes to stay in the village, he should marry a local woman. Ayat, in return, asks for Ra'na's hand. The villagers reject the suggestion, but Ra'na accepts his proposal. In deep focus shots—which Beizai employs very rarely—Ra'na is portrayed in the foreground against the villagers, who are shown in a foggy background. The deep focus shots and the foggy setting create a mysterious atmosphere. Moreover, as Naficy notes, this type of camera work represents Ra'na's isolation and distance from the rest of the villagers (279). Ra'na and Ayat are both strangers to their surroundings. They are not at home either on the land or in the sea. Therefore, they start fighting with each other on both land and sea. As critics including Naficy (277) and Behzad Eshqi (293) indicate, Beizai has rehearsed Iranian and Japanese rituals in this film. In *The Stranger and the Fog*, Beizai's meticulous gaze reconstructs these rituals. In fact, in this film, conventionalized and conventionalizing rituals of any kind are abandoned in favour of crafting new conventions. As a deviation from the hierarchy of power and privilege, the hegemony of male dominance—here represented by the village council and Ra'na's in-laws—is problematized. Through rejection of behavioural conventions in personifying Ra'na, traditional and patriarchal codes of behaviour are being questioned.

This inclusion of the female perspective becomes increasingly visible in Beizai's films. For instance, in his next film, *The Ballad of Tara*, made just before the Revolution, the leading female figure, Tara, rejects subordination as a rural widow. There is even a tendency toward adventure in her characterization as she finds out about a mysterious sword in her grandfather's belongings and faces the Historical Man in the woods. Thus, refashioning conventionalized gender representations becomes more controversial in *The Ballad of Tara*. Unlike Ra'na, Tara has no match among men in her village and thus becomes a heroine without an equal hero.

As a cultural production, cinema is both a reflection of and a response to the society that it represents. It is therefore all but impossible to investigate films without considering their social and historical implications. Although analyzing the formal elements of films is instructive, a purely formalist approach, one that studies film as a self-contained vessel of immanent meaning, would not represent the significance of, for instance, Beizai's historicizing practices in *The Stranger and the Fog* and his subsequent films. It is only through exploring films in their historical and sociocultural contexts that we can fully appreciate their meaning. Iranian cinema, as a cultural and artistic discourse, interacts with other cultural discourses and with institutionalized and noninstitutionalized systems. Beizai's different gaze and his attempts to reimagine women in urban, rural, historical, and modern settings have been a response not only to the Iranian film productions of his time but also to the written, official history of modern Iran that excluded women from historiographical accounts. In Beizai's films, this reappearance of the female segment of society redefines the relations between men and women.

Historical narratives and the collective national memory depend upon history as *construed* by historians. For the most part, these historians have been men, who have no stake in questioning the foundations of patriarchy. As a result, it has been the historians' particular gaze that has constructed the history of gender relations and, to a certain extent, social gender arrangements. In a general sense, it could be argued that all historical accounts are ideological products. Ana Maria Alonso proposes this idea when she states:

> All histories, whether spoken or written, are produced in an encounter between a hermeneutics and a field of social action which is symbolically constituted. . . . Much of this encounter takes place "after the fact"; histories are retrospectives because the contours of the past are finally delineated and fixed

from the vantage point of the present. Thus, the contingency of history-as-action is always mitigated by the backward gaze of history-as-representation which orders and explains, which introduces teleology hardly evident at the time of the original events. (34)

Alonso's contention holds true in terms of Iranian historical accounts. As Afsaneh Najmabadi points out, "what is considered in those narratives as unimportant and what is thus lost in those histories becomes productive of national forgetting" (174). The history of modern Iran was self-consciously a history of men. Najmabadi demonstrates that Mehdi Malikzadih, in his account of the Iranian Constitutional Revolution, presents a male-oriented history.[2] This emphasis is conveyed through his use of the words *man* and *men* (*mard* and *mardan*), "which in Persian do not carry the potential meaning of 'generic human being(s)'" (Najmabadi 180), with reference to the main focus of events. In Malikzadih's account of the Constitutional Revolution, the exclusion of women, except in brief digressions, is justified on the basis of his belief that women were socially excluded from the revolutionary activities. Other sources of history are not drastically different from Malikzadih's text in this respect. As a result, women in general seem to be absent from the collective national memory.

In *The Story of the Daughters of Quchan: Gender and National Memory in Iranian History*, for example, Najmabadi revives a narrative that had disappeared from the cultural memory. She tells the story of women and girls who were sold by "needy peasants to pay their taxes in a bad harvest year—1905, the year preceding the Iranian constitutional revolution" or "taken as booty in a raid by Turkoman tribesmen against a village settlement" in northeastern Iran (1). For a few years after the event, ordinary people, Muslim preachers, and social democratic militants remembered this story in the form of poetry and prose, street songs and satire. However, the event vanished from subsequent narratives of that Revolution and was thus erased from the cultural memory (Najmabadi 1–9). Since the story of the daughters of Quchan was not categorized with "histories of grand ideas and great men," such as the ones written by Fareydun Adamyyat and Malikzadih (Najmabadi 174), it became the victim of national amnesia. Ironically, the notion of gender was a central structuring category in the making of Iranian modernity in the beginning of the twentieth century. As Najmabadi states:

> Concepts central to the imagination and construction of a modern Iran were envisaged in terms related to concepts of femininity and masculinity. Nation

> (*milat*), for instance, was largely scripted as a brotherhood—at least until the first decade of the twentieth century, when women began to claim their space as sisters in the nation. The modern notion of *vatan* (homeland), on the other hand, was envisaged as female—as a beloved and as a mother. Closely linked to the maleness of *milat* and the femaleness of *vatan* was the multiple load of the concept of *namus* (honor), which shifted in this period between the idea of purity of woman (*'ismat*) and integrity of the nation. (182–83)

By remembering the story of the daughters of Quchan, Najmabadi carries out "a recuperation of women into the national narrative and of gender into historiography" (8). In the process of writing a different account of Iranian history, scholars such as Najmabadi "rewrite" women into the history of Iranian modernity that previously excluded women. What made earlier Iranian historiographical texts women-free zones was the political culture of the society.

Cinema as a cultural form of expression was no exception to this cultural norm. As discussed earlier, in many popular and art movies, women were subject to dehistoricizing practices that excluded them from the national memory, an exclusion that was reinforced by the artistic media. More recently, women have been represented more realistically in films such as *The Stranger and the Fog* that take a different approach toward gender issues. Beizai's reconstruction of national memory became even more significant in his post-revolutionary productions. His films depict the hidden layer of modern history ignored for decades. His filmic version of "history" of culture, however, does not rely on the official or canonical version of history. On the contrary, Beizai challenges the long-standing segregation of *mythos* (myth) and *logos* (truth) through the prominence of mythology and popular arts in his aesthetic sensibilities. Thus, the main emphasis in his films is on the recovery of a gender-oblivious history. In this recovery process, Beizai reimagines women not through factual narrative but through metaphorical language in fictional situations that are deeply rooted in the realities of Iranian society.

In a society where women are depersonalized and viewed collectively, Beizai's filmmaking is an oasis for female personal expression. In his films, concepts such as revolution or explicit social concerns are set aside in favour of a more imaginative and private artistic vision that examines gendered issues in the light of questions related to modernity and identity. Beizai's films highlight women's issues of the sort that had, in the past, rarely been allowed to surface. In *The Stranger and the Fog*, notions of masculinity and femininity, which are absent both from previous Iranian films and from national memory, are interrogated and redefined. Unlike the women in films such as *Gheisar* and *The Cow*, Ra'na is not relegated to a secondary role. On the contrary, she is a powerful figure who is able to decide her own destiny. When compared to Ayat, Ra'na has equal opportunities for domination and subjection. The representation of women in *The Stranger and the Fog* is somewhat different from Beizai's previous films. Although *Thunder Shower* portrays a woman (Parvaneh Ma'sumi as Atefeh) as a central character in the film, she is depicted as a physically attractive but vulnerable woman who needs to be protected and loved. Atefeh's ultimate fate depends on the psychological battle between her two lovers—a teacher who is a stranger to the community and a butcher who is considered an insider and a legitimate patriarchal power in the neighbourhood. In a radical move from the character of Atefeh, *The Stranger and the Fog* shows an independent woman who ignores the authoritative words of the village council, marries a stranger, and initiates a search for the truth in a misty maritime bay. The foggy setting of the film metaphorically suggests the complications in the journeys of women and men who strive to discover the meaning of life.

The Stranger and the Fog established a new gendered discourse in Iranian cinema, but it is in *The Ballad of Tara* that gender identity and power truly come to the fore. Here, Iranian film culture is completely transformed in the portrayal of Tara as a mythic woman who faces the battle of life completely on her own. The powerful performance of Susan Taslimi, as Tara, in a primitive setting evokes the power of nature, love, fertility, and pleasure. Nevertheless, Tara represents more than a force of nature: she also embodies a multi-dimensional human being who is capable of working, thinking, and making choices on her own terms. In one scene, Tara says, "I work for every single bite that I grab, each breath that I take. My life is all about working hard and doing it all by myself. So why shouldn't I laugh my head off or act silly when I wish?" In this film, the exercising of power, a male commodity in the national memory, is delegated to Tara. The dependent femininity of Atefeh in *Thunder Shower* is now replaced by a sober independence in the representation of Tara. In contrast, the male figures in *The Ballad of Tara* are either immature (such as the boy who falls in love with Tara) or insignificant (such as Qilich, her brother-in-law). The most important male figure in the film is the Historical Man. The inverted gender depiction in *The Ballad of Tara*, however, results in an unexpected softness in the personification of the Historical Man, despite his ironically ferocious physical appearance in his war outfit.

This deconventionalizing of gender representation, which began with *Thunder Shower*, is further developed in Beizai's subsequent films. As opposed to Kimiai or

Taghvai, both of whom employ expressive actors with obvious physical presence, Beizai's leading actors are not physically powerful figures. For instance, Parviz Fanni-zadeh, a short, slim man with thick spectacles, who was cast as the leading figure in *Thunder Shower* (the teacher), does not represent the conventional masculine attributes of vigour and sexual energy. Other examples of Beizai's deconventionalizing of gender representation include his casting of ordinary-looking men (e.g., Hussein Parvaresh in *The Crow* and Parviz Pur-Husseini in *Bashu, the Little Stranger* [1989]) next to dazzling and powerful actresses such as Ma'sumi and Taslimi.

Male figures in Beizai's films, including *Bashu, the Little Stranger* and *Dog Eat Dog*, are generally more vulnerable and less sophisticated than the female figures. In a number of post-revolutionary films, such as Ibrahim Hatami-kia's *The Glass Agency* (1998) and Kimiai's *Snake's Fang* (1990) and *Protest* (2000), the emphasis is on masculine energy and power in combat in the absence of female agency or even a female presence during the Iran-Iraq war and the post-revolutionary social chaos. Beizai's aesthetics does not follow this patriarchal model. The male figures are not portrayed as morally or physically superior to their female counterparts. The male dominance that is illustrated in films such as *The Glass Agency* is, in some cases, replaced with a kind of male weakness in Beizai's films made after the Revolution. This weakness is represented in *Bashu* when Na'i's husband, a farmer, is shown as a disabled man, returning from (apparently) the war front. In *Dog Eat Dog*, the moral weakness of Mu'asir, in contrast to Golrokh's honesty and strength, depicts a problematic masculinity. In his post-revolutionary films, Beizai tends to depict men as lacking maturity and/or morality; at times, they are shown as having childish sensitivities. This immaturity is portrayed in the personification of the Historical Man and Qilich in *The Ballad of Tara*.

Through a "recuperative practice," Beizai's cinema portrays women with a rule-breaking dignity and boldness. From Tara to Golrokh, women are not camouflaged within a culturally approved rhetoric of home, marriage, and motherhood. Tara, for instance, a widow who shows a reluctant tenderness toward her two children, is not depicted as a conventionally nurturing and concerned mother. Similarly, Asieh in *The Crow* does not embody a self-sacrificing wife absorbed in the household affairs but rather a woman involved in her career as a teacher of the deaf and in her growing plants in a greenhouse of which her husband is not aware. Na'i's striving in the rice paddies and at home is more in harmony with nature than culture; she is a single mother with two children who has to work hard to survive.

The moral power of these women is not based on their sexuality but is grounded in their work and their mystical and psychological journey of self-discovery and self-exploration: this makes them groundbreaking strangers in their surroundings. Although Tara is at times portrayed as eager and sensitive in relation to men (especially in the romantic incident with Qilich in the woods), on other occasions, she is capable of acting without feeling in her encounters with men.

In general, gender identity in Beizai's films is not embedded in cultural practices or social reality. Furthermore, Beizai's gender representation does not rely on the collective Iranian memory or on established cinematic conventions. His films map out different relations of power and gender in the Iranian cultural system in terms of masculinity and femininity, gender dominance, subordination, and resistance. The filmic treatment of women in Beizai's films rehistoricizes and remythologizes relations between men and women by representing a more liberated gender identity that does not match the gendered behaviour in the official Iranian history and mainstream cinema.

NOTES

1 For more on a similar movement in other artistic media, see Shayegan.

2 Malikzadih's study is regarded as one of the canonical texts of Iranian history, along with works by two other early-twentieth-century historians, Ahmad Kasravi and Firiydun Adamiyat.

FILMOGRAPHY

Beizai, Bahram. *Uncle Moustache* (Amu Sibilu). 1970.
———. *Travel* (*Safar*). 1971.
———. *Thunder Shower* (*Ragbar*). 1971.
———. *The Stranger and the Fog* (*Gharibeh va meh*). 1974.
———. *The Crow* (*Kalagh*). 1977.
———. *The Ballad of Tara* (*Cherike-ye Tara*). 1979.
———. *The Death of Yazd-gerd* (*Marg-e Yazd-gerd*). 1983.
———. *Bashu, The Little Stranger* (*Bashu: Gharibeh-ye kuchak*). 1989.
———. *Perhaps Some Other Time* (*Shayad vaghti didar*). 1988.
———. *Dog Eat Dog* (*Sag-koshi*). 2001.
———. *While We Are Sleeping* (*Vaghti ma kahbim*). 2009.
Dariush, Hajir. *Bita*. 1972.
Golestan, Ibrahim. *The Secret of the Treasure of the Jinn Valley* (*Asrar-e ganj-e darreh Jenni*). 1974.

Hatami, Ali. *Mr. Simpleton* (*Aqa-ye Halu*). 1970.
———. *Touqi*. 1970.
Hatami-kia, Ibrahim. *The Glass Agency* (*Ajans-e shishei*). 1998.
Kimiai, Mas'ud. *Gheisar*. 1969.
———. *Reza motori* (*Reza, the Cyclist*). 1970.
———. *The Deer* (*Gavazn-ha*). 1974.
———. *Snake's Fang* (*Dandan-e mar*). 1990.
———. *Protest* (*E'teraz*). 2000.
Mehrjuei, Daryush. *The Cow* (*Gav*). 1969.
———. *The Postman*. 1972.
Shahid Sales, Sohrab. *Still Life*. 1974.
Taghvai, Nassir. *Sadeq, the Kurdish*. 1971.

WORKS CITED

Akrami, Jamshid. "*Gharibeh va meh*, jahd dar gharib-nama'i" ["*The Stranger and the Fog*, Striving to Make It Strange"]. Qukasian 294–96.

Alonso, Ana Maria. "The Effects of Truth: Re-presentations of the Past and the Imagining of Community." *Journal of Historical Sociology* 1 (1988): 33–57.

Bazin, André. "The Ontology of the Photographic Image." Trans. Hugh Gray. *Film Quarterly* 13.4 (1960): 4–9. Rpt. in *What Is Cinema? Essays Selected and Translated by Hugh Gray*. Berkeley: U of California P, 1970. 9–17.

Beizai, Bahram. *Majles-e shabih: Dar zekr-e masa'eb-e Ostad Makan va hamsarash Rokhshid Farzin* [*The Tragedy of Professor Makan and His Wife, Rokhshid Farzin: A Passion Play*]. Tehran: Nilufar, 2005.

Chappell, Crissa-Jean. "*Muriel*: The Time of Return." *Senses of Cinema* 37 (Oct. 2005). 10 Feb. 2010. http://sensesofcinema.com/2005/37/muriel-2/.

Eshqi, Behzad. "Darbareh-ye *Gharibeh va meh*" ["On *The Stranger and the Fog*"]. Qukasian 288–94.

Malikzadih, Mehdi. *Tarikh-e enqelab-e mashrutiyat-e Iran* [*A History of the Iranian Constitutional Revolution*]. 3 vols. 1949–54. Tehran: Elmi, 1985.

Mehrabi, Massud. *Tarikh-e sinama-ye Iran: Az aghaz ta sal-e 1357* [*The History of Iranian Cinema: From the Beginning to 1979*]. Tehran: Nurani P, 1985.

Naficy, Hamid. "*Gharibeh va meh*" ["*The Stranger and the Fog*"]. Qukasian 277–85.

Najmabadi, Afsaneh. *The Story of the Daughters of Quchan: Gender and National Memory in Iranian History*. Syracuse, NY: Syracuse UP, 1998.

Qukasian, Zaven, ed. *A Collection of Essays on Bahram Bayzai's Films*. Tehran: Agah, 1992.

Shayegan, Dariush. "At the Cutting Edge of Intersecting Worlds." *Iranian Contemporary Art*. Ed. Issa Rose, Ruyin Pakbaz, and Dariush Shayegan. London: Booth-Clibborn, 2001. 9–12.

Tavakoli-Targhi, Mohamad. *Refashioning Iran: Orientalism, Occidentalism, and Historiography*. New York: Palgrave, 2001.

CHAPTER ELEVEN

Technologies of Memory, Identity, and Oblivion in *Persepolis* (2007) and *Waltz with Bashir* (2008)

William Anselmi and Sheena Wilson

In an age of instantaneity, memory can appear within the array of technological options as a gratuitous act, unnecessary to the creation of an individual presence in the world. We use the terms *age of communicative instancy* and *age of immediate gratification* to refer to the socio-cultural conditions created by current technologies of communication. Not only do these technologies enable individuals to be present, simultaneously and instantaneously, in multiple spaces, virtual and real, but the grand narrative of postmodernism has transformed history into a plethora of diluted and deluded narcissistic performances and commercially packaged identities that can be gratifyingly selected, donned, and discarded with a click or hit but that lack the narrative coherence necessary for meaning making both in the present and in relationship to the past. Given the ubiquity of opportunities for technologically mediated self-assertion, memory's primal role in forming a sense of social belonging and identity is slowly but surely disappearing from the cognitive map. Although this frees us from our attachment to the grand narratives of the past, it also risks constricting existence to a present that is not anchored within any social-temporal construct other than that provided by the plethora of techno-communicative devices that surround us.

As a result, participation in everyday life is not only mediated but also conditioned and thus in fact limited by whatever informs the viewer or reader. Memory making is not simply a question of soliciting the mnemonic device as a cognitive agent; memory and the individual and collective identities it produces are fundamentally linked to how memory is preserved, stored, recuperated, and used in our everyday interactions. For any society, the particular mnemonic coherence that exists within specific cultural and linguistic groups situated in a given place and time is dependent on a sense of belonging that ties one individual to another in terms of social responsibility.

What happens when those ties that bind a common memory are substituted by technological representations that make claims to be able to encompass our existential selves? This question remains pertinent with regard to the epistemological sedimentation resulting from the transformations that have occurred throughout historical periods, shaping present social conditions in terms of identity paradigms. Can the experience of living be an eternal present, a mindset, in which everything is all-consumable in the moment and consumed by the moment? Does it suffice for us to be gratified by the instantaneity and immediacy of images that delimit the sphere of a shared social memory? Can social memory even exist in a contemporary narcissistic, monadic world where information is targeted to consumer profiles and segmented into commodification grids? Two animated films stand out as recent destabilizers within this general framework.

Persepolis (2007), by Vincent Paronnaud and Marjane Satrapi, and *Waltz with Bashir* (2008), by Ari Folman, both reclaim different social memories with a similar intention to disrupt and reformulate individual identity paradigms in relationship to conceptions of national histories and the impacts of those histories on the ways that national narratives are consumed and interpreted globally. These two animated films challenge official narratives, not only because they propose political engagement but also because they confront head on what can only be called the restructuration of memory within the mediatic circle, that is, the interpretive constellation formed by the economic, social, and political forces that circulate in media spheres and through which experience is configured (Anselmi and Wilson, "Performative" 46).

SELF-REFLEXIVITY, AGAINST THE MEDIUM

Persepolis and *Waltz with Bashir* resist and subvert the history that is visually offered to us today via the media circuit. Folman's film contextualizes the discussion of the protagonist's search for personal—and, by extension, national and historical—identity within a criticism of the cinematic medium itself. This film makes blatant Folman's awareness of the role of technology and the media in, at best, creating a false community and, at worst, effacing history and any sense of participation in the world. He, like Vincent Paronnaud and Marjane Satrapi, subverts the media's obliviation of history-as-it-happens by indicating that everyone belongs to a global community—beyond borders and passports and beyond the reduction of history to an eternal present. In other words, these directors use cinematic narrative techniques to reassert that history is a process of individual and collective meaning making that exists in contrast to image-history, that is, history as constituted by a staccato series of alluring images and sound bites that appear on the screen, are consumed by viewers, and then vanish before becoming integrated into a cohesive and meaningful cultural narrative. *Persepolis* uses segmented narration to recuperate personal identity into an organic whole. History, in contemporary reality, has been transformed from a chronological sequence of events into consumable, fragmentary images of events that detach us from a sense of living within a continuous historical process. The kaleidoscope of images that has become our naturalized habitat can easily disenfranchise us, depriving us of the opportunity to participate in and share responsibility for the social actions of individuals and groups.

Both *Persepolis* and *Waltz with Bashir* challenge the viewer to question the media-kaleidoscope of direct images that has become the norm in contemporary life. Both films illustrate that aesthetic avenues still exist whereby we can resist the loss of history that leaves us individually and collectively unmoored from the past or the present, reduced, in our consumptive quest for immediate gratification, to accepting false but ready-made identity kits that soothe us, if only fleetingly. Satrapi and Folman illustrate, literally, how we can either exist only at the synesthetic level, responding like programmed automatons to the images and information flashed onto the screen in the age of communicative instancy, or instead ground ourselves as spectators and reassume the responsibility of historical participation. The latter option provides opportunities to engage in social cultural transformation—to provide new form to the malleability of an entity, whether it be the self or the collective—and to resist accepting prefabricated, media-ready identities available for immediate consumption.

PERSEPOLIS (2007)

The film credits for *Persepolis* begin with white on black animation composed of a series of vignettes linked together by a floating flower, a symbol of genealogical continuity, which ties all of the events together and functions as a parallel for the life of Marjane, the film's central character. The continuity achieved through the floating flower that binds the different vignettes together (and that reappears in the final moments of the film) reflects on an existential fragmentation and dispersal that is given unity by the story. In a sense, what the film provides is a graphic representation of displacement that highlights the events of Marjane's life as the *fabula* framing a continuous *mise en abîme* wherein the telling of Marjane's personal story is also a recounting of the Iranian cultural revolution—a story within a story, a plot sequencing that reflects a strategy already successfully employed in *The Thousand and One Nights*. This technique of telling stories creates social cohesion, so as to avoid obliviation as a mechanism of social control deployed by oppressive systems. Storytelling, in this case through animated film, thus resists the centrifugal power of the entropic event: the downfall of the Shah of Iran. Paronnaud and Satrapi's movie is a depiction of resistance through artistic means; as such, it produces political resonance through time.

Oblivion, from the perspective of any individual, is a negative concept: it is associated with a loss of personal and communal history. However, from the perspective of sociopolitical systems looking to exert absolute control, the use of obliviation is a productive method of dissolving social ties. The fragmentation that occurs at the social level both atomizes and automatizes individuals. This process renders us insular, bereft of co-constructed definitions of self and community relations in the past or present, responding in automatized ways to the stimuli of a system that can (perpetually) start anew. Reinventing the future based on neo-histories, it can shape and reshape any chronotope—any time-space perception, world view, and/or narrative frame—as it deems beneficial to its own perpetuation and credibility. In *Persepolis*, this reinvention is particularly significant, since central to the movie is the idea of a revolution—the overthrow of the Shah—which was seen as the beginning of a progressive egalitarian society. The hijacking of this process by religious forces ended up transforming the hopes and dreams of a liberated society into an authoritarian structure that forcibly gendered power relations through populist means. In telling her story, Marjane, like Shahrzad, threads together the stories of many people and restores unity to the social community that has been disappeared—silenced either individually, through imprisonment, torture, and ultimately death, or on a mass scale, through fear tactics and discourses that obliviate history and enforce an anti-historical present.

The nine vignettes that can be extrapolated from the dynamic framing sequence back-dropping the credits at the outset of the film through white-on-black (negative space) animation present several topoi that constitute the narrative: voyage, birth, guidance (of angel figures), the idea of centrality, overcoming barriers, and ultimately finding a home (symbolic of personal identity). The strategy of opening the movie with very brief sequences that are traces or clues of what is to come in the film provides a determined mode of self-reflection. The movie is constructed in such a way that the introductory strategy reflects the subsequent plot developments that explain the complex identity formation process that the character undergoes. This animated Bildungsroman does not follow in a linear fashion but is diffused, like light through a prism, into various storylines that the viewer can reconstitute only at the end of the film, when all the narrative sequences have been provided. Through the film, viewers are detached from their own condition and identify instead with Marjane and her process of self-discovery, with the stories becoming instruments by means of which it is possible to make sense of the world at large. Iranian history can stand as a model for the struggle and affirmation of identity in communities where oppressive forces operate, and this is consistent with world history—whether East or West. Marjane's quest for integrity and sense of social responsibility requires her to understand her place in her genealogical and sociopolitical reality. By the end of the film, even though the viewers know that Marjane will never return to Iran, it has become evident that Paris is not the ultimate destination. Given that the beginning and final sequence of the film foreground Orly airport, this liminal space fulfills the ultimate mandate of the animated movie—what we would term a *critical imagination*, as deployed by Paronnaud and Satrapi.

Seen in the context of critical imagination, the beginning sequence of the film, which is in black and white, juxtaposed with the first of the four Orly sequences, all of which are in colour, cues us to the use of colour (or the lack thereof) to codify the temporal disjunctures and to maintain cohesion: the animation-narrative strategy creates a juncture that encompasses the existential present, as well as the past and potential future(s), providing, ironically, a neo-Aristotelian unity of sorts. By "neo-Aristotelian unity," we are referring to the recuperation of classic notions of time and space that have been dispersed by postmodern communicative strategies, reinforcing a nihilistic tangential dispersal.

In the introductory airport scene, Marjane is wearing a bright-red coat and her hair is exposed. In that same scene, she reads the arrival-departure board:

Cincinnati, Tehran, and Singapore. Tehran is squarely situated between East and West in this geophysical and cultural configuration. Viewers do not yet know, however, who is travelling and whether they are arriving, nor do they know whether Marjane is departing. We soon come to understand that the in-colour airport scenes represent the temporal-spatial present—from which she is telling the story—and the recuperation of history is presented through sophisticated usages of black, white, and grey. Only by the end of the film do we fully understand that Marjane is neither arriving nor departing from Orly International; instead, the airport serves as a Bakhtinian chronotype, a space that designates a specific narrative spatial-temporal matrix, linking story to place. Marjane goes to the airport to find herself by taking time to detach, to reflect, and to reassess her identity.

Each of the four colour airport sequences in the film is a mnemonic device that links the present with an earlier memory of significance usually associated with displacement, change, transformation, and an airport. These airport scenes anchor the viewer in the present by demystifying the present as we have experienced it in the postmodern condition through the narrative strategy of colluding a different previous airport memory with Marjane's current moment of detachment and reflection as she orients herself in her present—Paris. The first colour sequence takes Marjane back to an early childhood memory of the Tehran airport in 1978 when her family greeted a female relative who had arrived home from exile in Paris. From there, we follow the protagonist through the narrated highlights of her younger life. When a second colour airport scene is introduced mid-film, it allows Marjane to introduce the viewer to the next most important stage in her identity formation: when she originally left Iran for Austria, sent away by her parents because her teenage rebellions were attracting dangerous attention from the regime. In the third colour scene, she returns home to Iran after losing her identity and thus, temporarily, her way in Vienna. In the fourth and final colour scenes, the recent past, the present, and the future collude when the viewer is presented with her final departure from Tehran airport, shown in black and white, juxtaposed with her arrival at Orly airport, also in black and white (which indicates a past arrival). This scene morphs into the colour scene outside Orly, as Marjane leaves the airport in a taxi. The narration reveals, at that final moment, that her arrival in Paris is a thing of the past. The various airports throughout the movie are symbolic of defining moments and liminal experiences in her life.

Orly airport, in this film, illustrates the material aspect of the dispersal process present in the age of immediate gratification. At the same time, the film shows how this process can be subverted through reflection, which, in essence, allows Marjane to gather together multiple times and selves in order to reconstitute and reposition herself in relationship to her history and to orient herself—and thereby, viewers—in relationship to a complex representation of Iranian history.

To choose an airport as a departing point for the narrative is then to introduce the viewer to a form of resistance that deals with the depersonalization of people in particular geographical spaces. An airport, according to Marc Augé, is a non-place, in comparison to what Victor Turner, in *From Ritual to Theatre*, would characterize as a liminal space. Given these two paradigms, Orly International functions in the film as a way to introduce the viewer to the protagonist's displacement and her reflections on transience that resist a formulation of completion, of being at home, of finality. Both the non-place and the liminal space reinstate a nomadic reading of power relations. As such, the airport becomes a location out of time—where time is mechanized and reduced to arrivals and departures, where travellers mill about carrying with them their different time zones that bump up against one another. Each traveller manifests his or her own time-aura as a permeable and relative construct so that the sense of being disjointed is foregrounded by this non-place that contains all possible times and no time at all. Where there could be correspondence, the airport effaces any potential stories because everyone is in a transitional process. If time comes to a stop in a non-place, such as the airport, and each departure and arrival is the beginning and ending sequence of micro-history, the airport is then incapable of containing macro-history. This spatial-temporal relationship points to the fact that this form of modernity has produced the absence of time-history: the airport, therefore, becomes symbolic of oblivion within Paronnaud and Satrapi's narrative construction—an oblivion that they resist by transforming the airport into a critical chronotope.

While the other travellers in the airport are transient—awaiting arrivals or departures and therefore suspended from time, a form of temporal absentia—Marjane fully immerses herself in the space and uses her time there to re-collect her self/selves, her memories: who she was and who she has become. As she reassesses her life as an Iranian expatriate, she takes on an Odyssean vestige, familiarized in *The Odyssey*. The link between Shahrzad's storytelling strategy and that of Odysseus erupts in a repositioning of one's self in the world through a narrative that encompasses a multiplication of identities, including the Other and her listener, who is now a participant.

In the Homeric tale, Odysseus does not have a compass but nevertheless finds his way home—Ithaca was the guiding point for his return. In Paronnaud and Satrapi's film, the shifts between colour and black and white posit for the viewer a compass of sorts that segments the overall story into identity paradigms within precise moments of reassertion and re-dressing. It is not only a matter of a chronological rendition of identity but rather a segmentation of the experience of memory into meaningful parts that end up constituting precise identity-formation moments. Each of the moments of the compass—in other words, each of the four colour airport scenes at Orly—are linked to previous memories associated with other airport events that are transformative moments in Marjane's life. Through the process of recollection, the viewer is prompted to focus on these narrative partitions, which both subvert the flow of a continuous chronological narrative and disrupt the typical airport experience and the airport as a non-space, all the while reaffirming the character's inexplicable essence of existence that transcends the dynamics of displacement.

Marjane, by grounding her narrative in the airport, chooses the most uncharacteristic of places—a place that reduces the complexity of human interactions into an amorphous flow of continuous displacement-passages. The airport thus becomes an apt synecdoche for the role that media, especially television, play in effecting identity. The airport stands for the dispersal that occurs through fluidity and that dissolves our responsibility to actively engage with the world, while at the same time providing the illusion of permanence by allowing us to be in all places at once: the gratification of the desire for immediacy. This film employs a cinematic practice that allows for self-reflexivity and the use of representative images to procure meaning and social criticism, exposing the magic casement of television's environments. Television projects onto the passive viewer a steady flow of images that ultimately produces no direction, no sense of where the information is coming from or going to, thus creating the conditions for identity dispersal. What is apparently a very dynamic medium is comparable to an event horizon, the edge of a black hole, beyond which light cannot escape. Displacement-detachment—as a critical tool that allows for a vantage point on events, so that participants can engage in them and observe them at the same time (participatory duality)—is best rendered by the trope of irony: simultaneous detachment from and participation in the event at hand.

The introductory scene in Orly is juxtaposed with a black and white reminiscence from childhood in which Marjane's family greets the woman arriving from

Paris in the Tehran airport in 1978. Before this memory is shown, we are introduced to Marjane via her feet, which solidly base her in a material reality and which foreshadow her past-punk life in Vienna that we learn about later. Wearing bulky, black, thick-soled, asexual shoes, representing the leaden weight of transience and shipwrecks, she moves through the crowded airport toward the arrival-departure board. The international airport immediately presents the viewer with cultural juxtapositions signalled by dress codes, behaviours, and lifestyles: a shopping mall window onto fleeting and fleeing identities embedded in an ever-vanishing temporality.

In the various colour scenes, Marjane's identity transformations are narrated through the visual language and code-switching metaphor of the scarf that she puts on in the opening colour scene. She has loosened the scarf to reveal her hair a bit before she intentionally removes it in the second colour scene. It remains off in the third and the fourth and final closing colour scenes. As Marjane moves from the arrival-departure board to the washroom, the artificial cultural contrast implicit in the binary of East-West (them-us) is further reinforced when she dons the headscarf and becomes representative of a politico-religious tradition, whereas the other woman in the washroom scene, her Western counterpart, who applies lipstick, becomes a symbol of Western sexual opulence: Felliniesque figure, short red hair, bright-red lipstick, choker-style neck scarf, chain belt, black dress with shoulders cut out, and low-cut neckline (front and back). The scene sets up the two women as reflections in the mirrors over the public sinks, and we see Marjane looking first at herself in the mirror. She looks frightened and pulls her headscarf further down around her face to be sure it is covering her hair—almost as a defensive measure to hide herself. Once she has adjusted her scarf, the shot shifts to a wider perspective, and we see Marjane, through her reflection in the mirror, peeking at the woman next to her, who liberally applies more lipstick and shoots Marjane a nasty look as she walks away: a look of distaste for the Other that the woman recognizes in Marjane.

While the red-headed woman sees nothing of herself in Marjane, the protagonist recognizes herself in the Western woman. (Viewers are able to understand Marjane's expression in the washroom only in retrospect, once they have reintegrated the segments of plot within the chronology of the *fabula* by the end of the film.) Marjane, we later discover, was once perceived as a Western tart (à la woman in the washroom) when, upon her return to Iran from Vienna, her friends discovered that she was no longer a virgin. Later in the film, scenes when Marjane was earlier in Iran reveal that the images of sexy femininity adopted by her girlfriends in Tehran, which had to be cloaked publicly by the materiality of religious-normative discourse, simply disguised another layer of ideology—that of Western feminism, which the Iranian girls equated with a disproportionate amount of freedom. While adopting the tropes of Western sexual freedom via their fashion choices, these practices are merely epidermic, demonstrated by the fact that the girls are shocked by Marjane's practices of sexual choice and freedom. While their own clothing suggests resistance, it is actually only a mask for their conformity to the praxis of sexual reproduction, because they exercise no governance over their own bodies. These girls refuse the liberation of their own bodies and sexuality, as they will still produce children for the Revolution. As Marjane understands—given the trajectory of identity tropes she has tried on over time and in different social and national contexts—Western liberalism is merely another code that allows for the sexual objectification of women. Marjane does not conform to the dictates of Western fashion. To do so would mirror the process whereby women within specific politico-religious ideologies are constructed as sexual objects only to then be cloaked and repressed, thereby reproducing the regime.

In fact, in the washroom scene, Marjane perceives that, in both East and West, women risk succumbing to roles that are merely the extension of men's desires. She is able to recognize her commonalities with the woman next to her, whereas that woman's gaze keeps Marjane at her periphery, betraying a lack of solidarity or genealogical correspondence. The Western woman renders herself an object of desire and, by opting to fashion herself according to a prescribed dress code, reveals her own oppression within a limited system of identity tropes. Her absence from history is exposed through a lack of awareness: merely adopting a predefined social role does not equate with sexual freedom, or with the pleasure of the body per se, but simply entails obedience to different modes of governing the female body that are as oppressive as Marjane's scarf. In this, the role is merely an embodiment of the superficiality of the non-place of the airport in the age of immediate gratification. The red-headed woman, like many others, is unable to reflect critically on her identity and instead chooses to fulfill one of a limited number of roles dictated to her by the male gaze: a codified performance for the voyeur. The Western woman prepares herself in front of the mirror—as if on camera—again highlighting the film's criticism of camera-performative identities trapped by the event horizon of television environments.

After the scene in the washroom, Marjane proceeds to the Iran Air ticket gate, only to bow her head in defeat when asked for passport and ticket. The shot then cuts abruptly, substantiating uncertainty as to cause-and-effect trajectories, to her sitting on a bench in the airport, at which point there is a convergence of selves: the young childish Marjane runs through the frame and leads us back to a black and white reminiscence, set in Tehran in 1978, linked to Orly airport, where the young woman who returns from exile in Paris to Tehran becomes, culturally and politically, a synecdoche for the return of the Ayatollah Khomeini. By the end of the film, the viewer is able to understand that when Marjane approached the ticket gate, there could be no return to Iran. Of course, the irony is that the return is denied in Marjane's case but is historically substituted by the Ayatollah's own return in 1978. This, however, is not clear until the viewer has pieced together segments of plot to reconstruct the *fabula* and then situated Marjane's life story in the context of Iran's recent history.

The black and white flashback leads us into Marjane's childhood, where we learn of several significant formative experiences, such as Marjane's love of Bruce Lee, her desire to become a prophet, and the ambition to shave her legs, eventually. These identity tropes are an attempt to claim the active fighter steeped in the wisdom of belief paired with the mature woman and her own individuation. Through Marjane's memories of childhood and young adulthood, the viewer is exposed to the trajectory of the Iranian Revolution that leads up to the second colour scene in the film, where Marjane's departure from Iran to Vienna and the associated airport scene again land the viewer momentarily in Orly.

Here, Marjane, dejectedly sitting in the airport, takes off her headscarf and lights up a cigarette: these acts represent her current reality, far removed from the constraints of either childhood or Iranian social codes under the regime of the Ayatollah. In this scene, smoking aggravates another woman in her proximity, but Marjane is unaffected by the woman's attitude, a visual echo of the woman primping herself in the washroom. Marjane smokes her cigarette impudently, to the woman's disdain, while contemplating the past, the cigarette acting as a stimulant for recollections. The smoke, a symbol of the hazy and ephemeral memories that she is recollecting, is also a parody of the speech bubble in cartoons, establishing a direct connection between print animation and moving animation. Of course, the cigarette also contains an element of transgression, both in the here and now in Paris and in the then and there of Tehran, where friends and family partied in secret as a form of resistance risking imprisonment and/or death.

The black and white airport sequence that is linked to this colour scene is of Marjane's departure for Vienna from Tehran when her father tells her never to forget who she is and where she comes from. As she walks away, she glances back over her shoulder only to see through the glass partition that her mother, having fainted, must now be carried away by her father. The glass division is an irreparable caesura from innocence: Marjane will never again be the same person that she is when she departs from Tehran for the first time. This is the moment of the original displacement. Linked to her mother's fainting, this symbolic death foregrounds the sacrifice of all of Iranian youth that have, over time, resisted oppression and/or that were sacrificed in the name of religious nationalism in the war with Iraq.

The next scene switches to colour. The removal of the scarf at Orly airport that had been so meticulously donned in order to approach the ticket gate symbolizes Marjane's resituating herself in the present space: Paris. This act also acknowledges the impossibility of a return to the comfort of childhood. If the scarf is a symbol of who she once was or might have been, it is also the false umbilical cord embedded in oppression and domestication. At the same time, removing the scarf and freeing her hair—a marker of Western freedom—is now a freedom relative to time and place that comes with a price. The time in the flashback is 1982: the knowledgeable viewer will know that, by this historical moment, Khomeini had consolidated his hold on power while regaining most of the territories lost during the beginning of the war with Iraq.

In the third colour scene, Marjane is having coffee in the airport café. There, she reminisces about her return from Vienna to Tehran, rediscovering a transformed Iran through the narrations provided by her parents, which constituted her new horizon. This brief interlude in Orly is paralleled with her airport experience in Tehran upon her return. That airport sets up a repressive encounter: the male agent sitting at a table, a guard of the Revolution, asks for her passport and reprimands her for her scarf being askew. Her feminine identity is checked by the figure of male oppression both through his exercise of power over her physicality and through the language he uses to recuperate her through a revolutionary-familial language, calling her "sister." In retrospect, the viewer can recognize that this was the moment upon which Marjane was reflecting when she originally donned the scarf in the introductory washroom scene before approaching the Iran Air ticket counter. As the viewer also understands in the final moments of the film, her actions in the present Orly airport are the re-enactment of an oppressive process that traumatizes her return and that she is working through via the process of the narrative.

When she originally went home to Tehran from Vienna, it was with her parents' understanding that they would not ask her any questions upon her return.

Consequently, the necessity for oblivion was acknowledged, in order for the return to occur. Instead of expecting Marjane to recount her experiences, her parents report the transformative events that have taken place in Iran during her absence. Her possibility to reflect critically on Iranian society via her displacement, perhaps as her Uncle Anoush had done, is truncated both by the guard and by the expectations of her family. Failing to obliviate her past leads to incessant sleep, TV watching (another reflection on the medium as entrapment), and the consumption of alcohol and pills, all of which allow her to spiral temporarily in an ever-present denial of past events, a condition that cannot be responsibly sustained. This depressive behaviour is part of her response to the sense of guilt for having missed out on the experiences of her generation—experiences (such as the war) that had maimed some friends of substance and robbed others of their identity through cultural oppression. Through the illustrative power of representation, the viewer is shown how her girlfriends focus on the vaporous aspects of hedonistic Western society by dressing the part of Western beauty, veiled under the black scarves and coats dictated by the religious Revolution. Her rise out of this depressive process illustrates a way out of the television environment that *Persepolis* is eager to illustrate. The way that Marjane recuperates the plot of her life indicates that both at the time she excised herself from her depression in Iran and in the present in Paris, no degree of oblivion can be curative.

Near the end of the movie, just preceding the final colour scene, Marjane is in Orly; she has just arrived from Tehran and said goodbye to her family, with her mother forbidding her ever to return to Iran for the sake of Marjane's own freedom and safety. While the movie plot tricks the viewer into thinking of this as the present, the colour code allows the viewer to unravel the yarn: the sequence is in black and white, which, according to the narrative strategy, indicates the past. In the final moments of the film, the past and the present intertwine. It is only when the black and white incarnation of Marjane exits Orly and morphs into the present version of herself—the colour version wearing a red coat and driving off in the backseat of a taxi—that the viewer is able to understand that she has not just arrived from Tehran but has actually spent the day in Orly Airport. No destination other than the airport itself is revealed: it is the point of aggregation for all memories and identities. In the end, the day at the airport became part of an exercise in liminality and impossible returns. The taxi driver asks her, "Where are you coming from?" and she replies, "Iran," despite the fact that viewers know that she has not been anywhere but the airport itself. Her response indicates that she has not forgotten who she is or where she comes from—following from the advice of her father and grandmother. Marjane has been able to reconstitute her full identity, which was segmented by various displacements, so that the person and the *fabula* become one. Reconstituted, she is her-story.

The closing sequence of the film is again white on black animation, as with the beginning nine vignettes, and the images are again linked by floating jasmine flowers, which are reminiscent of Marjane's grandmother, thus drawing a connection to her genealogical line. As such, the device metonymically encompasses Marcel Proust's madeleine: if what guided Proust back to his life in *À la recherché du temps perdu* is the sense of taste, for Marjane it is the sense of smell. Her olfactory and mnemonic device connect to her relationship with her grandmother, which grounds her own identity but also hints at the fallibility of the visual as the one and only sense in the contemporary age of the image.

WALTZ WITH BASHIR (2008)

Ari Folman, in *Waltz with Bashir*, calls the viewer to reflect on the image by consistently weaving into the film's animated narrative technological apparatuses, mirrors, and lenses. This style opens up to a critical understanding of how the various technologies that surround the image create and manipulate identities that are fully removed from history. In one of the defining moments of the film (whence the title is derived), the Christian Phalangists in Beirut respond to their leader, Bashir, only as a constructed image. In this sense, the Phalangists are not individuals but rather extensions of an image environment that is void of individual responsibility. Finally, the film illustrates that such image environments have no ethical purpose despite often being constructed around narratives of moral and ethical obligation or action.

In the opening sequence of the film, a vicious pack of dogs—twenty-six of them, we later learn—is raging through the streets. At one point, we, as spectators, are watching the dogs rampage through the city via a reflection in a convex street-corner mirror. The director uses the mirror symbolically to connect to the notion of memory and surveillance. This introduction to the convex lens in the street at the outset of the movie resonates with the concluding moments of the film, in which "real" television footage of the Sabra and Shatila massacre is used to illustrate the limitations of the anti-historical media representations provided to viewers about history-as-it-happens. As viewers, we continue to follow the trajectory of the dogs running wildly through the urban landscape, eventually stampeding through a puddle that covers the painted image of an adult and child holding hands: a horizontal street-sign that indicates pedestrian traffic to oncoming drivers. Then, from the flat dimension of the street, we move from the horizontal to the vertical: from memory to reality. A mother stands, hugging her toddler to shield him from the pack of dogs that represent the eruption of chaos and the wild into the cityscape. All traffic flow is disrupted: cars stop and people flee and are separated from one another as the dogs race through their existence, creating social fragmentation. The link between recalled images and repressed traumatic memories becomes apparent during the course of the film. Because memories have a disruptive effect that threatens civilized society, they must be repressed by regimes exercising control. However, this film asserts that through the ability of art and/or narrative to provide context and origins, trauma can possibly be reintegrated into a healthier whole.

As the introductory sequence continues, further reflections on screen media are revealed. Suddenly, the focus shifts to a character looking down at us, the spectators, from the upper-storey window of an art-deco-style building. Despite the fact that the viewer will soon become aware of the fact that the film is set in contemporary time, the style of the building is reminiscent of a time before the Holocaust, again drawing the parallel between the two genocides: the Jewish Shoah and the Sabra and Shatila massacre. The bespectacled figure in the upper-storey window represents the alienation of truncated memories and the separation of the social body into inchoate shards. The window through which the figure is gazing becomes a frame onto the world, reminiscent of a television or film screen. Then suddenly, our perspective as viewers shifts, and we assume the position of the twenty-six dogs; we become a part of the dynamic chaos that the man in the window is observing. Outside the window from which he gazes is a spotlight or camera that the viewer presumes is pointed at the entrance to the building. Then, perspective shifts again, and we see the dogs in the street, barking up toward our viewing I/eye (the man in the window). This shift in perspective creates a striking tension: the man awaits an answer, the dogs await an answer, and we, viewers imbricated in this scene, await an answer. The foreboding associated with the anticipated answer is due, in part, to the animation choices in the introductory sequence: it is predominantly black, white, and grey, but it is mitigated by splashes of colour—the dogs' yellow eyes, the yellow backlight, and the yellow lettering of the credits playing at the outset of the film. The black and yellow colouring, combined with the dogs' foaming at the mouth, invokes a suggestion of madness, morbidity, and the uncanny.

As a framing device, this prenarrative sets up the negative displacement of the narrator, Ari, from his own memory and history and presents society's political dissociation or amnesia as a form of occultation. The interplay between image and word is where meaning is created through visual-textual punning, an ironic mode that illustrates the viewer's potential for critical participation. At this point in the film, no dialogue or narration has yet been introduced. The long scene following the wild dogs galloping through the city is meant to pique the viewers' curiosity and incite a connection between the unconscious as the prenarrative of dreams and the memory recollections that follow. The prenarrative scene, then, is filled with a strong beat of adrenaline-evoking music that backdrops the barking of the dogs and the multiple sounds of chaos erupting: chairs being overturned, tables falling, cars stopping. This soundscape provides an ominous threat that agitates the viewer into a fight-or-flight survival mode. It anticipates the narrative of military experience. The barking segues into the human voice but remains as a background soundtrack to the narrative, creating a doubling effect that allows for a contrast between civilization and savagery, the domesticated and the wild.

The first phrase of dialogue in the film, provided by the character of Boaz Rein, the man in the window, iterates the haunting horror he feels about the dogs: "I see them standing there: all twenty-six dogs, barking. Through the window, I see the hunger in their eyes. They are here to take a life. They threatened the life of my boss, Bertold: either give them Boaz Rein's head or we'll eat your customers." The passage suggests that the dogs speak, which is a transition from animal to human, and ultimately the message is that the dogs want justice. The fact that the dogs request the head of the boss or threaten to eat the customers evokes the biblical story of Salome and John the Baptist (the horrific fickleness of power) and the cannibalism of the Other (the unmediated power of the Phalangists), since the twenty-six dogs each have a precise identity, paradoxically becoming human by naming and therefore reconstituting and exposing the synecdoche of beast-terrorist for what it is.

The visual scene contextualizing the narrative voice then shifts from its perspective in the window above the dogs in the street, hierarchical in showing tension, to a dialogue taking place in a pub between two characters (Ari and Boaz), a horizontal engagement that suggests reciprocity, working through fragmentation to form a conscious responsibility critical of history. In this free-flowing social setting, alcohol consumption allows for the trauma to start unfolding. Fragments of memory come through, and drugs bring about the de-automatization of recall through the dulling of pain. (Similarly, in *Persepolis*, cigarettes stimulate recollection, and pills and alcohol provide the necessary respite from trauma.) However, meaning is achieved through the dialogical interaction that, from this scene on, ironically moves closer to the ground zero of what has been cut off and left suspended from the Israeli social body: the responsibility for the massacre. In this sense, then, the dialogical is not only a Bakhtinian communicative strategy but also a Buberian resolution, a taking of individual responsibility. Interaction between the unconscious (what is obliviated) and the conscious (what is known) is an ongoing dialogue. As the individual becomes known to himself or herself, personal and social histories can be re-established (reintegrating the shadow) so as to claim back individuality and identity. As far as the film confirms this, war is a denial of identity that subverts the dialogical, that fossilizes the Other into a picture of barbarism that, in turn, renders the "I" a rigid construct. Within the narrative paradigm, war can only be a polarization that ultimately indicates genocide: the extermination of the Other. War is the struggle of a monologue to re-place another monologue. As such, it is the caesura with life and ourselves. As Tzvetan Todorov has demonstrated in his analysis of the European conquistador's encounter with the Other in *The Conquest of America*, it is possible to identify with the Other, especially when doing so serves the purposes of domination and exploitation of the world at large.

Once the dialogue between Ari and Boaz begins, another layer is visually introduced to the viewer: in the top left corner of the screen, there are names written in both roman and Hebrew lettering. This cinematic strategy reaffirms the constitution of the film as a narrative reconstruction based on interviews with actual participants. Through this visual layer, the movie is self-reflexive about being a medium to capture, still, and distill life-memories that have transpired before the movie was created. The names are a reminder and a remainder of something that has already taken place.

At least three memory lines intertwine in the film: the memory contained within the movie, the memories of those outside the movie that were gathered through interviews, and our memories as spectators who know something about Sabra and Shatila. What is introduced in the beginning sequence, after the dream is discussed, is the function of the narrative. Ari asks Boaz:

Have you tried anything?
Like what?
Therapy? A shrink? Shiatsu? Anything?
No. Nothing, I'm reaching out to you.
I'm just a filmmaker.
Can't filmmaking be therapeutic?

One of the functions of this dialogue is to bring into focus the scope of the film itself. Through interlocution, the viewer is brought to reflect on one possible role that the film can have and its therapeutic potential. At the same time, however, this role is but one aspect of this complex film; the film is able to reach the viewer on many levels. The therapeutic process first targets the Israelis themselves. As well, the narrative is constructed and based upon *The Iliad* and *The Odyssey*—the two texts upon which all of Western literature is based, according to Italian critic Franco Ferrucci, who argued this point in *L'assedio e il ritorno*. Notions of return target a much wider international public. Also, the film touches on the way in which history and the media are at odds: the reintegration of history touches the world in general, since in the film, history is absented by media mechanisms.

QUANTIFIABLE PROXIMITY: OBLIVION AND THE ANGEL OF HISTORY

As the dialogue between the two characters of Boaz and Ari unfolds, it becomes evident that Ari has distanced himself from the memories of his military experiences as a youth—memories that include the Sabra and Shatila massacre. However, Ari's metaphoric distance from and uncertainty about the past is questioned by Boaz, who quantifies Ari's participation in the event: Boaz cannot understand how Ari cannot remember, given that he was only a hundred yards away. Proximity to the event, from Boaz's perspective, seems to suggest a measurable relationship to history. Boaz remembers various events quite well and quantifies many aspects of his experiences, such as the twenty-six dogs in the opening scene of the film. Nevertheless, this does not equate with being able to integrate his experiences into a coherent existential narrative. For Boaz, the war remains a series of quantifiable fragments, much as it would be for a viewer watching a war as a series of news clips. The empirical objectification of the events that we typically receive as spectators via news media—ten bombs dropped, one hundred civilians killed, three soldiers dead, and so on—serves the purpose of allowing viewers to embrace the image-reality of events with a false conception of understanding: titillating with the horrors of reality from a safe distance while inhibiting or prohibiting any empathy with victims or sense of responsibility for events. Ari, however, contradicts Boaz's claim that Ari was a hundred yards from the event. Ari says it was "more like two hundred, three hundred yards—the truth is, nothing like that stays in my brain." While Ari has no memory of the massacre, he claims less physical proximity than Boaz's estimate, which seems to imply that for him, the physical distance of a few hundred yards means the difference between memory and oblivion. As a signification of what is to come in the film, when the two characters separate after the bar scene, it appears that one is a shadow separating from the other. As Boaz walks away from Ari and stands looking at the tempestuous sea, Ari looks over his shoulder (à la Benjamin's Angel of History) as though to look back on his past, which will allow him to move forward by retrieving memories that are integral to a sense of identity.

This visual representation of the men as dividing from one another is indicative of the film's dynamic, whereby Israel must reclaim itself (and reintegrate its multiple identities) through the recuperation of memory: this happens in the film through Ari's reintegration of his past, which is linked to the recuperation of national history. Through interviewing former members of his military unit in order to reconstitute a lost generation that is part of the body and identity of Israel, Ari becomes the material thread that weaves together the different fragments of a dispersed and displaced community. The conversation in the bar with Boaz is the moment that begins Ari's own quest back into his past: he suddenly becomes aware of his lack of memories about his own experiences in Lebanon as a young military man. The film then travels back through memory and time to uncover what happened. This mimics *The Odyssey* insofar as it records Odysseus's voyage back from the Greek war on the Trojans and the siege of Troy. Odysseus's journey home takes twenty years, which corresponds to the time it takes for Ari, a synecdoche for Israel, to bring to life the historical context: it has taken twenty years for Boaz to begin dreaming—in other words, to begin the process of remembering—and to incite Ari's own journey.

Waltz with Bashir and the combined narratives of *The Iliad* and *The Odyssey* intersect at several levels. First, both narratives revolve around a siege and a war. Second, in both narratives, the protagonists undergo transformations of identity that result from the traumas of war. War wounds the protagonists by displacing them from their identification with the Other, which prevents their identification with humanity and, ultimately, with themselves. Third, the reintegration of both Odysseus's and Ari's war-fragmented identities are realized and made possible through the creation of a narrative that reconfigures their histories and memories.

One of Ari's first encounters with the city of Beirut—once popularly considered the Paris of the Middle East—is through the airport, which, for a moment, he imagines as a hub of cosmopolitan life, only to be shocked out of the reverie to realize that it is an abandoned war-devastated location. As we follow his discovery, the broken carcasses of planes are foregrounded, much as in the scene of the slaughtered horses in Beirut's hippodrome, which produces a moment of negative epiphany for one soldier/patient. This trauma, the absurd death of the horses, collapses the ex-soldier's grasp of sanity because the distance he had created between himself and the horrors of war, by using the camera, is dissolved when he sees the dead animals. Whereas Paronnaud and Satrapi use the airport as a symbol of oblivion, Ari Folman uses it to illustrate a confrontation with oblivion.

What *Waltz with Bashir* suggests, and herein lies the contradiction, is that oblivion—Ari's oblivion, the oblivion of Israel, and the oblivion of the international world of spectators—has been rendered possible by the image-based media environments that saturate contemporary culture. In other words, as a result of mainstream media's focus on satiating their consumers' thirst for immediacy, memory is not a collection of dynamic images strung together into an ideological narrative. Rather, the memory of strife must constitute a critical recounting that encompasses the participants in the strife and that can bring back a sense of responsibility to everyone (at every level of participation or inaction) for the dehumanizing process of that strife. To extend Martin Buber's premise, it is only when "I" recognize the Other's dead as my dead as well that "I" find my humanity and "I" am again, possibly, able to recover the person that "I" was before the trauma. By naturalizing scenes of terror and despair, whereby suffering becomes spectacle, the world of images has succeeded in eliminating the sense of social responsibility that is, in large part, the basis of engagement with others in a democratic society. Such a process is able to convey the illusion that we have acknowledged the strife and trauma of Others. More than words, images have the power to suspend death in time and render it available for immediate consumption via worldwide networks of communication, which at the time of Sabra and Shatila would have been largely televisual but which are now available in perpetuity via the Internet. Folman is now using animated feature-length film to recuperate the meaningless spectacularization of history. The ironic aspect to the movie's intentionality—what could be called "critical humanism"—is its ability to establish a parallel with the Holocaust.

In the case of the Holocaust, pictures were the testimonials of the dead: pictures became necessary to narrate the Shoah. The denunciation of today's power of the image throughout *Waltz with Bashir* is a denunciation of the passage from the role of the image before the end of the Second World War to the role that the image has acquired in the contemporary world: that of removing the sense of responsibility of human beings in the world while granting them the power of oblivion because of the transitory nature of life. In other words, what contemporary static and dynamic images through media environments have accomplished is to create a false sense of catharsis while releasing the emotions of their historical context and development in order to gratify the desire for immediacy as the lowest common denominator of any formulation of identity.

THE REFRAINS OF MEMORY: ONE IN THREE

The anthropological device used by Ari Folman—the actual interview with participants—retrieves the individual voices that had no authority and were silenced by the magnitude of the event and the official reports that erased history. This is not to say that these formerly young military men were not responsible for the massacre in which they were voyeuristic participants; rather, they were secondary characters in the staging of the event, and the narrative ultimately exposes the chain of command and responsibility that orchestrated the event.

In the process of recollection, Folman resorts also to other narrative techniques and strategies, one of which is the use of the visual refrain of the tragedy that acts as a silent chorus. In this refrain, which occurs three times, the naked young male bodies rise out of the water; the viewer eventually comes to realize through the repetition of the scene that this flashback is of Ari and two members of his military unit who walk out of the water onto the beach of war-torn Beirut. These scenes, with the young men first seen floating and then slowly standing and walking out of the water, completely naked except for the automatic weapons that they are carrying, represent the birthing of these youth into war by the sea. Although no word is spoken, their sense of purpose is the military mission that awaits them. As they dress on the beach, the viewing "I" anticipates their encounter with an enemy, only to be displaced from anticipation by the fact that when these youth enter into the streets of Beirut, they do not find "the enemy" but are instead encountered with fleeing civilians. The young Ari finds himself moving against the flow of people: silent, open-mouthed women and children running away from what we will later come to understand is the location of the massacre. This cinematic commemoration, a compassionate rendition piecing together the massacre, occurs three times during the movie, and in each instance, the viewer moves one step closer to the ground zero of the event, as though moving one hundred yards closer in a series of concentric circles that focuses and refocuses the viewer on the disappearance of the event through television images.

Given that Ori Sivan, Ari's therapist friend, in another moment in the film, addresses the notion of water as representing fear, the rising of the three young male bodies naked and armed from the night waters of Beirut has several functions apart from embodying the militarization of life through the male body: it provides a sense of importance and anticipation for an ominous moment; it sets up the space of the event; it gives the viewer the culpability of innocence; it brings out a sense of resurrection and/or mortality; it sets the origin of the oblivion as fear; it recuperates the fear as an instrument that can lead to knowledge; it sets up the metaphor for liquid reality (the flow of people but also the flow of media images); and it denounces the fact that if a person (or a nation or the world community) denies a trauma, the trauma will reoccur unmitigated, over and over again. In other words, these concentric circles of the repeated silent chorus of the three men rising out of the water and revealing a bit more of the actual sequence of events each time brings us closer and closer to Sabra and Shatila (and all television-mediated events). In the third and final repetition and elaboration of this cinematic syntagm, the viewer arrives at the climax and final scene of the film, which segues into live television footage of the massacre. Epistemologically, the event is dissolved by the act of zooming in on the women who lament the carnage of their dear husbands and children in such a narrow way as to obliterate the perspective of the viewer and the larger context of the event, turning a political massacre into a television drama of select women and children similar to the spectacle of reality television. The process illustrated is Folman's attempt to renegotiate Israeli identity as a responsible and critical identity, given Israel's background (the Shoah). The unstated denunciation is that those who have undergone a trauma and have not come to terms with it are condemned to repeat the cycle of violence.

During the anti-climactic finale, Folman intentionally conveys both his criticism of television and the public's misplaced faith in its power to render "real" lived events that form and inform identity. The use of "real" footage in the final moment of the film, rather than providing credibility to history and the viewer's acknowledgement of past events, dissolves the horror of the event into a recyclable amalgam of hate and violence. Those moments of footage cannot convey the context of the 1982 war in Lebanon. Instead, the images reduce it to a moment of spectacularized pornography of grief that ironically conveys a less complex understanding of reality than does the preceding animation, with its highly charged process of self-reflexivity. Ultimately, the footage is unveiled as both a parody of itself and the sublimation of the trauma.

SUBVERTING THE PARADIGM

Both *Persepolis* and *Waltz with Bashir* use narrative strategies to recuperate lost personal and national identities by subverting mainstream representations of history-as-it-happens through free-floating images on mainstream television (and new media). Both films subvert "real" images by using the media of animation and feature film narration, drawing on techniques inherent to grand narratives of culture and history to illustrate the caesura that postmodernity has imposed on individuals when it alienates them from themselves and from their context. In *Waltz with Bashir*, Folman is specifically critical of television's potential to erase active participation in the world. In *Persepolis*, Paronnaud and Satrapi criticize the fragmentary image-constructions of either individuals or nations provided by television and associated new media technologies that make people and nations ever-present consumable commodities. By reverting to narrative strategies grounded in history, both film narratives redirect the active gaze back onto constructions of history itself and call the viewer to question the contemporary notions of history-as-it-happens that is being offered to us, the orphans of critical humanism.

The animation in these two films works to take back the "image-" prefix of image-history in order to deliver us to history. In a sense, these films are cultural antibodies. By freeing the image-history, these films provide us with a vocabulary that redelivers our presence in time. Perhaps the penned image—the drawings and animation—is somehow able to represent reality more accurately in the contemporary world than "real" pictures, since everything around us reminds us of our presence in the image-based media environments and associated pathos, with neither a link to critical distancing nor the ability to process beyond sensorial gratification. However divergent the styles and representational strategies instrumental to the narratives in these two films, the self-reflexivity, intentionality, and repositioning of image-making processes (film, graphic novels, television, media reportage, animated movies) produce similar communicative goals.

Persepolis is focused on informing the world at large of the repression that has shaped recent Iranian history and the subsequent displacement of various classes. The communicative strategy is one that foregrounds the concatenation of different voices so as to show that Iran is not just one homogeneous system—the oppressive system—and that an array of voices are linked together by their individual identities that do not conform to the imposed norm. At the same time, the reacquisition of voice through the many characters that arise in the process of *mise en abîme* points to the destruction of the Western stereotypes that qualify all Iranians as homologous to the oppressive religious and political system presently in power.

As a case in point, in the uprising in Iran after the elections in June 2009, Satrapi granted permission to two Iranian students who requested access to her graphic novel so that they could update it to include the actual events of the protest that ensued after the elections. Overall, it is clearly the intention of these artists to demystify the constructions that have made of Iran a prototype of a medieval tangent, taking Iran completely out of the trajectory of modernity. In the film *Persepolis*, the voices that are embodied by the animation represent a dynamic, enlightened, and cultured society that has been decimated by torture, imprisonment, and systematic elimination. This foregrounding, we think, is very important in Paronnaud and Satrapi's work. We have already hinted at Satrapi's efforts to deconstruct the stereotype that has gained common currency in the Western media: Iran as an Islamo-fascist regime run amok with the power of nuclear devices.

Waltz with Bashir, until the final scene, scrutinizes the unhealed wound of the Sabra and Shatila massacre with an Israeli audience in mind. Faced with an event that denies narration, just as the Holocaust is beyond narration, Folman's film proposes that it is our social responsibility to recuperate that traumatic event from oblivion, from those individuals who have been co-responsible for both the historical occurrence and its subsequent erasure. The proliferation of images projected internationally at the time of the event functioned as a reductive mechanism; the media coverage projected horror and trauma but failed to encompass the context, the meaning, or the viewer's implication in the event of the "real." Television—another medium in which Folman works—is re-viewed under Folman's scrutiny and is found incapable of offering perspective. According to the representation of television and media images offered throughout *Waltz with Bashir*, which culminates with the incorporation of "real" (not animated) media footage at the end of the film, television makes available only flat images that provide the viewer no context. And in the absence of context, television images projected to viewers are merely free-floating signifiers that allow spectators to abdicate their responsibility.

Both films strive to engage the viewer with history-as-it-happens in order to illustrate and resist the process of obliviation that has been naturalized by contemporary media practices. This process is characteristic of a world that insists on instant gratification, that aims for forgetfulness of the present and erasure of history, and that prefers what we term *post-political participaction*, in which potential political agency is transformed through televised images into a spectator sport and thereby rendered inert. Although both movies refer to specific geopolitical realities, the reverberating messages comment on the underlying conditions of present societies where the fulcrum is oblivion. Yosef Hayim Yarushalmi asks, "Est-il possible que l'antonyme de « l'oubli » ne soit pas « la mémoire », mais *la justice*?" (20; "Is it possible that the antonym of 'oblivion' is not 'memory,' but *justice*?"). If the answer is yes, then the project of these two films in recuperating national histories is to ground identities in the dynamics of interlocking narratives, embedding the protagonists and the viewers in history through an ethic of responsible presence. *Persepolis* does so by illustrating how to maintain a sense of self and personal dignity by avoiding the traps of oblivion. *Waltz with Bashir* is a complex warning about what happens to nations and ultimately to the individuals of whom these geopolitical spaces are composed when the lure of the sirens of oblivion shipwrecks them in Time, by capturing them within their media environments.

NOTES

1 "Marjane" is also the first name of Marjane Satrapi, the author of the graphic novel *Persepolis* on which the film is based. In what follows, we will use "Marjane" to refer to the character in the animated film and "Satrapi" to refer to the author and filmmaker herself. Similarly, in discussing *Waltz with Bashir*, we will use "Ari" for the character and "Folman" for the filmmaker.

2 Dispersal refers to both Marjane's centrifugal exile and the actual historical dispersal of community memory that is bound to particular participants who envisioned a different revolution with the fall of the Shah—communists, progressives, anyone who did not support a religious revolution—and also to people who were eliminated from the Iranian future through torture and death.

3 "Shipwrecks" here references her near identity-shipwreck in Vienna, where there was temporary caesura from her genealogical line because she forgot what her grandmother told her before her departure: "In your lifetime, you are going to meet a lot of jerks. If someone hurts you, just say that it was because of their lack of intelligence. [. . .] never get bitter. Don't lose your sense of dignity. Don't lose sight of yourself."

4 Within the framework established by the film's critical reflections on female identity, including sexuality and a sexually liberated female body capable of giving and receiving pleasure, becomes impossible to represent within the confines of Western historical conceptions of sex and power relations. As with Roland Barthes's *Le plaisir du texte* (1973), the pleasure of the actual, physical body is forever postponed within the mediated textualization of the body, a conceptualization that is possible within a post-structuralist world's riposte that has been embraced as a naturalized state.

5 Folman, too, engages with smell as a guiding sense both through darkness (of space, of the soul) and as a link to personal past events, as our absolute and dangerous reliance on image and visuality is finally revealed. In *Waltz with Bashir*, Ari suddenly remembers why patchouli oil makes him feel sick: it is connected to his memories of his wartime roommate Frenkel, for whom patchouli was not just a fragrance but a way of life, just as Frenkel's present life as a martial arts instructor is guided by a specific philosophy and regime: hierarchy, discipline, and order. These three elements correspond to the way he used patchouli to guide his men on the battlefield, and these elements, combined, are also one of the ways by which history is recuperated.

6 We have chosen to quote directly from the narrative voice-over, given that the subtitles abbreviate the words spoken.

7 The term *post-political participaction* makes reference to the Canadian ParticipACTION campaign, established in 1971 with the goal of motivating Canadians to get physically active. In December 2011, Kelly Murumets, president and CEO of ParticipACTION, told the House Standing Committee on Health: "We're a pioneer in social marketing; we have become internationally recognized for our compelling communications to promote physical activity" (http://www.parl.gc.ca/HousePublications/Publication.aspx?DocId=5326379). The irony, of course, is that to see the ParticipACTION campaign TV commercials, one has to be sitting in front of the television.

WORKS CITED

Anselmi, William, and Sheena Wilson. "Performative Radicalism in Contemporary Canadian Documentary Film." *Film International* 7.1 (2009): 44–53.

———. "From *Inch'Allah Dimanche* to *Sharia in Canada*: Empire Management, Gender Representations, and Communication Strategies in the Twenty-First Century." *From Solidarity to Schisms: 9/11 and After in Fiction and Film from Outside the US*. Ed. Cara Cilano. New York: Rodopi, 2009. 237–72.

———. "For Whom the *post* Tolls Beyond Technologies of Feminism: Postmortem of Transnational Communicative Environments." *Journal of Critical Studies in Business and Society*, Special Issue: *Critical Perspectives on Gender* 1.1–2 (2010): 138–72.

———. "For Your Glaze Only: Imperfect Divinity." *International Journal of the Image* 1.3 (2011): 73–86.

———. "When We Dream, Do We Accumulate Capital? On Christopher Nolan's *Inception* (2010)." *Bright Lights Film Journal* 74 (November 2011). http://www.brightlightsfilm.com/74/74inception_anselmiwilson.php.

Augé, Marc. *Non-Places: Introduction to an Anthropology of Supermodernity*. 2nd ed. Trans. John Howe. London: Verso, 2008.

Bakhtin, Mikhail. *The Dialogic Imagination*. Trans. Caryl Emerson and Michael Holquist. Austin: U of Texas P, 1981.

Barthes, Roland. *Le plaisir du texte*. Paris: Éditions du Seuil, 1973.

Benjamin, Walter. "Theses on the Philosophy of History." *Illuminations: Essays and Reflections*. Trans. Harry Zohn. Ed. Hannah Arendt. New York: Harcourt, Brace, & World, 1968. 253–64.

Buber, Martin. *I and Thou*. Trans. Ronald Gregor Smith. New York: Charles Scribner's Sons, 1958.

Ferrucci, Franco. *L'assedio e il ritorno: Omero e gli archetipi della narrazione*. Milano: Bompiani, 1991.

Homer. *The Iliad*. Trans. Rodney Merrill. Ann Arbor: U of Michigan P, 2007.

———. *Odyssey*. Trans. Stanley Lombardo. Indianapolis: Hackett, 2000.

Payman and Sina. *Persepolis 2.0*. http://www.flickr.com/photos/30950471@N03/sets/72157620466531333/show/.

Persepolis. Written and directed by Vincent Paronnaud and Marjane Satrapi. Film SAS and France 3 Cinema SAS, 2007.

Stories from the Thousand and One Nights. Trans. Edward William Lane. New York: Collier, 1963.

Todorov, Tzvetan. *The Conquest of America: The Question of the Other*. Trans. Richard Howard. Norman: U of Oklahoma P, 1999.

Turner, Victor. *From Ritual to Theatre: The Human Seriousness of Play*. New York: Performing Arts Journal, 1982.

Waltz with Bashir. Dir. Ari Folman. Arte France and ITVS International, 2008.

Yarushalmi, Yosef Hayim. *Usages de l'oubli*. Paris: Éditions du Seuil, 1988.

Contributors

Mostafa Abedinifard holds a PhD in comparative literature at the University of Alberta. He currently teaches academic writing courses in the Department of English at MacEwan University. His research interests include comparative and world literature, masculinities studies, and humour studies. He has translated into Persian Charles Bressler's *Literary Criticism: An Introduction to Theory and Practice* (Tehran: Nilufar), and has articles and book reviews published in journals such as *Social Semiotics, Iran Nameh, Cultural Sociology, Journal of Graphic Novels and Comics, Journal of Men's Studies,* and *Literary Criticism* (Tehran).

William Anselmi is professor in the Department of Modern Languages and Cultural Studies at the University of Alberta. He has co-edited and co-authored a number of books on ethnicity, multiculturalism, and media representations. His work addresses a broad range of areas, from Italian and Italian Canadian literature and culture to cinema, media, and television studies. Recent projects involve the exploration of narcissism and immortality in the deployment of post-human technological apparatuses.

Blake Atwood is assistant professor in the Department of Middle Eastern Studies at the University of Texas at Austin. His research interests include Middle Eastern cinema, contemporary Persian literature, and Persian language pedagogy.

Babak Elahi is professor of English and associate dean in the College of Liberal Arts at Rochester Institute of Technology. He is the author of *The Fabric of American Literary Realism* (2009), as well as numerous scholarly articles in *Iranian Studies, Cultural Studies, Comparative Studies of South Asia, Africa, and the Middle East, Symplokē, Middle Eastern Literatures*, and *MELUS: Multi-Ethnic Literature of the United States.*

Goulia Ghardashkhani is a teaching associate in the Department of Iranian Studies at the Centre for Near and Middle Eastern Studies, Philipps-Universität, Marburg. Her research interests include contemporary Iranian prose literature, emigration and diaspora literature, and cultural identity. Her recently completed doctoral dissertation focuses on issues of space, mobility, and identity in Goli Taraqqi's short fiction.

Farideh Dayanim Goldin was born in 1953 in Shiraz, Iran, to a family of dayanim, judges, and leaders of the Jewish community. She studied English literature at Pahlavi University and earned an MA and an MFA (in creative nonfiction) from Old Dominion University, in Norfolk, Virginia. Her first book, *Wedding Song*, concerns her struggle to reconcile her Western education with her deeply rooted Iranian Jewish upbringing. A forthcoming volume, *Leaving Iran: Between Migration and Exile*, chronicles her life as a new immigrant to the United States. She teaches literature and is the director of the Institute for Jewish Studies and Interfaith Understanding at Old Dominion University.

Manijeh Mannani is chair of the Centre for Humanities and associate professor of English and comparative literature at Athabasca University. In addition to numerous scholarly articles, she is the author of *Divine Deviants: The Dialectics of Devotion in the Poetry of Donne and Rumi* and the co-editor of *Selves and Subjectivities: Reflections on Canadian Arts and Culture*.

Laetitia Nanquette is a lecturer and Australian Research Council DECRA Fellow at the University of New South Wales, in Sydney. She holds a BA in philosophy from the Sorbonne and a PhD in Near and Middle Eastern studies from the School of Oriental and African Studies at the University of London. Her interests include the circulation of literature and culture between the Middle East and countries of the diaspora, the relations between the West and the postcolonial world, and literature and globalization. The author of *Orientalism Versus Occidentalism: Literary and Cultural Imaging Between France and Iran Since the Islamic Revolution* (2013), she is currently working on a comparative study of contemporary Iranian literature in a global context.

Safaneh Mohaghegh Neyshabouri is completing her PhD in comparative literature at the University of Alberta. She has a BA and MA in English language and literature and is a published translator of English to Persian. Her research interests include women's writing, Iranian women's memoirs in English and Persian, Iranian diaspora literature, and minority and exilic writing.

Khatereh Sheibani is assistant professor of Persian language and literature at York University. Before coming to Canada, she studied at Shiraz University and at the University of Tehran. She completed her doctorate in comparative literature at the University of Alberta in 2007 and is the author of *The Poetics of Iranian Cinema* (2011). Her essays on modern Persian literature and the relationship between Middle Eastern cinema, poetry, and the conventions of the visual arts have appeared in a number of journals, including *Iranian Studies* and the *Canadian Journal of Film Studies*. Sheibani has been consulted and interviewed on issues regarding Iranian visual arts by global media services such as the CBC, PRI, and the *New York Times*. She has taught courses on Persian literature and cinema, Middle Eastern cinemas, postcolonial literatures, and documentary film and television.

Veronica Thompson is dean of the Faculty of Humanities and Social Sciences and associate professor of English at Athabasca University. Her research interests include Canadian and Australian literatures, postcolonial literatures and theory, and women's literature and feminist theory. She is currently researching representations of terrorism in postcolonial writing. She is co-editor of *Selves and Subjectivities: Reflections on Canadian Arts and Culture* (2012).

Madeleine Voegeli graduated in Middle Eastern studies and English literature and linguistics at the University of Basel. As a former academic assistant and lecturer in Persian language at the Universities of Bern and Basel and now an independent scholar, she has concentrated on Persian literary criticism and contemporary prose literature, especially works by Simin Daneshvar, Mahshid Amirshahi, and Zoya Pirzad.

Sheena Wilson is the director of the Bilingual Writing Centre at the University of Alberta's Campus Saint-Jean and the co-director of Petrocultures, a research group also based at the University of Alberta. Her interests include the relationship between the written word and the image as discursive referents in sociopolitical contexts. Specifically, her research involves the interdisciplinary study of human and civil rights abuses and minority rights as expressed through cultural representations, particularly as they pertain to gendered and other forms of marginalization within the context of global oil cultures. Wilson has published extensively in these areas and is also editor-in-chief of Imaginations: Journal of Cross-Cultural Image Studies. She is the co-editor (with Anna Chilewska) of *Writing After the Gaze: The Rupture of the Historical* (2007), the editor of *Joy Kogawa: Essays on Her*

Works (2011), and the co-editor (with Andrew Pendakis) of *Sighting Oil*, a special issue of *Imaginations* (2012). More recently, she co-edited (with Diana Davidson) a collection of creative non-fiction, *Telling Truths: Storying Motherhood* (2014).